Healing Journeys

Paul Williamson

CAPALL BANN PUBLISHING

Healing Journeys

©1999 Paul Williamson

ISBN 186163 100 6

Cover design by Paul Mason

Published by:

Capall Bann Publishing
Freshfields
Chieveley
Berks
RG20 8TF

Acknowledgements

I would like to thank several people who have been important influences in the creating of this book.

Firstly, I'd like to give special mention to my friends Marjorie and Reg. My relationship with you has formed a foundation for much that I have written. Thank you for your confidence in me.

For Lynne, I'd like to appreciate very much your tireless efforts in typing the manuscript, sometimes retyping and modifying text several times. Thank you also for your honest feedback with my questions and doubts and your continuing affirmation concerning the worth of what I was writing.

To all my clients and friends whose stories and inner processes are included, I give thanks for your permission to do this, and for helping me to clarify details of my case work with you.

I would like to acknowledge Penny and Paul for your constructive suggestions and feedback which came at a crucial time.

Moira, I'd like to thank you for helping me to gain the confidence it needed to start to undertake my own inner journeys. And Roger, I'd like to thank you for all the therapy skills which you taught me.

For Linda, I'd like to honour your kindness and support in providing illustrations. To my Healing group, I'd like to express my appreciation to all of you for your enthusiasm and encouragement with this project - especially Carol and Stella for your contributions.

I would like to acknowledge the peace of Viittakivi in Finland, with its beautiful lake and nature. This setting inspired me to write several chapters in a short space of time. Thank you.

I feel that I have been guided to write this book, and so I would like to honour all the Spiritual beings and unseen presences who have contributed to what I have written.

Thank you also to Julia and Jon for accepting this book for publication.

Finally, but not least, I would like to thank my wife Dorothee and sons, Julian and Johannes, for tolerating and accepting the long hours when I've needed to be writing *Healing Journeys* on my own.

Illustrations

Linda Pope is a psychic artist and Channel. She is also a member of our Healing group. The sketches of the Spiritual guides 'Sojah', 'Sebastian' and 'Dagmar', have come to her as visions while she has been meditating. She has tried to be faithful to these visions with her drawings. Checking with Marjorie, these drawings have been confirmed as accurate representations of how she sees these guides and they correspond well with the impressions I have gained of them too.

Preface

In writing this book I want to help people who wish to know themselves more deeply and who are interested in exploring experiences from their inner consciousness. The subjects about which I am sharing include Past Lives, Inner Child therapy, Channelling, Spiritual Healing and Earth Healing. With each of these topics I will be offering explanations and describing the process involved in exploring them.

I feel that all these subjects are interconnected, blending into each other and operating together. With the experiences I relate, I hope to show how this is so. In the way that I have experienced them, they are all aspects of learning about inner Truth and Spiritual life.

By interweaving my own story of how my interest in these various subjects has developed and discussing in depth case studies from others who have worked with me, I aim to show how therapy and healing processes in all these areas can dramatically change people's lives for the better, and perhaps ultimately even bring more peace to our world.

The journey to connect with our inner Self or 'Soul' may be quite challenging. Often this core of our being is obscured by fears, guilt and various limiting beliefs that colour how we think and feel. To reach our soul we usually need to work through these limitations first. But, as each inner impedi-ment is removed, we may feel increasingly free, and our inner Truth can radiate more brightly. My approach when working with people has been to 'help them help themselves'. Deep inside, I believe that people know what they need to experience in order to find peace and inner freedom. I have tried to support people to do this and support my own inner quest in this process similarly. Through my work, I have been witness to many interesting experiences and transformations.

For people who have had inner experiences that they have struggled to understand, I hope that this book will provide some 'maps' which can help clarify some of the possibilities that exist. By writing personally, I hope this will help people to recognise some of the potential that exists for inner exploration, and realise that with this, you don't have to feel alone or frightened.

I know that some people may not accept all the belief systems that form the main tenets of this book. However, I have tried to be sincere and truthful in what I have related as I could be.

I want to start by outlining aspects of my early life and how I became interested in past lives and reincarnation. The rest can follow from that.

Contents

Part 1

Past Lives and Psychotherapy

Chapter 1

The Healing Path

I believe that we each have a path through life which our soul has chosen for us to experience. In as much as we can live in accord with our deep inmost Self, then we can find peace and fulfilment by going on this path. However, it is not necessarily easy or obvious to know our path and to live by it. There can be many pressures, both internal and external, that prompt us to stray and go in other ways. If we are not living a life true to ourselves then this can bring much suffering and unhappiness to our experiences.

For some people, finding fulfilment in a personal relationship may be most important. For others, it could be about making a success of a career or raising a family. There can be people who need to learn through coping with a particular tragedy. Many, many possibilities exist about what may be most central for a person's life. This can be unique for each individual.

Sometimes people can be occupied with things not really connected to the core of their life path. They may feel through obligation or sense of duty what they should be doing even though inside they may not really want to do those things. Alternatively, a person may feel trapped by circumstances, feeling afraid, helpless and unable to escape. Through letting selfish desires and greed rule over them, people can ignore inner promptings about what they really need to be doing in life.

In these situations, people are living more superficially. They may not be aware that they are not acting in their own interest. But if they could listen and act from what their Soul wants them to do, their life may start to move in quite different ways, and they may be happier.

I feel that we can know about our personal life path through our hearts. In our hearts we feel love and joy. When we act with love and joy in our hearts, then we feel strength and confidence. When we listen to our hearts and we do what we know we have to do, then this is another indication that we are going the right way.

Sometimes we may be able to envision our path unfolding in front of us, knowing how our life wants to be. At other times, it may be as much as we can do to take the next step and we may feel blind about what wants to come next.

My Life Path

In my own life, I have come to realise that my path is about healing and trying to help others. This is not something of which I was aware when I was younger. But it has become stronger and clearer to me as the years have gone by.

As a child living in Australia, I was rather dreamy and shy, and I was uncertain of what I wanted. When I moved into adolescence though, I became more determined to find out what I wished to do in life. Yet, I felt 'out of place' with other people around me. They seemed to be concerned with having a car, a job that paid well, getting drunk in the pub, competing to have the best stereo system, having a girl friend..... Something was missing from my life with them. I came to feel how frustrating it could be for me to try and do what other people wanted from me. I could never find happiness that way. It was vital for me to learn to be true to myself.

As a young adult I came across people, groups and organisations who helped me. I found that I loved working with children and helping them to express themselves and do what they wanted.

However, I still did not know in what ways I wanted to dedicate my life. I sensed that the path for me would not be a conventional one and that what I really needed to do may go beyond the normal expectations of my family. With this awareness came the growing yearning for me to make a trip away from Australia. I needed a space where I could manifest my own identity. There was a need for me to create a physical distance from those influences with which I had grown up, so they would not continue to affect me so strongly and restrict me.

From this, I feel I began my own healing journey when I left Australia. The changes that have come into my life since then go far beyond what I had imagined. Once I was away from Australia, I felt I had the freedom to explore. Initially, I found fertile ground for this exploration in living within the Findhorn Foundation in Scotland, and then later in many other communities I visited throughout Europe.

As well as learning more about the ways of the world and relationships with people, I felt the urge in me to learn about myself and to know myself from deep inside. I wanted to know about the inner mysteries of life, and I was interested to learn of this through other people's experience as well. This inner searching became very rich and exciting for me.

The more I explored the inner workings of myself and others the more fascinating this became for me. I wanted to go into this more and more. As I proceeded, my faith and belief in a Spiritual reality grew. Being occupied with these matters gave me much happiness, and I felt that at last I was going in the right direction in my life. Gradually though, there came a time of change for me, a transition, where the focus of my attention shifted from following my own desires, wanting to seek excitement and adventure for my life, to trying more to care for others and serve other's needs as much as my own Accepting this change was not always easy for me, and at times, parts of me rebelled. This was a slow process of learning extending over many years.

In my personal life, signs of this change manifested them-selves in my marriage and the birth of my children. In generating a family of my own, I had to learn to be more responsible. That helped to ground me more in life, and I needed this. From having been a 'free Spirit' doing what I liked, I had to learn to consider others in my actions, and not just me. Although this felt like a loss of freedom, this change was also very positive for me and my life felt enriched by it. Now, more than me mattered, and there were substantial elements into which I could channel my love, creativity and passion.

With my work, this change corresponded to a time when I started facilitating groups and leading personal development workshops. From there I went on to attend various trainings to become a therapist, and later on I became a healer.

Actually, I found that as I focused my attention on helping other people, this gave me joy and energy. The more I engaged in this type of work, the more satisfying it became for me. Of course, I had much to learn. But I could listen. My main challenge was for me to really put my desires to one side so I could be there for others and open myself to help meet their need. I had to gain life experience so I could really understand the needs of others. Along the way, I have made mistakes and I have been confronted with inadequacies in my own character. My life has had its crises which have been sometimes very difficult for me. But for me to try to help other people sort out their lives, I needed to apply those principles to myself as well.

In healing people with healing or therapy, I have had to learn not to expect any rewards. Many people are either uninterested, afraid or hostile when it comes to considering the importance of inner realities. Also, when people have received help, they have often moved on in their lives without offering any acknowledgement. I have had to let them go. It is not a work for forming close personal attachments, even though the love shared during inner work can be very intense. This has formed part of the learning process for me. I have had to try to give help unconditionally and let people make their own choices. Occasionally though, I have made friendships through my work and this has been a bonus for me.

As time has gone on, the 'knowing' inside of me has grown that the 'Healing Path' is the right way for me. I have gradually learnt to trust that the Universe is supporting me and not be afraid. At first this was rather shaky. But with time, I have become increasingly confident.

Chapter 2

Exploring Past Lives

The Awakening of My Interest in Reincarnation

As a child I was taught conventional Christian beliefs and values. I was told that when I died, if I was a good Christian, I would go to Heaven and be looked after by God and the Angels and Jesus. If I was not so good in my life then when I died I may end up in a place that was not so nice.

My parents attended Church regularly and I was expected to go with them or to Sunday school. Although part of me rebelled against these teachings, from an early age, I did not know any differently.

Then as a teenager, when I was introduced to the concept of reincarnation by my friend Stephen, at first I tried to dismiss these ideas because they were so strange and unfamiliar to me according to my conditioning. The idea that we could live more than one life on Earth was contrary to the beliefs that I had been taught. However, I was already very sceptical about the claims of conventional Christianity and did not feel I could be part of it. Christianity seemed to be set up like a form of exclusive club to me, where only if you conformed to a particular set of beliefs and values could you be sure of salvation. This did not seem right or true to me.

The aspect of Christianity which appealed to me though, was its Spiritual side. I longed to find a deeper meaning to my life and a sense of belonging and Spiritual purpose. With my friend Stephen and other friends, we had many discussions about this and about the inadequacies of the materialistic society around us.

Eventually, when I was 18 years old and living in Sydney, I heard a radio broadcast from the Theosophical Society and Spiritually it felt like a 'coming home'. I did not agree with everything I was told by the Theosophists. Many of them seemed to have different opinions from each other anyway. However, through the Theosophical Society, this was like a gateway for me to be able to explore different religions and beliefs about Life and Death. I could learn about various experiences people had had journeying on a Spiritual path and trying to find their own way to a God or Spirit. It was like breathing fresh air for me and I no longer felt constricted by teachings I did not believe in.

I felt that I needed to test in myself the beliefs that could be true for me, those beliefs that felt most right and filled with hope and love. After much studying and reflecting, that belief which gave me most peace and felt most true to me was a belief in reincarnation. This is what I settled on.

My Belief in Reincarnation

I came to believe that we are Spiritual beings, and that our physical body is a vehicle for our soul to express itself. Life is such a miracle and filled with marvellous mystery. I could not imagine that when we die, that this is the end of existence for us. Neither could I imagine that as souls we could experience and learn all that we need to learn on Earth in one lifetime only, especially when some people's lifetimes are very short or limited in circumstances. It seemed much more logical and true to me that we are on a continuing journey of experiencing, learning and assimilation. So, if something is unfinished for us in our experience from one lifetime on Earth, then we could have the opportunity to go further in another lifetime.

I could soon accept the Law of Karma, cause and effect, where what we projected out of ourselves through our free will would return to us in some form or other, sooner or later. It did not seem that this balancing could always be accomplished within one lifetime, but it could be part of a larger process. Thus, if someone was very cruel to others, it was maybe important for that Soul to experience what it is like to receive that cruelty, to learn from another perspective about the energy he was projecting outwards. Likewise, a person who was very loving and caring could be rewarded with love from the Universe for these actions.

It seemed that the journey of the Soul on Earth was not an easy one. Often we needed to experience suffering to gain self-awareness and compassion. Because we could easily become lost from the needs of our Soul, inner listening and forms of Spiritual practice like meditation were important. Such practices could help us connect with our Inner Self. I felt that many of the rhythms of Nature around us were like symbols to help us understand the greater meaning of life. Thus the rhythm of needing to sleep after a day's activities could have a correspondence with the life of a Soul so that after our life's effort, when we are tired and old, we would need a time of replenishment to be ready for a new life. The functions of the seasons- winter, spring, summer and autumn with their qualities seemed to have a correspondence with our journey through life and even the greater journey of our Soul towards liberation from Earthly experiences.

As I looked at a tree with its deep roots, strong trunk and branches, leaves reaching form the sky, bending with the wind, this seemed a beautiful symbol for how we needed to be as human beings in our lives. Even the animals had their qualities which we could embrace to become fully human and living out our potential. I believed there was a logic and a meaning in the ways how life functioned on our Earth to help teach us. The more in harmony with this we could be, the happier we would be.

On the other side, human beings could also be destructive. When people's personality acted from greed and self-interest rather than being aligned with their Soul purpose, then great damage and hurt could be caused. In our world there seems to have been a perpetual struggle between those forces where people have deliberately behaved selfishly and greedily rather than aspiring to do their best, concerned with greater needs than just their own. This struggle appears to be a task for each one of us to confront in ourselves as well as what is played out between people and nations.

14

One indicator of reincarnation could be with people who have come into the world with pronounced abilities of one form or another. Often our scientists attempt to explain this in terms of genes and what has been passed down through the blood line of inheritance. But this is not always so obvious. Could it be that a Soul has spent many lifetimes developing a particular talent or gift? Then, with a small opportunity, these abilities which the Soul has already gained, could be activated so that the Soul in the new body could go further in developing this.

There may be occasions where we meet somebody and feel strongly inside that we already know that person. This may be expressed as 'love at first sight' or an instant dislike. In some of those meetings it could be that through that person we are reminded of someone else with whom we shared such strong feelings. However, for some cases, one explanation may be that as Souls we are already familiar with each other through having spent time together in other lifetimes. Another possibility is that we may know this person as a Soul from our Spiritual sojourns while we have been asleep or before we were born.

People can visit places which evoke strong feelings, thoughts and memories that defy normal explanations. Could these places be where those people have lived before in another lifetime? People may be sensitive to energies that linger in a particular place without it having any personal connection to them. But I have met many people for whom reincarnation is the only explanation that satisfies them with these kinds of experiences.

The main problem I have encountered when considering whether reincarnation is true has come when I have thought about the world's population. There are certainly many more people living on our planet today than there have been at any other time in our recorded history. So, if we have all had past lives, are there enough bodies in history for this?

One theory is that some of us may have evolved from animal Souls. I tend not to believe this as I feel that the human king-doms and the animal kingdoms do not mix in this way. Another idea is that souls are tending to 'split' to experience several bodies at once. I do not accept this very easily either. What seems to be more likely to me is that Souls can 'live' on many other planes and even other worlds than our Earth plane and that there may be a substantial number of 'new' Souls on Earth at the moment, Souls who have not experienced human life on Earth previously. My belief in reincarnation is a personal belief. I do not claim to have all the answers. However, there have been many experiences that have come to me and which I have witnessed in others to support the hypothesis for me that this belief is true.

The Beginning of My Own Exploration

As my interest in reincarnation grew, a longing and curiosity arose in me that I wanted to know about my own past lives. Yet, as this desire became stronger it was hampered by messages I had received in my childhood.

From the Church, dabbling in the Occult was dangerous, and investigating experiences of reincarnation certainly came into that category. But in general, there was an attitude that it was better not to go too deeply into things with people. If we looked into ourselves too deeply we might find something unpleasant that would be difficult to live with, like a Mr. Hyde beneath our civilised respectable exteriors. The message I received as a child was that it was better to leave these aspects of life alone, and concentrate instead on getting a decent job, house and family as soon as I could.

Even some of the Theosophists were not entirely encouraging. Some of them argued that the reason we 'forgot' our previous lives through being born into this one was part of the Plan, to help us focus on our present life. Besides, what if we had killed someone in a past life, or if something horrible happened to us? Wouldn't it be wiser to leave it alone in case we became too upset, or even that it may affect our sanity? Against this came my inner urge that I wanted to know myself more deeply. I wanted to know about my Soul and its history. When I listened to my own inner promptings about this, I felt that I did not need to be afraid.

My journey away from Australia represented a break for me, almost like some Rites of Passage, and as part of my exploration, I carried the desire that I wanted to learn more about reincarnation and my own past lives.

Psychic Readings

As I embarked and went further with my inner searching, I came across people who claimed through various forms of divination to be able to tap into the 'Akashic records' and gain knowledge about people's past lives. I was very interested in this and thought that this could be a method through which I could discover about my own past.

Soon I arranged to receive some readings. From the first person with whom I did this came the revelation of a certain life it was claimed I lived in Sweden. In this life I had suffered from alcoholism. As I studied this and reflected inside myself, it felt as if this reading may be accurate. It was true that I was very sensitive about alcohol in my present life and I tended to stay right away from it. Could the residue of this past life be affecting me now?

Eagerly I asked for more readings and my imagination went to work with all the information of different lifetimes that was given to me. These other lifetime readings did not resonate with me as strongly though as the Swedish life information.

Eventually, I sought further help from other psychic readers. I thought that doing this would test the consistency of the information I was receiving. However, although there were one or two past lifetime experiences that 'rang true', there was a lot of this information which was less convincing to me. Disappointingly as well, many of the readings seemed to contradict each other.

Soon I became disillusioned with this method. Although I felt some truth could come through with talented psychic readers, there was much which felt to be misleading and inaccurate too. I felt that somehow if I was going to discover about my past lives, I needed to find a method whereby I could find this out from myself rather than being told by other people who were not necessarily so tuned into me.

Hypnotherapy

The next stage of my search led me to explore hypnosis and hypnotherapy. I wanted to learn about this, not only for my own personal reasons but also for its potential as a possible profession for me so I could help other people. There was much about hypnosis which fascinated me. I learnt about the existence of our subconscious mind. It interested me how easily it was possible to move people's normal rational critical mind to one side and thereby relate more directly to the inner consciousness of the person.

The subconscious mind was that part of us which held our beliefs, our habits, our fears and expectations. Our behaviour was very influenced by what was in our subconscious mind. With our normal consciousness we could not control this. Our subconscious mind was like a sponge which through the course of our life could absorb much input from how we interacted with our environment and what came to us from others. Typically, those experiences which had with them a high emotional content were the ones etched most deeply upon the subconscious mind.

For instance, a child who was told repeatedly that he was stupid or that he could never get anything right could grow up with this belief and expectation etched in his subconscious mind. Then as an adult he may continue to live out situations where things do not work out for him despite his best efforts to do otherwise.

This was where hypnosis could be so helpful. I was impressed how through the implanting of some suggestions or the release of some blocked feelings from within, remarkable results could be gained to help people. The beliefs we had acquired in our subconscious mind were not always the ones we wanted or needed most in our lives, and it was possible to change those beliefs.

However, I discovered through my work with others what I believed to be a wise and loving inner core to our being that did know very well what we needed to experience in our lives. So, if I could enable people to gain access to this, they could learn a lot about themselves from within. Thus, it could be an educational process to help these different parts of ourselves learn how to live together in harmony.

My attitude as I worked with people with Hypnotherapy was that I did not want to play 'God' and decide for them what was 'right' or 'wrong' for them in their lives. It seemed much more helpful for them to make these discoveries for themselves. Our sub-conscious mind, once it was pulling in the same direction as what we wanted with our personality consciousness, had a lot of power to support us in our actions. Yet our personality consciousness still had to learn what was wise for us and what we really needed to achieve and attain in our lives. Therefore a course of Hypno-therapy could be like a Spiritual quest.

So, with Hypnotherapy, I aimed to help people find a greater harmony between their outer and their inner self. It felt vital to me that my clients would feel empowered so that they were consciously agreeing to every stage of the process and thus contributing to helping themselves be healed.

Some people did not want this. They preferred to have like an inner operation such as a Doctor would perform on a patient in a surgery. There were perhaps circumstances where this approach could be necessary. But people did not learn very much if it was all done for them, and it did not help people to become more responsible for their lives, or attuned to their inner purpose.

Regression

The most interesting phenomena which I learnt about, relating to hypnosis, was regression. Using this technique, people could be guided to recall events and experiences from their past. This was more than just a constructed 'remembering' which our rational critical mind could elicit. With regression, people would be feeling and knowing and sensing their reality as if they were in this situation from the past. This process could allow people to recall details of experiences which had been long forgotten to their normal consciousness. This was how our subconscious mind stored experiences, so it seemed that everything that we had ever experienced was there somewhere within our consciousness.

As a phenomenon, regression was very convincing. Often the experiences it brought forth, especially of childhood memories, could be verified by others as being real and true memories. However, the subject's perceptions, beliefs and prejudices could colour how a particular memory was experienced. Then the therapist working with someone in regression also needed to be careful about what questions were asked. It was important not to ask questions where the subject's response would be implied in the question that was being asked. The inner consciousness of a client could be only too willing to do its best to please the therapist, and this was OK as long as what was being expected would not compromise the truth. So questions needed to be asked so that the answers would come from the inner truth of the subject concerned rather than the expectations of the therapist.

However, for many people when they were in a hypnotic state, a simple suggestion for them to regress to a time before they were born in their present life would lead to experiences where they were relating about a past life.

When I first witnessed this, I was amazed about how strong an emotional experience this could be for people. The quality of past life regression was very similar to the experience of regression to childhood. The experience was just as real for people, except that now they were experiencing themselves in another body, acting out a drama and a story from another time, feeling and sensing it as if they were there, yet knowing this was quite another reality from the life of the person they were in their normal state of consciousness. These experiences could be very surprising and unexpected for the person receiving them and also for the therapist.

Therapeutic Aspects of Regression

Through simple questioning when a person was in a hypnotic state, if the person had a particular problem, then it was possible to ask that person's inner consciousness to go inside that problem and let the person gain access to the source of this problem from the past. Then, the person's consciousness, as far as it could, would do that. So, this was a direct therapeutic application of regression, where the experiences that come to the person in response to this question could come from anywhere, including past lives.

Let me offer this hypothetical example. A woman may come for some sessions of therapy, complaining that with a specific person in her life, a man with whom she shares a close relationship, there may be instances where she gets severely depressed when she feels she does something to upset him.

As we go inside the feelings associated with this, what emerges may be an experience from a Past Life. In another time period and setting, this woman may sense herself to be closely together with a man who she loves very much. Through some action of hers, he may get very upset with her. While still suffering this upset, he may have an accident in which he dies. She then feels much guilt, fear and abandonment, and blames herself for what has happened. These feelings may want to come out strongly.

By letting her express these feelings and encouraging her to do so, she may then sense that the man from this past life is the same Soul as the man with whom she shares a close relationship in the present life. This realisation and the release of feelings involved may be enough then to lift her depression and resolve the problems she has had around him.

Of course it can be much more complicated than that, and I will discuss some of those possibilities later.

The PoweR of Invocation

There were some important lessons for me in the early stages of my career as a therapist working with past life regression.

I found that it was generally relatively easy to guide people into the experience of another lifetime. Some of the results could be quite spectacular. I even tried doing this with members of my own family. As I gained experience with this I became convinced about the reality of past lives.

Sometimes when I went inside a problem with a client there were instances where the person would spontaneously start to experience a past life without any prior mention of the subject. Clearly, many people had experiences of other lifetimes in the memory of their psyche, whether they knew it or not! Everyone was different in this respect.

With some people there seemed to be indications of only a few lifetimes from quite recent times. Others seemed to have numerous lives extending right back to very ancient times. One person who had a very clear and open access to his past lives became aware of a 2000 year gap during which time he seemed to have no lives on Earth, although there were lives before and after this time. As we explored this further, we discovered that during this time, his soul had been exploring life on other worlds away from Earth.

As I thought about it, I realised that it was quite a big step for people to open themselves to experience another lifetime. Most of us had quite enough to do just to cope with our present life without opening to more than that. For many people, such experiences were a lot for them to integrate. I learnt to respect these experiences, that they were not an exploration to be undertaken superficially.

People asked me to regress them to the lifetime before now so they could know what they were in their last life. When I tried to do this, the results were not always clear. The more I tried to manipulate people's consciousness to try and engineer some particular experience often then my work was less effective and people were not helped as much. Sometimes the lifetime immediately before the present one was not an experience that wanted to emerge very easily. In that case, trying to force it to come into a person's consciousness was not a helpful thing to do.

I learnt that I needed to trust in the energy system of the person with whom I was working. From my time living within the Findhorn Foundation I had learnt about the power of invocation. If I asked for protection and inner guidance then I would be given it. Spiritual help would be given when it was requested. It grew stronger and stronger in me that I needed to apply these principles in my work with past lives.

I felt that when a person came to me seeking to explore past lives, there was a reason for this, although it may be hidden. People sensed when they needed to do something like this and I needed to support them in their exploration. I found that I could not help everyone. Maybe some people were not ready for this kind of work with me. With others perhaps I could not attune sufficiently with them to meet their needs. But I could learn from my failures as well as my successes.

I found that if I asked the person's consciousness to choose the lifetime which that person most needed to access for their healing, rather than me trying to control it, then often the results were much better. Usually there was some teaching from the past life which presented itself that could help the person with their present life. With my intuition I needed to guide the person to access the essence of this teaching and let the person experience this as fully as possible. This was where I needed help and I needed to ask for that help from within.

I grew to know that there were two main purposes for my work with people exploring past lives. The first of these purposes was to help people to gain inner awareness. The second purpose was to help people release psychic blockages relating to the past which could be interfering in that person's life now. Paradoxically, it seemed that once people had gained the learning they needed and integrated this from a particular past life experience, then it actually helped them to live more fully in the present. If I could allow this and invoke this, then past life exploration was a means for the Spiritual Self of the person to teach the personality Self about deep inner needs that were there.

I encountered very few kings or queens or important figures in my regressions with people. What I did find were many ordinary lives with significant events where people struggled with fundamental human issues with choices that needed to be made. I needed to help people face the main elements of the dilemmas brought up by these important turning points. The person's inner consciousness could help me find them.

Often, people would encounter moments where they made mistakes or misjudgements. As they could forgive themselves for this, they could let these moments go and learn from these experiences. But letting go was not always easy and there could be quite a drama about this.

Past life experiences could be very emotional and going through a past life people may experience strong sensations through many parts of their body. Gradually I learnt not to fear this.

I knew that some therapists preferred for their clients to experience past lives in a detached way, like looking at a projector screen. So if the client came across some traumatic episode from a past life, then he wouldn't get upset. However, I found this approach to be quite inadequate.

If a person was confronted, as an example, with a past life situation of loss where the feelings of grief were somehow suppressed, then it would be important in the therapy to create a safe space so the tears could flow. To look at the situation mentally and then move on was just insufficient.

I gained confidence that if I asked for Spiritual help and protection and I was well attuned with my clients then I felt that past life experiences which presented themselves to them would be ones that they would be ready to confront. If I trusted this inner process then I could let the person experience fully what they needed to face and they would benefit from this. I needed to emotionally support my clients as best I could and ideally they needed support from others with their experiences too.

Past life experiences could reach into quite vulnerable places in people's being. They would need support to feel OK about this. Sometimes the integration process to assimilate these experiences could need considerable time.

It was important for me to try to co-operate sensitively with my client's feelings so I would not step over their boundaries about what felt safe. Sometimes time would be needed before a person was really ready to allow a painful trauma to surface.

Some time ago I had a young woman come to me with a problem needing regression. She went with her consciousness to a life where she was a young girl helping an older woman make herbal mixtures as medicine for people. She seemed happy in this life. I asked her to go forward in time to find out what happened next. She went blank. I continued to try to move the story of her life forward. Finally, an experience came to her where she felt herself moving through a tunnel very quickly. She had died and was leaving her body. I persuaded her to look back, and the house where she lived with this old woman had been flattened. Her body was in the midst of it.

I knew then that there had been a trauma around this death. Her consciousness had not wanted to face this, but had skipped over it instead. Before proceeding any further, I checked with my client, telling her what I supposed to be there. She told me that she felt it was enough what she had already done. So we left it at this. She can come to me when she feels ready to go further with that. In the meantime I trust that she will be guided to know when that time is right, and that she will have the courage to respond to that. However, I knew that in this instance, if I had tried to proceed without her permission, it would have been inappropriate. Later though, she shared with me how useful the session had been for her.

The Psychic Body

In completing a training of Past Life Therapy with Dr. Roger Woolger I learnt many more aspects about working with Past Lives.

I realised that for us as human beings there was a fundamental need and wish from within for us to be whole and to feel united with ourselves. This meant that our Spiritual Self wanted to be functioning in harmony with the different facets of our personality Self as one. However, it seemed very rare for people to be actually doing this. I noticed in myself as well as others how different parts of the personality were often struggling and even pulling in different directions. It was not an easy task to find inner peace. This picture became even more complicated when bringing in Past Lives.

For instance, from a traumatic past life a person may act in a way to decide that 'I can never forgive myself for that'. Such a belief and the energy of feelings attached to it could lead to one self-punishing lifetime after another. This thought would just not go together with other thoughts from that person's soul where he wishes to be happy and successful. Such a situation may lead to an inner life for the person in his present life that is like a battle, with one part wanting to be happy and successful and the other part wanting to under-mine that all the time.

Sometimes traumas could result in some essential part of people's nature being split off from the rest of them. As an example, a person who is abused by a man in childhood or in a past life may decide 'I'll never feel safe to trust a man again'. This part of the person then, the part which is open, innocent and trusting may be removed from the functioning personality and not express itself anymore. Our thoughts and inner decisions can make such a difference for us.

In these cases, the most healing thing to help may be to access those trapped feelings and inner decisions from memories and let them come to the surface. The thoughts and decisions from those past times may not be appropriate any more, and once this is acknowledged and the withheld emotions brought into the open, then the person can be more free and whole.

What happened in the past cannot hurt us anymore unless we hold it inside and let it do so.

Once there has been a 'split' or a trauma to cause a disturbance in what would otherwise be a natural harmony between the Spiritual and personality Self, then this usually leaves a wound in the psychic body of the person. This wound could then have a particular association with some part of the physical body. For instance, a person who in their past felt rejected in love and unworthy to be loved, may find it difficult to express love and this may be felt as a tension around the heart area of the body.

I learnt that there were many ways of accessing past lives besides using formal hypnosis. Once people become sensitive to their psychic bodies the memories of past lives can emerge spontaneously in many different ways.

By breathing into the place in the body where the wound is situated, this can quite quickly and dramatically bring associated thoughts, feelings and memories to the surface. By applying the breath to these areas it would be acknowledging what is there and giving permission to open the channels to gain access to those parts of the self that need healing. Our physical body then could be the mode for the release of trapped energies. Because these energies belong to the past and not the present, it is quite safe to let them express themselves through our body now to let them go.

Even an experience like a gruesome death relived from the past could be felt and sensed in full bodily and emotional detail. It does not need to hurt the person going through this. In fact some people would find this an enjoyable and exhilarating experience! The aim would be to release our attachments to the past. Our past has contributed through our inner growth to where we are now. But where aspects of our past are frozen or interfering with our present self they need to be freed and the energy withheld released for us to find greater wholeness.

Again, my main lessons with this were to learn to know and trust the psychic body and Spiritual Self of people. If I could learn co-operate and support people with this when I was wanting to help them, then the healing that was needed would take place.

Meeting My Own Past Lives

As I developed my work as a therapist, I was fascinated by what experiences lived inside of people.

However, I still had my quest to uncover knowledge of my own past lives. Hence, I looked to find someone who would be able to regress me. Sporadically, I made a few attempts with different people and achieved quite inconclusive results. Sadly, I doubted whether I really had the ability to be a good subject. I had heard it said of therapists that oftentimes they could be useful at helping other people but not so easily able to receive help themselves. I did not want to be like that.

Through my investigations it became clear to me that most regression processes were very biased towards visualisation and seeing inwardly. In my meditations and when I was in a hypnosis state I would hardly see anything. This mode of operating did not suit me. What I could do more easily was to sense the tone of an experience rather than see it.

Just when I was beginning to despair that I would never succeed with this, I met Moira. Now, Moira was a much more lively personality than me. To begin, I think that we were quite wary of each other. However, because Moira had experience of working with past lives and had spent time in Australia, this brought us together. We both wanted to explore our past lives, so we set up an exchange.

Included as one of Moira's many abilities, she had a strong psychic gift. She was also in communion with her Spiritual guide who used to teach people and offer personal guidance. Moira's psychic gift proved to be very helpful for me.

At the beginning, when it was my turn to be regressed and she led me into a meditative state or a light trance, I was only aware of the vaguest of sensations in response to her questions. So much did I feel lacking in confidence that I did not feel able to do it at all. Yet Moira was very patient with me. She gently encouraged me and gradually I dared to express what I sensed was happening. I came to trust her.

Moira was able to follow what I experienced with her psychic gift. She confirmed to me that what I conveyed was accurate. This gave an enormous boost to my confidence. It helped me to believe that maybe I could do it.

Gradually the impressions I was getting in my sessions became stronger and more detailed. I had to learn to go with what was happening for me. The more I did that, the better it worked. Yet, I still did not see very much. I had to rely more on a sense of feelings or the tone of a situation, express that and let my body feel that. As the process unfolded, I felt considerably surprised by what emerged. The lives that I was able to access with Moira generally felt much more real and true to me than what I had been told in Psychic readings. Because I was now going through my own process to explore my past lives it helped me to feel greater compassion for others who would go through their past lives with me.

These sessions of exchange with Moira became very precious to me. So, I was very sad, when six months after we started, Moira made a sudden decision that she needed to go to Australia. It was hard for me to let her go.

The lives I accessed with Moira brought together a mixture of different teachings and learning for me. Together, we spent many hours sharing and processing.

Not all of the lives that I accessed were lives of which I could feel proud. I realised that our souls want to find their way through the dark side of human nature as well as the light. What could be most difficult, was to admit to an experience where I felt I had done wrong. If I had been violent to someone, left someone I loved, avoided some important responsibility or some other wrong doing, it could be very hard to come to terms with that. It was easier in some ways to be a victim where at least it would be possible to blame someone else . But there were situations where I had made mistakes, where I needed to let go and make up for it now. It was not always possible to find easy solutions. Sometimes, with experiences I accessed of my past lives I needed a lot of contemplation to adjust to what had happened and what I may have done.

I learnt that I had done healing and therapeutic work with people in the past. This was not the first time. There were resources from these experiences that I could use to help me now. Although with some of these lives I felt that I had failed or been defeated, the flame of determination in me wanted to go further this time.

Later on, I went through more past life experiences while training with Roger Woolger. These experiences tended to be more emotional and cathartic, but were also helpful. Working with him, I learnt more to allow my body to be an organism to facilitate emotional and psychic release. For instance, if I was going through a Past Life experience and my body wanted to shake, I needed to let it shake until it did not want to shake any more. If thoughts and feelings came to me while this was going on, I had to let those thoughts and feelings out. It could feel quite peculiar at times, with my body wanting to do this or that and just letting it happen.

Sometimes I wondered if my past life experiences were just in my imagination. I recognised that they were revealed to me through the imaginative faculty of my mind. But from wherever they originated, I came to respect these experiences because they had a lot to teach me. Finally I reached a point where I felt I had done enough exploration of my own lives. I could sense there are more there that could be explored, and I could gain more detail from those with which I have already made contact. However I did not want my seeking past lives to become addictive, like wanting an emotional 'fix'. I felt that this work was something very precious and sensitive. At the right time, when there was a real need, this work could be very healing.

Leading a Past Life Session

Each past life session can be very different and I believe that there can be no formula for working with past lives that will be satisfactory for all cases. However, I would like to suggest some guidelines for working with people with past lives that I have found helpful.

Firstly, when people enter a past life, it may appear to them like watching or being part of a still frame. The image of this could be quite vague. This then needs to be focused and the person needs to be helped to be connected with the body and being of the past life personality as much as possible. This is really a process of 'grounding' the person in the past life.

To achieve this, questions can be asked about clothes that are being worn, what the ground is like under the feet, about the body- male or female, big-small. Then the person can be asked to relate to the surroundings, whether inside or outside, with others or alone, whether the temperature is hot or cold. Then more can be asked about the person's relationship with that which is around him. What is he doing? If there is some aspect of the scene that draws his attention, then questions need to be asked about that, to go with the energy of what is happening.

Finally, once a sense of identification has been established with the past life character, it is possible to ask the story of this life to go into motion, asking 'What happens next?'

It is much better if the person can really feel themselves and sense themselves living out this life from the past, rather than viewing it in a rather detached way. However, this cannot be forced and allowances need to be made for what is possible for the person concerned. Sometimes if a person is unable to connect fully with the past life character, there may be some tension or numbness in the body indicating some aspect of the experience where there is fear or hidden emotions. By breathing into these parts of the body may help get the process moving.

People going through past life experiences do not need to lose connection with their present life Self. The present life Self is voluntarily allowing the psychic/emotional experiences of the past life to come into consciousness. I feel that it is important for the process to go ahead, and that they are aware of what is happening at all times. Then if something feels too much they can say 'no' and stop the process as well as feeling some sense of control. With this approach people can be aware of a kind of dual consciousness where they know their present life body is sitting or lying down in the therapy room with their therapist, while at the same time they are allowing this inner experience of a past life to fill them.

It is quite common that the moment in the past life where the person enters the experience is quite a crucial moment although this may not be obvious at first. If it is difficult to move the story forward this may be a sign that the person is not ready to face fully whatever comes next. In this case, I usually ask the person to go back earlier to fill out details of the story of how the person got to that point. Sometimes much patience may be needed, especially in the early stages, as necessary details are gathered.

Then by asking the inner consciousness of the person to go to significant and important moments in the life, this will generally happen. It may need time before the main thrust of what the life is about emerges. But to ask questions to establish what are the person's strong emotional attachments and concerns, it is possible by going through the main moments of the life to find out what happens with those. The drama around this is usually where the main teachings or lessons of the life are held.

Very often, there is some unfinished or unresolved aspect to the past life, the facet of the life where the energy of this may have carried over into the present life. I have found that it is best to really allow the person to experience this as fully as possible - not to try and fix it up and make it better straight away. The truth needs to be faced in this instance, if the person is able to do that.

It is also important to try to bring out the inner feelings of the past life character. Questions like 'What are you really feeling that you are not saying?' may help the person to unburden himself of withheld feelings and decisions. Very often there can be an inner and outer clash between the person's actions and how he feels about this from inside. This is where guilt, shame and secret regrets may need help to be acknowledged.

Then, it is also important generally for the person to go through the experience of dying in that past life. The actual process of dying may be quite difficult or painful especially if the past life personality is resisting it. It is sometimes this moment where the person will be most aware of the achievements of the past life or the failures. So there can be a lot of trapped energy and emotions around the dying process. But by asking the consciousness of the person to go right through what happens until it is all over, or until after the last breath, this gives permission for that dying experience to come through and for the person to experience what it is like to die.

Usually, once the person has died the feelings are much more peaceful. People may find themselves going up to the light or floating around the body. I usually ask the person to refer to the body and how he feels to be leaving that body. Often death can be like a welcome release.

In the Spirit world following death, much healing can be achieved. It may be possible to meet wise Spiritual beings who can shed light upon the purpose and meaning of the life, or provide comfort where necessary. It may also be possible here to confront difficult unresolved conflicts or meet people with whom there are things to be worked out. It is important in this Spirit world to encourage as much communication as possible. The Spiritual realm is the place where people can gain perspective about that life they lived.

Then questions can be asked linking the past life with the present, asking the consciousness of the person to help him to learn how they are related.

There may be parts of the past life that need to be gone through again to complete a catharsis process and to allow hidden feelings and layers to surface.

To finish a session I often ask the consciousness to suggest to the person an experience that would be very healing. The result is usually much better than any idea I could have managed.

Then after a session I like to talk with my client, check how he is feeling and go over important issues that seemed to emerge. I generally suggest for my clients to write down their own recollection of the past life soon after the session has ended. This can help with the integration process and serves as a conscious acknowledgement, so the person can let the process go. Sometimes, follow up sessions can be useful and helpful but I leave this for the person concerned.
I recommend that for anyone wanting to lead people through Past Life sessions that you invest in a thorough training for this kind of work before venturing too far with trying this out on others.

At the completion of a session it is important to allow space to bring people fully back into their present life body, and as much as possible to round out issues from the experience so that these will not then be coming up after it is all over. With this in mind, it is not always possible to confine a past life session to a neat time frame. Some sessions need longer than others and it is not always possible to anticipate this in advance.

In the following chapters I will present some case studies and further explanations of various aspects of this work.

Chapter 3

Janice and Her Fear of Spiders

Janice's Problem

Janice was in nearly all respects a happy, well-adjusted young adult. She had a good and stable relationship with her boyfriend. Also she had a close relationship with her mother and father plus a satisfying social life. She enjoyed the job she was doing and was generally pleased with the way her life was going. When I enquired about her past there were no major traumas, and apart from a couple of moves of residence and some bullying from her early years in secondary school, she had had a happy upbringing.

There was only one main problem, a problem that others may not regard as significant. However, for her, this problem caused much anxiety and disquiet from within her. And it was getting worse. Janice was afraid of spiders.

With all other animals she felt OK, but with spiders she could not cope with them. If she sensed there was a spider around, she would do all she could to avoid it. When she saw a spider, she would sometimes be so fixated that she felt unable to move until the spider was gone. With spiders in her vicinity, her heart would race, the adrenaline inside her would pump. She could feel sick in her stomach. If there was somebody with a spider she could really feel violent towards that person.

Janice felt that this fear was starting to rule her life. It caused her panic and she was becoming very anxious about going into situations where there may be spiders. This was especially difficult concerning visiting her parents.

She needed to stay with her parents quite often because of her work. Also though, she wanted to spend time with them because she felt close to them. But their house bordered onto a field. With the change of the season, particularly at the end of summer, the spiders would come into the house. She couldn't keep them away. This was terrible for her.

From the time she decided she needed help with this, it took her six months to come and see me. She had never had hypnosis and she was rather anxious about what it may bring out.

As we talked, I tried to reassure her. But when I explored her life history with her, I could find no traces of where this phobia may have come to her. She remembered that she had been anxious of spiders even as a child. There was no incident where she could remember a spider having harmed her or attacked her in any way.

I discussed with her that if there was a specific event that had triggered the phobia then her subconscious mind would be aware of that, and we could ask her subconscious mind to bring this memory with its associated feelings to the surface.

Janice was willing to do this. She knew that her fears were irrational, and she wanted to release them if it was at all possible. She trusted me.

Before we started, I asked about her religious background. She told me that she had no particular religious beliefs and she did not adhere to any specific theories about life and death. She was happily absorbed in her life as a young woman and had no great concern for these larger questions of life's mysteries.

Finding the Source of Her Problem

In working with Janice, I decided that the best first step would be to locate if we could, the origins of the phobia.

Janice proved to be a good hypnotic subject, although she continued to be aware with her own thoughts of what she was experiencing right through the process.

I asked her inner consciousness to select one finger to rise as a 'yes' indicator and another as a 'no' indicator. Her fingers gave a clear response to this question. I then suggested for her inner consciousness to recall her experience at different ages in her life, asking the question 'Are you afraid of spiders at this age?'

As I regressed her with this question right back through the different stages of her life - from age 20, 15, 10, 5, 4, 3, 2, 1, ..., her fingers kept giving a clear affirmative response. I asked the question for her first year of life, and then for when she was in her Mother's womb - still 'yes'. So finally I asked from her experience before her present life began, is this when the phobia began?

Her finger remained still. But her body began to feel very heavy as if she could not move it. Only her head and neck remained mobile. The rest of her body was like a dead weight. Everywhere was dark. The temperature was cold. Her arms felt exposed and they were cold. My intuition told me that she had entered the experience of a past life.

I instructed her consciousness to go back a little earlier from this, when things were still all right. Her body from the neck down continued to feel like a dead weight. However, now she could see the sun. She was outside in a garden. A boy was nearby playing. It emerged that she was a young woman in a wicker wheel chair sitting under a tree. She was paralysed from the neck down.

As I uncovered her story, she was living in Victorian England. Her name was Sarah. She lived in a well-to-do house with servants taking care of her basic needs. Her Father was her guardian. Her Mother it seemed, may have died at around the time of her birth. Sarah had not been born paralysed but had caused this to herself through a horse riding accident when she was a young girl. Now as a young woman she was accepting her circumstances as best she could.

When I asked her consciousness to move to the incident concerning the spider, it seemed that one day she was sitting in the sitting room on her own. A big black spider with hairs on its legs crawled onto her lap. Then it kept crawling across and up, coming right up her neck towards her face. Of course, being paralysed, she could do nothing about it. The spider caused absolute terror. She screamed, shouting for help. Finally when help did arrive she was very badly shaken and scared by the experience.

She did not live so long after that, and died with the fear of the spider, the utter feelings of powerlessness of not being able to move the spider away or do anything to help herself in that situation.

Emotionally, Janice had lived right through Sarah's experience. I helped her to experience that she as Janice was no longer paralysed. Any spider now crawling about her, she could move it away and didn't need to be afraid.

Letting Go and Moving On

When we met for our second session Janice told me how shocked and surprised she had been by what emerged in the first session. She had not believed in past lives and certainly had not expected something like that to come to the surface. But she could not deny what her own consciousness had produced for her. She recalled how during the session there had been part of her wanting to fight and dismiss what she was experiencing. But she admitted that it was not within her normal imagination to come up with such a story. After talking it through, she could accept, that at least for her psyche, this past life experience was the source of her phobia about spiders. As she accepted this, it would now be possible to take steps to let this go, to put it in the past and begin a new life free of this fear.

In hypnosis, I asked all the different parts of her to come together and make a decision to be willing to let go of this fear. The fear was based on an experience from the past when she was paralysed. She was not paralysed any more. Besides, spiders were little creatures, mainly afraid of human beings. They could not harm her. Janice accomplished this and felt the fear burning up in a fire. I then got her to continue to affirm that she liked spiders. She could imagine them crawling on her hands. She could take them off herself if she wished. Then she could also imagine herself enjoying the rooms of her parent's home, feeling quite calm to be there.

I decided to provide one test for Janice. I told her about the spider in my therapy room, the one that lived under the chest at the end of the room. Momentarily, Janice felt uncomfort-able. She said to me she felt as if she was paralysed! It was clear where this was coming from. I suggested for her to move her arms and hands. As she realised that she was not really paralysed the fear eased away. She felt much more relaxed.

At the end of this session she could say that she liked spiders, and know that she felt quite happy about that. She was ready for a new life, free from this fear.

Chapter 4

The Case of Edith

Beginnings

My work with Edith began during an Inner Child workshop I was leading. It was a particularly gruelling and intensive workshop with much emotion and cathartic releasing. The group was lively too, with some strong personalities making their presence felt.

During a session of the workshop, one of the men was involved in a process where he was hitting a cushion with a long stick. This enactment was relating to some earlier incident in his life, and was linked to feelings of anger. However, although he was hitting the cushions with his stick rather violently, he was making light of it as if he had no strong feelings about it at all. There was a very visible contradiction here. I wished I could find a way to help him show what he was really feeling inside. I continued to concentrate upon this with him for some time until I noticed Edith.

Edith was very sensitive around men's anger. She could not cope with it very well. Now she had shrunk back into a corner. There she sat huddled with her arms around her knees, instinctively trying to protect herself, and hold herself still. Her skin was pale and she was shivering. She appeared fairly oblivious to what was going on around her and had gone into some form of frozen state. Her mind was somewhere else.

It was not a very convenient moment for me to begin an extended process with Edith. However, I had to find a way to help her out of this. Others in the group were looking on feeling concerned. I tried to communicate with her, and she could just about answer my questions after I repeated them a few times.

She seemed to feel herself to be at school. She'd been hit by her teacher and sent to the corner. All the other children could see her there. She did not want them to see her like this. She felt very frightened. I tried to detach her from the situation, reassuring her that she was not in the school anymore; she was in the room with all of us. But her consciousness would not shift forward into the present. Even with suggestions that she was safe now and she did not need to feel frightened anymore, Edith remained where she was sitting, frozen. I wondered what I could do to bring her out of this.

With Julian, one of her friends, we tried to move her and get her to stand up, to take her physically away from that corner. By continuing to reassure her, she tried to co-operate with us. Slowly she got to her feet. We led her further and further into the room.

Suddenly, her resistance became tighter. She became very emotional, agitated and upset. She could not believe when we told her she was safe. She could not trust men. They were telling her it was all right, but it was not all right. They were leading her to something really horrible and she did not want it. There was a crowd all around making an ugly noise. They were accusing her of being a witch. They were taunting her and tormenting her...

I had to think quickly. Edith had regressed into a past life. Firmly, I told her that she was experiencing the memory of a past life. We could not deal with it now. However, she could come and see me afterwards, privately, for some sessions and we could work through this past life then. She needed to return to our group now in her present life and we could work out the past life later.

It worked. Edith slowly emerged into her present day self. She was shaken and very surprised. We had not talked about past lives during the course of the workshop. It was completely new for her to have any experience of this sort come into her consciousness. Also, she had not been seeking in any way consciously to invoke past life memories. Her concern had been to heal her Inner Child. So this experience for her was a revelation.

For sometime afterwards, I had to explain to Edith about Past Life Therapy, and how it may be able to help. I told her that in an Inner Child workshop, it was inappropriate for me to start to deal with Past Life material. Otherwise, it would just start to invoke past life experiences in others, too. So, if she wanted to follow it up, she could contact me after the workshop. She did.

Edith's Present Life

About three months later, Edith travelled to see me for some sessions. She brought her friend Julian with her for support. It was obvious that she felt quite tense and nervous about what was to come. But she was clear that she wanted to go through with it.

To begin I needed to know more about Edith's present life background. It was important to establish present patterns in her life that may be influenced from the past.

As she talked more about her life, it was clear the Edith had many problems. Most of her life she had tried to hide these problems from everyone else. But now she could not do that any more.

Edith was the oldest child in her family. When her parents split up, she found herself in the caretaker role. Everyone in the family wanted her support. But there was no one to help her with the inner pain and turmoil she was experiencing. As she grew older, Edith became more and more driven to want to help the suffering and the underprivileged in the world. However, because she was not facing her own feelings inside, the pain that she was carrying took on other forms.

For a time, she struggled with bulimia and anorexia. By dedicating herself utterly to try to help others, she would not need to think about herself. Also she was intelligent and had successfully completed three university degrees. She went to America to help with people who had AIDS. For a year she was a hospital chaplain, ministering to the sick and dying. Many of the friends she made died. But this did not deter her in her crusade. Edith felt very attracted to all those who were outcast. Her passion was to reform establishments that did not care for those in need sufficiently.

On those occasions when she did give some space to her own thoughts and feelings about herself, she tended to feel very unhappy, and more than once she had contemplated ending her own life. She rationalised though that it was selfish to think of herself. There were always others much more in need than her. She had to help them all she could.

An event happened then to completely take away Edith's drive and purpose. Her younger brother, Graham, died. He had committed suicide by inhaling car fumes while in the Grand Canyon. Edith felt devastated. This was too close to home. She could not ignore her own feelings about this. Her life felt as if it was crumbling to pieces.
For so long she had been caring for the ill and the needy, spending all her time and energy on those causes. And with her energies so focused in that direction, she had not even given space to notice what was happening to her own brother.

Edith had felt very close to Graham and felt tremendous guilt that she had been unable to save him. With Graham's death, Edith went into deep depression. She felt overwhelming sadness and hopelessness for all the suffering in the world. It seemed not fair! But she also felt tremendously alone. Who would help her? Now she could no longer escape from confronting her own feelings towards herself and her own emotional needs. The wall protecting her from feeling her own vulnerability had to come down. In relationships, Edith had found it very difficult to open herself to feel intimacy and to trust anyone. But from this moment when Graham died, Edith knew that she needed to either give and allow some attention and love for herself, and with this, face the feelings inside her so she could become stronger - or else to die too!

The Sessions

After the initial interview, Edith and I met for a series of seven Past life sessions over a concentrated short space of time. Each session, except for the last one, was extended and emotionally gruelling for all of us there. Edith's friend, Julian, was also present for the sessions. He wanted to be available to offer Edith support throughout the process.

All the sessions were devoted to this one particular life - the life where she as her past life character, was accused of being a witch. Through the trauma of that life, she held suppressed experiences, emotions, thoughts and beliefs in her psychic body. It needed time and patience to let this come to consciousness and express itself so she could become free of it. From the Inner Child workshop where she had gone into such a deeply frozen state, it seemed there was much fear blocking the expression of what she was feeling inside. She would need to feel safe and strong enough to let this come out.

We worked in my outside room where Edith would lie on a mattress during our sessions. Often her body would be writhing around, shaking or showing other visible signs of torment. At other times her body was fairly still. I managed to record the sessions through hand written notes. With this, I was able to take note of nearly everything she said. Some key sentences were repeated a number of times and what she told was often interspersed with much emotional release.

In the following account, I will include some direct excerpts of much of what she related with some additional commentaries and explanations.

Session 1

The memory of her experience from the Inner Child workshop was still very fresh for Edith. However, rather than specifically directing her consciousness into that past life, we decided to leave it open and I suggested for her inner consciousness to go where it needed to go for healing. It is little surprise then that Edith's consciousness did indeed anyway start to reveal other moments from this particular past life.

Passing through a symbolic door, she was aware of standing on dark earth. Her feet were bare and felt cold. She was wearing a bodice, skirt and a blouse and carrying a basket with her. She felt herself to be a young woman walking through woods, collecting plants, feeling happy and alive. It becomes clear that she is collecting these plants for potions and for healing.

Later, she is in a cottage by a fire. She is with two other women. One is older and she is her teacher. Through this teacher, she's been learning wisdom, learning about plants and healing, about fire and the power of fire. With the teaching she's received, the fire is very important. For her, the fire has its own language. And the power of fire is used for transforming and for healing. All the plants and substances around her have their energy that is alive and her teacher helps her to feel the knowledge of this coming to life. Together, they worship the power and love of the Goddess as the great provider.

Through her teacher she has learnt about the energies of colour - the colours of different pain and wounds, colours that heal wounds and how fire changes the colours of plants and mixes them for making potions. Smells and sounds connected to stones are also important. She feels happy and fulfiled learning with this old woman.

There is a room at the back of the cottage, a secret room. This is where the old woman does her healing. The old woman is teaching a group of women the Arts of Healing. They are all close and sometimes engage in rituals together. Edith, as her past life Self, often assists the old woman when she works in this secret room.

On one occasion, she is helping the old woman to heal a man who is in a lot of pain. He has a deep wound in his arm. They are trying to put a poultice on his arm and get him to swallow a potion, a dark red potion.

The man is resisting though, and he is shouting and screaming. He is very frightened and unsure if he can trust the women.

A male friend of his has brought him. She knows that he'll lose the arm unless he accepts their help. This friend is waiting outside on watch. Somehow, there seems to be some danger. Suddenly he comes in. Other men are coming. The man receiving treatment will have to be quiet. They don't want to be discovered. But the wounded man is not able to be quiet. He keeps moaning. So his friend hits him to make him be quiet. They hope the men outside have not heard. These men come into the cottage. They don't see anything at first because the room is hidden. There is a small peephole from where she is able to watch the men in the next room. But then the men start tearing everything up. They can see the potions. Edith becomes very emotional....

'....I feel frightened......They're going to find us....They'll kill us .....don't understand...get caught...'

Edith is soon too distraught to continue. I want to give space for the story to unfold at a pace with which she can cope. So, after she calms down a little, I ask her to recall when she first met the old woman. Her demeanour changes and softens, becoming much more peaceful.

'......as a child by water....old woman puts her hand on my head - very hot....She kisses me on the head....There's a white light.....colours....so much happiness....'

Shortly afterwards I finish the session with this. It feels important to me to allow Edith to experience the light as well as the darkness when she goes through this Past Life.

Later Edith shared with me how in these first two sessions to the earlier stages of the past life, she could see colours much more vividly than normal. It was as though her past life Self had a natural ability to perceive what was around her with a psychic awareness that was far beyond what she could manage as Edith. These colours were very beautiful and moving for her to experience.

46

Session 2

As we met to continue, Edith felt very apprehensive about going further into the scene where they were discovered in the secret room. So I suggested for us to explore experiences from earlier in the life to build up a fuller picture of her character and how her life developed. This is what we agreed to do.

When she had once again entered into the past life experience, I asked her for her name. She told me that she was Antonia.

As Antonia, her life was full of contrasts. In one aspect, she was very sensitive to energies. Antonia enjoyed the freedom and richness of being outdoors. She loved animals and plants and felt a strong contact with the wolves. It was as though she shared a psychic link which seemed to her like a green light energy with the wolves. They were her friends. Also there were people who were important to her. There was a little boy who seemed to be her brother. She felt very protective towards him. There were a group of women with whom she was learning the Healing. There were men too, learning in different ways. Sometimes there were meetings and occasions for the men and women to come together. They were all closely bonded. This was very satisfying for Antonia.

In another aspect though, her mother was a woman of the Church. The Church was powerful and allied to the Castle. The authority of the Church and Castle generated much fear among the people at large. Representatives of the Church were deeply suspicious of activities like the kind of healing and rituals which Antonia enjoyed. So she had to keep these important elements of her life hidden from these forces. It was not easy.

From gathering this information, I led Antonia forward to the most important event leading up to the experience where they were discovered in the secret room. She started.

'I am with the old woman....There's something wrong with the baby inside the mother....It won't come out....The woman's in a lot of pain....We try to give her potions that usually help....It doesn't

seem to work....Someone wants to get the Priest....The Priest doesn't like herbs....She doesn't need that....The Priest doesn't know anything about birth....We're frightened that she will die....The woman's having trouble breathing....She's in a lot of pain....She's been hurt before by her husband....I'm doing what the old woman tells me....We're in her house....There are four of us taking care of her...the baby won't come out....It's caught.....'

(Edith's body is getting more and more agitated.)

'We try to pull it out....She can't breathe....She's screaming....The baby's going to die.....If the baby doesn't come out it will die....The baby's not going to live....The woman screams...She's screaming....'

(Edith's body gets very emotional, writhing about.)

'She dies....I feel really frightened....The father of the child...he wanted the Priest...The mother wanted us....He doesn't like us....He thinks we're dangerous....The baby that's dying is a boy....He forced the woman to have sex before the baby came....I feel very angry....He wants to say it is her fault for dying and the baby dying but it is his fault....If he loved his wife, if he wasn't so frightened of us, his wife would have lived...He's a powerful man...He was an enemy already....'

Edith's consciousness shifts quickly to another scene a little while later.

'He grabs me, shakes me to the ground....He has other men with him...So I can't fight back....He accuses me of killing his wife....There's nothing I can do....'

It seems that he sexually assaults her, exerting his power over her. Edith's body shakes while releasing fear. We finish this session here. Edith needs a break.

Session 3

Edith is now prepared to proceed and face the experience of what happens when Antonia is discovered in the room. She knows this may be painful and difficult. But she wants to be able to release the core limiting beliefs and the trapped emotions connected with this life. I undertake to support and to use various psychotherapeutic body techniques to help express mental and emotional energies that are being held within, associated with different places in her body.

We enter into the experience of the life at the point where she and the old woman are trying to help the injured man in the Healing room. Nearly all the words she says are filled with emotions and connected with much body movement. To my questions, she relates

'The man is very frightened....frightened of us....He's shouting at us...He's saying ëDon't touch. Get your hands off me'....I'm focusing on the old woman....She's telling me what to do....I'm feeling angry with the man....'

I ask her what she is wanting to say to him? She replies...

'We're trying to heal you. Why are you fighting us?....We're in danger helping you....It's not safe....They'll find us....'

Suddenly Edith tells how she experiences blackness rushing through her very fast. Her body shudders. I try to encourage her to express aloud what she as Antonia is feeling inside. She continues...

'Stop it....Stop it....Stop it....My head's sore....It's not safe....I should get out of here...It's not worth it....we need to go....This man's not worth it....He doesn't want what we have to give him....It's not like it used to be....She doesn't understand either.'

(Antonia is referring to the old woman.)

'It's not safe anymore...I feel pounding in my stomach....She doesn't understand these men....They don't respect anyone....'

Edith's voice is trembling with emotion. These are thoughts and emotions from Antonia's inner being that she never expressed openly at the time. She goes on.

'The man outside comes running in....He's frightened....He says they're coming....The man we're trying to help is making a lot of noise....The other man hits him and knocks him out....The men are coming in....They're shouting everywhere....pulling things apart...very angry....very frightening....I don't know if they've heard him or not....I'm frightened they'll find us....The man wakes up....he makes a noise.   There's a man from outside says "Over there"....I'm very frightened....I can't understand why the fire won't come....I'm getting agitated with the old woman....Why doesn't she come?....'

(Antonia is now referring to the protective Goddess.)

'We need her...She should be here....I don't understand....They are going to get us....The old woman is very calm....I don't understand why she is not doing something....

'Now they're coming in....everywhere....really rough....So many of them....So fast....I try to leave my body....These men are touching me....all over me....hands all over me....They're ripping at me....'

Edith's body is moving frantically....

'They are all shouting....They think it's funny....I don't even see them cutting the old woman's throat....I'm all on my own...I didn't want them to touch me....They won't stop touching me....I can't get out of my body....Can't leave it....I'm too frightened to do anything....I bite one of them....they hurt me more....They hold me down ....It's horrible....I can't do anything.....I want to keep them out...I don't want them near me....'

Edith now cries and sobs uncontrollably.

'I can't believe it....I can't do anything because they're holding my arms and legs....I've got to get out of here....They can't do this to me .....I don't know where she's gone...'

Antonia is again referring to the Goddess.

'This can't happen to me...no...no...no...no....I'm held down....It's disgusting....they're disgusting ....Oh God....no....no....no....no.... They can't do this to me....They're ripping me apart....They're disgusting men....Oh God....I know some of these men....They have wives....I know them....'

I ask what she wants to say to them

'They're filthy, filthy hypocrites....my body can't take this....It's too much....'

Something in Antonia is giving up.

'I should be dead....I knew we should have gone away....There's nothing else they can do to me now....I'm under the table...There's nothing to do....I don't understand why she's gone...'

Antonia's passion has subsided. Edith just sobs for a long while, letting go lots of emotion.

However it doesn't end there. The degradation continues. She's taken and dragged away, put in a cell. Then some men come to get her again.

'I'm really so sore...It's cold....walls are all damp....I'm all alone....I don't understand where everyone's gone....all sticky....can hear noises coming....It's men....They're laughing....They say they are taking me for a special treat....one of them is touching me again....They think it is very funny....so tired...can't take anymore....doesn't feel like my body they're touching....I can hear other women screaming....so frightened...

'They're taking me into another room....men disgust me ....I don't want them to see that...I don't want them to see me. They can't

hurt me anymore....dark room....flames around the walls....They can't do anything else to me....I don't know....I don't know....They're asking me questions....I don't know the answers....I don't know....They do something to me...no...no...no...'
I ask what they do?

'They kick me...hit me....bang my head on the wall....They have a hot thing....They threaten me with it....I don't know what they want to know....I want to go somewhere else...I don't want to be here....I see flickering lights....One of them is the woman's husband, the one who died....I don't know....They're shouting...I can't hear....They did something to me so I can't lift my hand....I can't feel anything...left hand....'

By now Antonia is quite delirious. Edith too is quite exhausted. She doesn't have energy for more recall or to be able to absorb more information or even to release any more emotion. In a fairly deadened way she relates how she is taken back to her cell. Then afterwards, she is dragged again out into the open and led to a hole in the ground where she is dumped and left alone.

To finish the session, I ask for her consciousness to experience a healing place within that can help replenish her energies....She says...

'Yellow, golden...like a cave....go in cave....There's an old man who holds me...'

This experience is indeed healing for her, and her body at last becomes more peaceful and her energy system settles down.

There is a strange quiet in the room when this is over. I know now why Edith was so reluctant to go on from the scene in the secret room. I feel she has shown a lot of courage to go through that. I am aware of how little intervention I needed to make during this session. It all came gushing to the surface, as if it had been waiting to do so.

I ask Edith about what happened to her in the fire-lit room. We were able to piece together that one of the men had a branding iron. Antonia was branded on her left hand with a red hot iron. To bring out the feelings of this trauma more fully, I realised that we may need to go through this episode again. I hoped that Edith would be up to it.

Session 4

We met again then just to continue from where we left. Edith entered quickly into the emotions of Antonia's experience. I continued to focus on body work, supporting different parts of her body to release physical, emotional and mental energy that had been held. She began....

'I'm down in a hole....There's light coming in....I'm on my own....I can't use my hand ...It's mangled, distorted....Can't do anything with it....Big stones around the walls....There's no way out....They pushed me in....My body's so sore...It doesn't feel like my body anymore....Nothing is....They've broken in, distorted it....invaded it....I can't feel things the way I used to do....I could have healed myself before....now nothing comes....doesn't work...My head hurts so much....doesn't work....I don't know what to do....I don't want to be alive anymore....This isn't my body anymore....'

Edith's body is just moving shaking from side to side.

'I can't even use my hands....They've burnt my hands....I can't feel them...They put a brand on my hand....It's not my body anymore....They can't do this to my body....I don't understand how they could do this....My head's really sore....so bloody and sore....I can't do the things I used to do....I can't see the things I used to see....'

(Much sobbing right through this.)

'It's all gone black....It's not me....I can't see things in my head anymore....No-one's there for me....My head hurts....'

I ask what's going on around her?

'There's lots of noise....They're shouting, laughing...like a party....It's fun....I want to be dead....I don't want to be dead like this....I don't want this....I don't see any of them....just see the hole at the top with blue sky...only men's angry harsh voices....No-ones come....No-one's there for me....They've all gone away....It hurts so much....'

I move Edith forward to where some significant change happens for Antonia.

'There's a man on a rope holding me...He's carrying me out of the hole....I'm not going to let them see me upset...I don't want to look at them...They pull me up....I'm on the ground and I hear them in the distance a little way away....They are not going to hurt me anymore....This isn't my body...'

The refrain of 'This isn't my body...' comes back as a denial over and over again - the wish of Antonia to split away from the situation she is in.

'....They can't do this any more to me....'

Suddenly Edith gets very agitated, moving and making noises.

'These men are touching me again....I can't stop them anymore....It doesn't matter....They can do what they want...I don't want them to see me hurting any more....If I can just feel my head, I don't need to feel the rest....They've done too much to me....They make me sick....These men touch me all over again...'

Edith splutters and coughs and is almost literally sick, spitting out material from inside her. I lean forward to support her until she settles a little, then I direct her to tell me what happens next.

'Some men come and take the man off me....They tell him to leave me alone....I want it to be over...I don't want to see anymore....They carry me....There's all these people shouting...all this noise....I don't want to feel it....So much noise....They can't do this to me....I can't do it on my own....I can't do it on my own....I can't do this on my own....'

Edith's voice becomes very resigned and despairing. The mode of her description is now quite flat. Because of this I sense that she is only yet accessing the surface layer of her repressed feelings regarding this part of Antonia's story.

We will need to go through this again for her to access and free her emotions about this more fully and deeply.

'They tie me to a stake....Its not my body anymore...My feet hurt....I can't feel what's under them....My feet hurt....sore....so sore....can't feel anymore....My body can't feel anymore....They can't do anymore to my body...'

She is going through the experience of her death.

'My eyes hurt....not going to feel anymore....can't breathe....My feet are so hot....Help me....Help me....I can't breathe....They're burning me....I don't want them to hear me....'

Edith breathes very fast and then the breathing finally slows down with groans.

'So much pressure in my tummy...It's all red...Can't breathe...'

I try to encourage Edith to breathe into her stomach to try and free the blocked emotions that are there But she remains stuck at this point, and is unable to move forward. She obviously needs a space to be able to assimilate the distress and fear that have already been released.

I decide to end the session here and I ask Edith's inner consciousness that she may receive some healing as a completion for our work today. With this, Edith experiences a rush of warmth and heat coming down through her head. This calms the atmosphere, and slowly Edith comes back to herself in the room with us.

Session 5

We have now reached an outline of the main features of the story of the trauma of what Antonia faced in her life. In some ways this is reassuring. But there are many places in the story where Edith's relating of it and description had been quite passive. This seemed to indicate a numbness brought on by fear was protecting and insulating her from experiencing the deeper more active feelings and associated thoughts that were there. The story of this life was complex with different levels and layers that needed to be tapped. And of course, there was also the experience of Antonia's death where the energies were stuck and needed to be freed.

I needed to check with Edith to find out how she was feeling and how she felt about going further. However, I sensed that by trusting in Edith's inner consciousness, that the experiences that still needed to be unfolded for her healing would emerge 'naturally' if we allowed a space for this to happen. As we talked about this, Edith was agreeable for us to continue with this approach.

So we began our next session by directing Edith's conscious-ness to go to the place in the story that she was ready to face and was most in need of further attention.

She went immediately into the situation where the men were attacking her in the healing room. I sensed that now, some of her more assertive feelings were wanting to come to the surface. I tried to encourage them. Again, this was another session where her body and emotions were connecting actively with the words she was speaking.

'I'm indoors...These men are grabbing me all over...'

I ask what she wants to say to them. She goes on.

'Get off me....I can't stop them....too many of them....I can't stop them....Can't stop them....too many of them....so many of them....can't stop them....no right to do this to

56

me....no....no....There's nothing I can do to stop them....It won't
stop....I can't do anything....They won't stop....'

Again I ask if she can relate directly what she wants to express to
them. This is difficult for her to sustain.

'You're disgusting...I want it to stop....They're hurting me so
much....Stop it...Stop....Don't do this to me....Don't do this to
me....Listen to me....Hear me....Feel this pain....Feel what you're
doing....Stop and listen...Let me breathe....Get away....They're
inside of me....Get away....They're so violent....so hard....They won't
stop....I can't do anything....all dirty....I can't get them out of
me....They have no right to do this to me.'

Again I urge her to relate directly to them.

'I hate you....you're scum....I hate you....Don't touch me....I hate
you....The more I say, the more they hurt me....I can't do
anything...just makes it worse....All dirty....I want to get them out
of me....My body's all dirty....Not my body anymore....I don't want
this body anymore...It's filthy now....I can't get them out....There's
too many...rolling in the dirt....with them pulling me...'

I move the story forward. After briefly relating about her
experiences in the cell, the energy and tension builds up again as
her consciousness opens to deeper layers of her experiences in the
interrogation room.

Here, she is aware of a man who confronts her.

'He's an evil man...He wants to destroy me...deep hate and evil...He
wants to destroy me....I can't do anything anymore...I'm not going
to let him see me....I can't do anything....They're kicking me...'

Once more, I try to encourage her to relate her feelings directly to
those that are doing this.

'Stop it....Don't do this to me....They're banging my head....They
keep hurting me more....There's nothing to do....I can't get them to
stop....nothing to do....I can't get them to stop....I don't know how

they can do these things and I be still alive....I can't be alive....They've chained my arms and my legs....They keep asking me questions....I don't know.... They've got these brands.... no....no.... They put them on my hands....They can't do this to me....They can't do this to me....'

Edith/Antonia doesn't speak anymore. She goes through a prolonged time of crying and sobbing, her body releasing volumes of repressed emotion - grief and despair. I support her to continue this until eventually it subsides.

By now, I sense that Edith is exhausted. Therefore I ask her consciousness to enable her to experience a peaceful place as a conclusion to the session. She experiences a space where she is aware of gold light, receiving it into her being. The energy in the room becomes still and more peaceful. It feels right to finish the session there.

Session 6

After a break and some rest, we met again. There was one part of Antonia's experience which was still waiting to be expressed and that concerned the events leading up to and including her Death. The first time we went through this she seemed to be stuck at some point in her dying. Now I hoped that she would be ready to go further, and deeper into this.

As we began, her consciousness went to the memory of where Antonia was being taken to the place where she would be burnt.

'....Lots of noise...I can hardly move my body....It's all pain....So much noise....shouting....Laughing....Cheering....I can't do anything....too tired....so humiliating, dirty....These men carry me....People throw hard things....I don't care....It hurts....women too....They look away....Some of them are crying....I don't want people to see tears....They're frightened too....I can't believe this....I want it to be over....I shouldn't be alive....I can't take in what's happening....So many of them...I see lots of faces...I can't take any of them in....I can't bear this....It shouldn't be like this...If I see the

eyes I feel the pain...They're not getting any more of me...I see eyes I know...I can't bear to look....Their anger stops them doing anything...I can't look...I want it over....

They tie me...My body is all so sore....can't be sore anymore...It's flat....Lots of sticks all around me...They can't hurt me anymore....It's all right....The fire is my friend....They're going to bring me the fire.   It's better than the men....I want the fire.....It's alive.....Somebody is shouting....Can't hear....A woman is shouting 'Let her go'.....But I want the fire....I don't want these men anymore....I want the fire....I don't want to hear her....The men get angry....It's a sport for them....I don't care....I would burn them with my eyes....'

I detect an edge in Edith's voice. It seems that Edith/Antonia is getting in contact with her anger. I wonder if she expresses this anger whether it will clear the block? I encourage her to direct these feelings to the men.

'I hate you....I despise you...'

She gets more and more worked up.

'feelings so big....I hate these men...'

She lets out a tremendous scream of hatred to the men. But then her voice softens and weakens. Something changes within her.

'...I want them to all go away....I don't want to hurt them....'

Now this is the crucial moment. After all the violence, abuse, torment and humiliation heaped on her by 'all these men' it would seem so easy for her to lust for revenge, to perpetuate the cycle of violence and want to give back to these men what they have done to her, thus carrying this energy in her soul for future lives.

I have opened the space in the therapy to encourage expression of these feelings as much as they may be there. But in this moment, Antonia decides she does not want to hurt them. It feels as though this is a big test for her Soul. What she chooses is to maintain her commitment to healing. Now she continues with renewed strength and purpose.

'They're crying too....I don't want to hurt them....I don't know how to heal them....I want to feel the fire....It's behind me....I hear the noise....I want to go home....don't feel anything....hard to breathe....smoky....I'm going to be proud....I'm not going to make a noise....I know the fire....I want the old Lady to come to me....She knows the fire too....My feet are hot...It's all right....The fire will burn me clean....'

Antonia seems to have reached a point of acceptance now where she is actively longing for and wanting to welcome Death.

'Take these men out of me....My feet are hot....All so sore....I want to be out of my body....They throw stones....I need to breathe in fire....'

As she does this, Antonia is connecting more and more with the Spiritual teachings of her Healing practice. She becomes aware of something above her head.

'....Stones are above my head....Something of the stones....Contact with the stones....Circle of stones....'

As she focuses more and more on the stones, her perspective changes.

'....I don't feel the fire.....watching it from above....I see the fire....burning the body....the clothes ....all red....red everywhere....It makes the dirt go away....So much dirt....all broken....clean....I want to burn up....It's good....'

Edith is breathing heavily while this goes on. I direct her to look at the people. This is what she relates.

'Hysteria....cheering....some people are going away....some are crying....so much anger....grey smoke....'

Antonia is becoming less and less attached to it all. She continues to be aware of the stones.

'...The stones are going away....I'm watching them go away....They took something of me with them....going away, up into the sky....I don't know who I am....I'm empty....I want the stones to wait for me....I don't want them to leave me here....I want to go with them....I'm going ahead....'

It seems that Antonia needs some purification before she can catch up and be united with that part of her that left with the stones. I direct Antonia to focus attention upon herself.

'....lots of blood....big, big wound....black inside....around my tummy....I want the black to come out....'

I direct Edith/Antonia to breathe into the black in her tummy, and let the energy of it express itself. She uses the words 'filth, anger, despair' to describe it. However, the black remains rather stuck. She has done enough cathartic expression of emotional release. This 'black' needs to be released in some other way.

Intervening on Antonia's/Edith's behalf I ask for inner help to deal with the blackness. Gradually there is a shifting of awareness. A female Spiritual being comes with her. She is kind and loving. The atmosphere in the room becomes more and more peaceful.

'A woman is holding me....Other Spirit people too....She's moving right through me....She's sprinkling sparkling light through me....She's stroking me....Stuff's coming out of me....pouring out of me....'

There's a long pause.

'....like I'm empty....a black river....It's all right now....She's kissing me....She's stroking right around me....She's very gentle....She's blowing away the bits of blood which aren't flowing....She blows them away....She knows I'm very tired....she just holds me....She's part of me....She's holding me....We're looking down on all the people....the fire has gone out, smouldering....Some of the men are drunk....She's stroking my hair....She says I was right not to hurt them....because they are children....They haven't really hurt

me....She's giving me a drink, a great drink....very soothing....The drink reminds me of the wolves....

My brother is in the house with other men....He's very angry....very upset....I want to send him green light....The man whose wife died....who had me burned....He's very upset....He felt that burning me would make him feel better....It hasn't....'

I ask about her women friends.

'....They're all crying in the woods....They are very frightened....'

'Now the old woman is there, looking over my shoulder smiling....She tells me 'I told you the fire's our friend'.....I didn't understand....She's looking at my head....She's beautiful....I see black at her neck....It was time....She lets me kiss her neck better....The black needs to be transformed into light somehow....She was holding black in her neck for others....not letting it go....doing things the way it used to be done....'

By now I sense that Edith has been through as much as she can absorb, so I ask her to experience what would be necessary to complete the session. She feels herself to be holding her hair under a waterfall. It is filled with purple and pink light.

As Edith brings her consciousness back into her own body awareness, it feels in the room as if we have survived a war.

Session 7

We meet together one last time for integration purposes. Edith is feeling saturated with all the experiences she has been through. It is good then that this session is gentle, simple and healing. I direct it in a way to help her make connections between Antonia's life and her present life as Edith and hopefully to be able to let the past go. Edith senses strongly that her brother in Antonia's life is the same soul as her brother Graham, who killed himself in her present life. Edith senses that there are stories of abandonment between her and him that have played out many times and still wanting to be fully resolved. But it feels as though Edith is ready to decide differently to Graham. She wants to live now.

I ask Edith to make contact with Antonia so that she may be able to dialogue with her former self. Immediately Edith feels herself in a place of light, that is bright. Then she is aware of Antonia's presence. The energy coming from Antonia is radiant. The atmosphere feels very peaceful.

I ask Edith if there is anything she wants to relate to Antonia. She says.....

'I want to connect with your passion with life, your deep, deep inner knowing and trust which opened up doors to be one with all around you. I want to share that wisdom you once knew.'

I ask if there is anything Antonia wants to give to Edith. Edith senses Antonia coming closer to her. There is a remarkable atmosphere of love in the room. Antonia places a hand on Edith's belly and one on her heart. Edith says.....

'...There's so much energy through my body....Her forehead's against mine....The energy goes further than our bodies...Beautiful, purple light....'

We stay with this for a while until I sense that Edith is ready to go on.

I ask if there is anything Antonia wants from Edith. Antonia speaks through Edith.

'I want for her to live without fear and to honour her wisdom....to know her own beauty and strength...and to trust....and to listen deeply....'

There is a meaningful silence while Edith absorbs this. Next, I ask for Edith to experience a vision of her future, knowledge her soul wants to unfold. Edith relates the following experience with intense feeling.

'There are beautiful colours from my hands around people....It's amazing....Love is so much bigger that all the pain....to let the colours soothe the despair....That's why we are here together....There are different things to learn from each individual....I need to...'

Her voice trails off into inner reflection.

Edith has gained a purpose for her life. I sense that she is now ready to go on from this. There is much healing energy in the room - words are not needed. As I reflect I realise there are a couple of the strands of the therapy I did not follow up. I did not trace what the stones had taken, or asked to find out the identity of the Spirit woman who comforted Antonia. But these details do not seem so important now. The main work had been done.

Outcomes

Two years later, I met Edith once more. She was now happy and very healthy looking. The change in her was quite remarkable.

I asked her how her life had been in the time since we met. She told me that life had continued to feel tough for her in the months immediately following our past life sessions. Not only did she need to integrate the experiences of our sessions but she was still suffering from the death of her brother and she struggled to find how she could live her life the way she wanted to live. But then she went to another country and found her way to a Spiritual Community away from any big cities or towns. Here she could do some simple work, but basically relax and enjoy herself and enjoy being with others with little extra responsibilities. In the way she described this Community, it seemed extremely gentle and nourishing for her.

Perhaps for the first time in her life, she was genuinely creating the space and allowing herself to meet her own needs, and put those needs first. It was good that she felt she could do this happily on Earth. She was not needing to try and cope with all the world's problems on her own anymore. This was a place where she could rest and rejuvenate her energies. She was planning to live there for some time to come.

When I mentioned having more Past Life sessions, she was not interested. She had done enough of that for now. Her attention was with the present. That was what she wanted to enjoy. Somehow, within me, I felt quietly satisfied that our work together had made a significant difference to her life.

Postscript

More recently I spoke to Edith again. Now she had sold her house and was travelling the world with a Spiritual Teacher. Doing this, she was dedicating herself to a spiritual quest to search for the truth of her essential Self. She seemed very much at peace with this. Edith's healing journey is contin-uing.

Chapter 5

Yvonne

Introduction

With Edith, there was one particular past life that we chose to work through thoroughly - and not more. There had been hints while I was working with her, that there was at least one other past life which may have been expressing a similar pattern to her life as Antonia. However, my intuition told me that Antonia's life was the most essential past life experience that Edith needed to bring to consciousness for her healing process. Certainly, afterwards, she did not feel a need to go further.

It has happened often though for me, when I have been trying to help people through Past Life Therapy, that there may be several lives with threads that can be contributing to problems that a person is facing. In these instances, going through one past life only, may not be sufficient to help a person substantially. At the same time, it may be important to apply judgement as to how many lives to bring forth.

For example, a person who has suffered a lot as a victim in his present life, may find, as he explores his past lives, that in life after life, he has been a victim of one sort or another in those experiences as well. So, to continue to bring out the suffering, what he could have done better, and the shortcomings of each of these experiences, may ultimately serve only to compound the feeling of misery and hopelessness, that nothing can be experienced any differently.

One of my important aims and intentions as a therapist is to try and bring more balance to my client's energy field and personality. So I will attempt to support and strengthen those aspects of my client's personality that are weak and discharge energy from those areas of my client's personality that are over emphasised. But I cannot make these changes happen for my clients. It has to come from within them. What matters then, is that people receiving help are sincere and really wanting healing and help. This means also that my clients must in some ways be willing to surrender some aspects of control over their inner life. This can be scary for some people. However, I try to support my clients to believe that if we ask for inner protection and guidance, it will be safe for them to open to what wants to emerge from within. It is only through this surrender that change can come. Otherwise, by keeping control, patterns of behaviour and the person's way of being will just stay as they have been. As people make inner shifts with energy patterns and awakening awareness, this often leads to outer changes too. So I generally encourage my clients to be sensitive to allow adjustments and changes to take place with different aspects of their everyday life alongside of the therapy. Changes though, cannot be forced into being, and will only occur easily when the person is ready to accept them. Often, this needs time.

Past life exploration often feels like working to reveal an inner tapestry of engrossing experiences. There can be many surprises and interesting challenges along the way. So, as people's inner journeys may lead through a succession of past lives, it is important to connect the past with the present, to let go of what is no longer needed from the past and learn lessons from those past experiences that can strengthen the present. Thus, the therapy then serves as a bridge between past and present, with the past no longer having some hidden dominance over present circumstances and behaviour, but more, that learning from the past can help people to live their present lives more fully, the way how they really want and need to live.

Meeting Yvonne

Yvonne came to me though her mother who had done some work with me that had been helpful to her. They came together from Scotland so that Yvonne could do a few days of intensive work with me.

Yvonne was a young attractive woman in her late twenties. Although, she seemed to have quite a bubbly personality with a smooth and confident voice, I sensed that inwardly she was quite nervous and edgy. She could talk about surface things like the weather easily, but she was obviously shy and not used to talking about herself.

As we began to share together, it emerged that her main problems were that she could not accept intimacy or tolerate affection being shown openly to her. Because Yvonne felt so close to her mother, and her mother had recommended me, she was able to open up to me. However, I could sense that 'lack of trust' was also a big issue for her in her life. She could not bear to be touched or hugged. Any kind of close contact was difficult for her. Lacking in self-worth, she tended to act in a way that others expected her to be, rather than being true to herself. She liked to be independent but her way of doing that was to have a wall around herself to protect herself. She did not really have any close friends and she kept herself emotionally detached from people.

With men, she had had three major relationships which had all proven unsatisfactory. Through these failures, she doubted that she had the ability to form a fulfiling relationship, however much she wanted one. With John, her present boyfriend who she had been seeing for about a year, she was very reluctant to let him get at all close to her.

I wondered if Yvonne may have suffered some form of abuse during her younger years, but I could find no evidence for this. Her father and mother had been kind and loving to her. Her upbringing had been largely uneventful in terms of disruptions or tragedies. The main trauma she had suffered was at the age of 16 when her father had died. This was a big loss for her. Somehow, her grieving for him was delayed in its expression until four years later, when something triggered her feelings while in a pub on Father's day. This grief was not suppressed in her, but I found it interesting how long she had waited until it came out.

In her relationship with men, she could cope with sexual inter-course. But she did not like to be seen naked, or to be touched when she was not ready. She did not feel able to accept compliments from people or to give them.

Deep inside she wished to start a family of her own. However, she felt repulsed by the idea of having to nurse and cuddle a baby. She also wanted to know more her own inner feelings and feel safe to express them so she could feel less isolated and more connected to others. Most of all, she wanted to overcome her intense aversion to touch and intimacy so she could feel comfortable with these aspects of her life.

Our sessions together

We did not know what to expect when we began our sessions. However, what followed was the recall of a number of past lives, one after another, a different one with each session. I tried to help Yvonne process through each of these as best I could. Although the outer appearance of the lives was quite dissimilar from one to another, the underlying themes in each had a consistent thread. They showed a past tendency from Yvonne's Soul to create situations where she would feel isolated, and where she would withdraw from reaching out for help when she needed it. They were lives with lessons of love, needing to give and receive love, to accept herself - and times when she had struggled unsuccessfully to do this. Somehow, Yvonne seems to have needed to be reminded of these experiences to help get her present life on a better footing. There were also many past wounds that needed healing too.

Life 1

This life came with very little prompting. It must have been very close to the surface in Yvonne's awareness. It was perhaps the experience that disturbed her most too. Yvonne felt some tension in her stomach. I asked her to close her eyes and breathe into this. Then I gently touched her on the stomach with my hand. Immediately, the tension hardened and increased tremendously. Emotions of anger and distress came to the surface associated with the tension.

'Get off me', she yelled at me, trying to push me away. She repeated this several times. But as I encouraged her to keep going with this, she realised that she was no longer experiencing herself as Yvonne, but as a young boy.

As I tried to stabilise her perceptions with this, the story of this life unfolded.

This poor boy was physically and perhaps mentally disabled. He was utterly dependent on others to feed him and look after him. His limbs did not work for him in any co-ordinated way. At some stage there was a pen where he was placed that had bars around it so he couldn't get out. One difficult memory came where Doctors were prodding him, trying to open his eyes, doing tests on him and he couldn't do anything about it. His mother didn't seem to care. There was no affection given to him. When people were around they were just coming at him, touching him, doing things to him whether or not he wanted it. He felt tremendous frustration at all this, and he tried to be as much on his own as he could. The only sense of control he could feel was with his dog. He could choose whether or not to pat his dog. The dog was his closest companion. He could hardly communicate to people apart from resisting them. It was a life of continuing, enduring suffering. No one valued him. He wanted to shut them out.

Leading him to his time of Death, he did not seem to be very old. He passed through this easily and then at last he felt free to move, and peace. The boy was so confined in that life. He then became aware of other Spirits wishing to speak. Finally the words came to him 'Love in every shape and form'. This life had been a lesson in love - learning to accept a body in a most grotesque form, when there was little or no support around. The boy had not done very well at accepting himself or the situation he was in. He had held enormous frustration inside himself.

But now, Yvonne was ready for something else. I passed her a cushion to represent the boy and asked what this boy needed. She replied that he needed a cuddle, affection and love.

As she hugged this cushion, floods of tears and sobs came from Yvonne as she released volumes of pent up frustration. It was a great moment of healing that subsided gradually into peace. She could now accept this boy and feel compassion for him. Thus, she was also then able to accept and love an important part of herself.

Life 2

After our first session, Yvonne spent many hours talking with her mother about her experiences. So, when I saw her again, she was ready to go on.

When she closed her eyes, I asked Yvonne to allow the image of a door to come to her consciousness. This door then, could lead her to what she needed to experience next.

As she went through this, Yvonne found herself to be in a garden. She felt her body to be very heavy and then realised she was experiencing herself as a man. This man's name was Sam and it became clear that this was the memory of another past life.

There was not much happening in this garden. Sam was moving very slowly and just wanting to go to sleep. There was a strong energy of resignation and giving up. I sensed that we had entered this life right at the very end of it. As I gradually pieced together the story of Sam's life and helped Yvonne to experience it, this was another very sad tale, a dull and ordinary life.

Sam had been born on a farm as part of a large family. He had initially felt close to his mother and wanted love and affection from her. But eventually there were too many other children wanting the same from her. Sam did not feel that he could get what he needed emotionally, so he cut himself off in this way and preferred his own company. He was not mistreated, but he felt the family to be 'too noisy' and that he 'couldn't be bothered' to try to be close to anyone.

When he grew up Sam got work on an Estate, looking after the grounds. This was quite a solitary occupation. To outer appearances Sam fitted in with the society around him, in the way he dressed and went about his business. But Sam kept himself very much alone.

One crucial moment occurred in Sam's life when a young woman with ginger hair wanted to be his companion. He found it difficult to admit that he wanted this too. So one day he was walking up a hill to go and meet her. A conflict raged inside of him. He had become used to being on his own and that felt safe but another part of him was yearning to break out of his self-imposed isolation. He did not reach her home. Before he could get to the top of the hill, he decided it was a waste of time and turned away.

That seemed to be a last chance for Sam. After that, his life went down hill, so to speak. He died in the garden which seemed to be on the grounds of the Estate where he worked. Like in the first past life story, his only companion in the end was a dog. He died feeling broken, depressed and unfulfilled.

This past life seemed to be set in the early twentieth century in Ireland, later than the first past life story.

Moving through the death experience, gradually releasing the heaviness, Sam could feel 'what a waste'. It was as if Sam had placed his life in an emotional prison.

I covered Yvonne with blankets and cushions to represent this prison. She did not want to stay that way and gratefully, with much energy, she enjoyed to break free. It was a relief.

Then Yvonne could experience Sam's life more alive. It had been so dull before. Sam had made his own life dull. Yvonne was glad to let that go. What Sam had really wanted was to open up himself to a full appreciation of the different aspects of life. This is what Yvonne wanted too.

Life 3

For our next session, I decided to begin in a different way. I asked Yvonne to repeat a phrase 'Don't come near me'. As she did this a number of times she began to feel more and more uncomfortable. Soon she did not want to say it anymore but by now she was starting to experience herself in the memory of being in another time and place. In this particular past life she again experienced herself as male. This was a more complex life from an earlier time, than the other lives, elaborating on themes we had already been exploring.

We entered the experience in childhood. As this boy, he was living in a family with a big brother and sister on a farm. As a child he was expected to help with the chores and work around the home, but he did not want to do this. What he wanted to do was to paint. All that he wished to do was to go out and explore and become an artist. However, his parents rejected this and sometimes refused to let him go out and do what he wanted. In turn, he rejected what they wanted and as time went on he fell into the familiar pattern of cutting himself off emotionally and preferring to approach life on his own. He felt that he was different to them and that they were not capable of understanding him. There was a clash of wills here and I could detect maybe some pride or sense of superiority in him that he was better than them.

It was a hard life though. Even with a fire in the house, it was cold often and his family were poor, having enough to survive on but not a lot more.

As a young adult, he decided to leave his family and go to town where he hoped he could make his fortune through being an Artist. For him to continue to be with his family felt like 'suffocation'. He did not feel that he could be himself with them, or that they would appreciate what he wanted to do. They wanted him to stay and help on the farm. They did not believe that he could manage as an Artist. However, they did not try to stop him from leaving. So he went without their blessing.

In the town, he did manage to paint and he did sell some paintings. So in his own way he was proving that he could do it.

But he was continuing to be on his own, without his family's support. Inside he really did want his family to support him. He wanted their love so that he could feel OK. But they did not value what was for him, his passion, so he was determined that he could get on without them.

This conflict manifested in his body as pains in his legs. This came from his childhood when he wanted to go out and paint and explore but he was not allowed to do so. Then as he got older, he became more and more restricted physically. As time went on, his painting became less rewarding too. He could express his inner feelings onto the paintings. However, it felt to him that with each painting he exposed more of himself, until there was nothing left. He hated his own weakness. It was his emotions, especially the more negative ones like aggression, fear, hatred that went into his pictures. There was a part of him that did not feel OK to be doing what he wanted because his family had not approved. What he really wanted was their acceptance and love. But he was not going to get it this way.

His life closed off and as with the other lives he became more and more isolated and physically sore, until he was bedridden and hardly able to move. Soon after this, he died. Death was a release which he welcomed. Yet it was another sad and unfulfilled life.

I pointed out to him that his family were not rejecting him as a person, only his interest in painting which they could not accept because they needed so much practical help. Probably they still loved him. Yet he had reacted by rejecting everything about his family, so he could feel able to do what he wanted. But inside, he still wanted their love. He was afraid of sharing his feelings and preferred to hide them away.

Realising that he needed to acknowledge this love, Yvonne went through a process with her hands to join together these different parts of her past life Self. As she did this, Yvonne had a strong awareness of light. Her past life self was now ready to meet his family in love. As she had the experience of him doing this internally, there was a great feeling of peace in the room.

This boy had suffered much guilt at rejecting his family. Again this rejection had been associated with a part of himself, the part that could not give and receive love. Yvonne realised that in her own life she had a tendency to blame herself excessively when things went wrong. Now she could begin to see a way through this.

As a final image in the session, Yvonne was given the experience of a red rose - a symbol of love. She was learning acceptance of love.

Life 4

Now that she had begun to open in herself to expressions of feelings of love, Yvonne was ready to experience an even earlier life, one which contained a painful wound connected with the heart. It could be that this was the time when Yvonne's soul decided that it was not safe to love. This past life story brought out even more strongly a polarisation between obligations of family duty and a wish to be and express herself.

In this past life Yvonne experienced herself to be female. She was a young woman living in medieval times. She lived in a castle or mansion and was the wife of a lord who had much power and influence. Her parents had also been quite wealthy and her marriage was arranged to enhance the wealth of both families. Her husband was big, rather overweight, smelly, gross and physically cruel and demanding to his wife. On the surface she appeared to be a dutiful, congenial wife. She did what was expected of her. However, internally she hated and detested him, keeping herself from him in all ways that she could.

Unbeknown to her husband, she also had a lover; a man she had known since childhood. They would go out riding together and when the opportunity was there, they would enjoy sex together.

She enjoyed very much to be with him, and had circumstances been different, she would have married him. Sometimes, in the company of her husband for instance, they were able to be more discreet, and managed to keep their relationship secret. However, in almost classic style, there came a time when she was betrayed and someone told her husband. He put her lover in chains and presumably killed him. She continued to deny the love affair to her husband and was eventually hanged.

In past lives where people are hanged, this is often also a symbol for a split that occurred for the person in that life, usually between head with its thinking and outer appearances versus heart and body and inner feelings. This was very true also for Yvonne's past life self. In this life, she had built a wall around herself so that no one would know her true feelings except her lover. And then, even he was separated from her. It left her all alone. She then kept her inner self and feelings totally hidden and cut off from others. Her husband had wanted absolute control over her. So with her feelings, to him and everyone else, this was what she could keep for herself.

The image of the scaffolding where her past life self was hung was very strong for Yvonne. By now, Yvonne had expressed as much emotional release as she could. But this scaffolding reminded her and helped her to become aware of the huge internal barriers she had erected inside herself to stop other people from hurting her, or getting in any way close to her, and at the same time keeping her own feelings locked in.

In that past life, the scaffolding had been very real, and it was from this that she had been hung and died. But it was as though in the other lives she had also created strong inner barriers to others. In each of these lives, although the barriers provided some protection, it also ultimately led to tragedy because her love did not want to stay locked inside. Now, Yvonne realised the same tendency had happened to her. This time there were no people building it for her, as in this hanging past life story. But she had created it for herself.

Integration

Each of the past lives seemed to have an opportunity that was missed. If the young woman in the castle had made some attempts to form an emotional relationship with her husband, if the artist man could have dared to share more of his feelings with his parents, if Sam could have made it up the top of the hill to meet his woman friend, if the disabled young boy had not so much totally rejected everyone coming towards him doing things to him, then maybe things could have been different as an outcome for those lives. So the pattern and habit of isolation had been compounded through these different experiences rather than resolved.

Now Yvonne could easily visualise this huge scaffolding as the barrier she had constructed around her heart to shield her from other people and the world around her. As we began to explore this, at first it appeared very daunting and she felt herself very small in comparison to it. I suggested to her to ask for inner help, which she did. In so doing, she was given a ladder from which she could explore the scaffolding more fully.

By breathing into her stomach, she felt as though she was in a cold and wet cave. It did not seem safe to go out. There were stones outside leading to different pathways that could take her into new futures. But these stones did not seem real or solid. It was very difficult for her to trust. I gently tried to encourage her with this, and eventually she was able to take a few steps.

The scaffolding did not seem so big now. She could climb to the top and she felt that she even had the strength to climb over it and to be free of it now if she wished. But Yvonne wanted to be free to choose.

She could only build up her trust gradually, and she felt she would want some protection sometimes. It felt important that she could stay behind the scaffold when she felt this was needed. But she also could acknowledge that her path now was going to be to venture out more and more.

Around her heart, she felt a fragile barrier like glass. She would need to be very careful with this. Then with her neck, when she focused on this she could feel a hanging rope. It was important for her to listen to both her thoughts and her feelings so these two parts of her would co-operate. Then she wouldn't need to go through an experience like hanging again.

Finally Yvonne experienced herself to be right on top of a mountain, with 'a wee flag'. She felt very smug and pleased with herself. She had conquered her mountain and she was now ready to face the world.

Afterwards

About three months after my sessions with Yvonne, I spoke with her mother. She told me that the change in Yvonne had been amazing. She seemed much more full of confidence and was coping very well, especially with work. Her life was flourishing.

Two years later, I talked with Yvonne again. She had got married to John, her boyfriend from when she came to see me. They were very happy together and had recently had a baby. With her baby, she had been happy breast feeding and being a mother. Yvonne felt at ease with this and also she felt much more at ease in general with people. In the meantime she had not sought any other form of therapy or help. She feels the work with me gave her a foundation and a starting point to move forward. She did not seem to want to do any more past life work with me. What she had done was sufficient.

In circumstances where she felt herself to be closing off from other people and when she was in challenging situations, Yvonne would still imagine the scaffolding as a symbol for her to find courage to overcome any barriers she felt. But also, she could use the scaffolding as an inner means to protect herself when she did not want to be open. However, now she knew it was her choice. She was in control of how she felt. With this she felt safe. Inside, this has helped her to feel much more happy and free.

Chapter 6

Healing the Inner Child

The Child That Lives Within Us

In the beginning, our life is full of wonder and love. As children we are open and curious to explore. At the same time we are sensitive to pain and we feel with our emotions very strongly. We like to play and have adventures, using our rich imagination. Yet we are also very receptive, absorbing experiences like a sponge, learning all the time. In our early years especially, we learn a lot through touch. From the feelings in our bodies we learn what we like and do not like. We enjoy that warm close feeling of being held by someone who loves us and wanting to care for us. As our will develops we want to express ourselves more and more and reach out. But we are also very vulnerable and dependent. We need adult people to help guide us and show us the way. We cannot survive without support and help. If we are hurt, we need someone to look after us.

Usually, our parents are very important to us. We tend to expect a lot from them. They are so big and powerful. Often we want to be like them. We follow their example. With our heart we want to be valued and appreciated by them.

Our early years go through many phases of development. At first, we approach life very instinctively. Then this finally changes as we learn to think for ourselves. Going through the adolescence years we become aware of our own identity as someone who is distinct. Our consciousness narrows as we become more self-conscious with the awakening of our sexuality. But then we still need support and encouragement to learn skills and to become more independent.

So what happens then when we finally reach adulthood? Do we merely outgrow our childhood consciousness so that it functions in us as no more than a fading memory? Or does our childhood consciousness continue to influence us and actively live in our psyche and contribute to the consciousness of who we are?

I feel that the answer to this question is obvious if we are honest with ourselves. When we observe children playing and having fun, if we are open to it, this brings joy to our hearts. This is because we recognise in the children playing, the experiences from our own childhood. The recognition implies that the experience of our own childhood is still alive inside of us and it is precious.

People who deny the importance or relevance of their childhood may be denying an important aspect of themselves. Such people may live, in some respects, cold and empty lives. Otherwise, the child within them may find ways to express itself through them of which they are not aware.

The Wounded Child

Of course, not all children are happy. Some people may look back on their childhood with a mixture of fear, dread and loathing. Much can happen to render childhood to be a miserable time.

People may feel a sense of helplessness when the circum-stances of their upbringing has been difficult, feeling as though it has happened beyond their control. From the model of reincarnation, this may not be the case. Spiritually, a Soul may have chosen its parents and the conditions for its upbringing as a child. There may be reasons for this. But that can also be hard to accept, and living through abusive circumstances can contain much suffering.

There are many ways in which the life of a child may be damaged. Mentally, the child may be affected through negative thoughts that are spoken or unspoken. The child can pick these up and the imprinting can be stronger when these thoughts are accompanied with loaded emotions or when they are repeated several times.

Negative thoughts can create negative expectations in the child's mind.

Emotionally, the child may be damaged when love and affection are withheld or when there is other deprivation. Rejection and anger can make the child feel very afraid. Absence can also affect children at times when they need support. On the other side, children may be damaged by having too many emotional demands thrust upon them. Children may also be conditioned into behaving in a particular way through emotional blackmail.

Physically, the child may be wounded through lack of touch or tenderness. Violence can have an appalling impact upon a child. Perhaps most damaging of all though, a child can be affected severely through sexual abuse, because this is confusing for the child on so many levels.

Spiritually a child can also be damaged. If when a child has important Spiritual experiences, these are ridiculed or dismissed this can be quite devastating for the openness of the child. Also children can be manipulated to conform to particular modes of behaviour when if they don't do this they are told they may be punished by God.

Once specific wounds have been acquired and say, passed down from parent to child, then it is quite likely that when that child has grown up, especially if the wound is not addressed, that it will then pass on to the next generation, thus setting up as a continuing cycle.

From another perspective, just as our physical body takes in food which is digested and assimilated through our bloodstream into our body to nourish us and help with our growth and development, so with all our experiences in childhood, as we digest and assimilate them into our emotional/mental and psychic being, we grow and develop according to the aptitudes, decisions and conditioning which have come to us and which we have chosen. Problems arise with those experiences which we do not manage to digest or assimilate properly. These may also be experiences that we choose to forget or at least try to forget.

The main element which causes experiences not to be digested is fear. When we are afraid, our emotional/mental/psychic body may become rigid or frozen. On a physical level, we may suspend our breathing. Our sympathetic nervous system can then be engaged for us to fight or flee. With this, the normal process of digestion and assimilation of our experiences is interrupted. So the thoughts, emotions and feelings we have in these moments may become detached energetically from the rest of our being, and may then continue to exist as an unintegrated experience within our psyche. Furthermore, if it is an unpleasant experience that we do not wish to remember, we may soon forget it so that it is removed from our normal consciousness and thus it can be beyond the control of our rational critical mind. Such experiences can then be quite destructive and influence us in ways which we do not want.

Helping the Inner Child

When we become adults we need to make decisions about how we want to live our lives. On a practical level this may involve choices concerning our career, relationships, where we want to live, selecting friends and interests as well as the values we want to live by. This is all part of learning how to take responsibility for our lives.

But we need to make inner choices as well. Some people when they grow up are quite content to follow in their parent's footsteps, do what society expects them to do or imitate how their peer groups are living their lives without much thought about doing things differently. For others, this may not be enough.

Like in my own life, there are people for whom it is not sufficient just to do what the crowd and everyone else is doing and live like that. Such people may feel the urge to find meaning in their life and search for what can truly make them happy. Living in this way can be like a Spiritual journey. In these cases people may end up living very different lives from how they started. Life can be full of surprises. These people are trying to listen to the needs of their Soul.

Sometimes there may come a crisis into people's lives as a means to encourage them to search for greater meaning in their lives. A death in the family, an illness, loss of job or ending of a relationship may serve to shatter people's inner sense of security and confront them with questions of what life is about and what is truly important. Such tragedies may be difficult, but they may also hold an inner purpose for people going through them to help them learn and adjust their values. Such opportunities are not always taken though. People can ignore them. But it is often from these critical moments that people may seek therapy for inner development and try to find inner peace and resolution from pain.

Once people begin this inner journey they may find that there are different aspects of their personality that are in conflict with one another. Although they may be wanting to make changes in their lives, they may find that there are parts of themselves that are resisting this. It may not be possible through use of the will on its own to do anything about this. But then by listening to these resisting parts more closely they may find that they can trace these resisting parts to their childhood and a child consciousness within them that may be afraid or suffering in some way.

When people begin a more Spiritual path in life they usually find there is a conflict between how they have been conditioned to act, feel and think and how they feel they really want to live their lives. Conditioning which has been entrenched over many years may not be easy to overcome. People need much support to be able to make progress with this. But sometimes people may discover some truth from deep inside of themselves that may enable some of this conditioning to fall away

With the child consciousness that may be blocking progress, there is a need for patience to help with this. First of all, that child consciousness needs to feel safe so that it can emerge. The adult Self needs to learn to listen and ask the child Self what it may need to feel safe. The adult and child self can form a relationship together.

Also though, that child consciousness is suffering from experiences relating to the past. Whatever the circumstances of those past events the child really is no longer there but is now with the adult in present time. Whatever is keeping that child consciousness trapped or attached to the past needs to be brought to the surface, acknowledged and released so that the adult and child Self can be united. In essence it is this process that will help heal the inner child.

The inner child may want to express some of those child like qualities through the adult Self. This may be surprising or even startling when it first happens, after some inner block has been released. The child within needs a lot of love but has a lot to give as well.

There are many methods for approaching Inner Child Therapy. I would like to outline my methods through different case studies of people that I have helped in this way. Firstly though I will present a hypothetical case study to show generally how I work with this and what may be expected to take place.

Hypothetical Case Study

Let me use this example. A girl may have done something to upset her father. He may then be shouting at her, threatening to hit her, calling her a 'naughty, bad girl'. The child in this instance may feel extremely frightened and bewildered by this enormous presence of her father so uncontrolled in his emotional reaction. She may not feel able to cope with it, and try to block it out.

But the message that she is 'bad' and 'naughty' may affect the energy system of her heart. She may feel very afraid that if she behaves like this, her father won't love her anymore. In turn, the terror of feeling and sensing his anger and judgement might make her 'freeze' inside. She may feel unable to cry or react for fear that his anger might become worse and he would hit her. This fear and dread of what might happen could easily then become locked into a psychic knot in her solar plexus region or stomach.

Years later, she may not even consciously remember the incident. But the effects would linger. In situations where she feels that others may not approve totally of her actions, she would probably also feel vaguely that she was 'bad' or 'naughty'. Then she may also be very cautious or inhibited about doing anything which may upset someone, because subconsciously she would carry the fear that the person may get upset like her father once did.

Repetitions where this kind of situation may happen many times in her early life may make the tendency for her to behave in this way even more pronounced and stronger.

As an adult she may recognise the pattern of how she reacts to these situations. However, at the same time she may feel powerless by herself to be able to do anything to change this. In a way, it is that frightened small child in her that is causing her to react in a way that she doesn't really want. She may not like this part in herself that is so lacking in self-confidence and insecure. But this rejection of the frightened child part of her will only add to her separation from this part of her and tend to make the problem worse. Unfortunately, this experience of her early childhood is floating unintegrated within her energy system because the child she was then couldn't cope with it.

This woman then, when she is ready and willing to face this issue, would be ripe to go through a process of Inner Child Therapy.

The first step in this process would be to find a way for the woman to make contact with the memory of the original incident that affected the girl from inside of her. This may not always be easy and I would want to go gently with this to be sure that the woman is really ready to face up to this. She needs to feel strong enough in herself to help her child Self.

There are different ways in which the memory could be contacted. One way may be through suggestion with hypnosis. I could ask her inner consciousness to reveal to her the situation when she first became frightened of doing something wrong or bad. Another approach would be for her to close her eyes and repeat a phrase like 'I'm bad, I'm naughty' several times, breathing into the feelings of this, until more feelings and perhaps memories start to arise. Alternatively, she could also recall a situation where she felt this nervous knot in her stomach, and just then breathe into this knot of feelings, going with the associations of what the knot is wanting to say, allowing the memories of the original incident to come in this way.

With any of these approaches the woman would feel that she has some control over the process, that she is voluntarily saying 'yes' to it. Then, if anything got too much, she could say 'no' if necessary.

There may be different layers of this pattern to uncover. Then as the memory of the original incident emerges, various things may happen. At first, she may start to feel fear and become aware of the energy of her father shouting. Initially she may not know what he is saying. The image may be frozen like the still frame of a picture. Here it is important for the woman to feel the fear through her body and to express it. The little girl may have had her reasons for not showing that she was afraid. It may have felt too much for her to comprehend the situation. So the adult part, with reassurance and love, needs to encourage and allow this suffering little girl in her to acknowledge these feelings. This may mean that her body wants to tremble or shake. There may be also hidden emotions wanting to gush out, perhaps associated with repressed thoughts she had at the time. The more of this that can be expressed, the better. It is a process where love is helping the little girl within to let the fear go.

As the fear and emotion begin to express itself, more of the incident may emerge. The memory may come alive. There may be fearful thoughts like 'Please don't be upset with me...I didn't mean to do it....I won't do it ever again' - thoughts she wanted to say to please her father.

Once these have come out, there may be deeper layers of thoughts and feelings wanting to come to the surface. The child within may have her own anger that she was holding inside, even defiance. Thoughts like 'It's not fair....I don't deserve this....I hate you for shouting at me like this' may be wrapped up in these feelings. For these deeper layers of feelings to express themselves is very important, because with this is included the child's feeling of self-worth and self-respect. The adult Self needs to help the little girl to be able to assert herself and assert her own sense of identity even in spite of her father's presence. With this asserting of herself, when she can do it authentically, it may appear to the woman that father is not shouting anymore. This is a very good sign because it generally means that the psychic charge around the situation has then been dissipated or dissolved.

Once this has occurred there may be other perspectives to the story that come to light. We may find out, for instance, that the little girl had been eating a chocolate ice cream and had got it over her hands and then wiped her hands all over father's brand new carpet. Perhaps father was already irritable as a result of other problems he was facing. Maybe the father had been a bit negligent in letting his daughter eat ice cream there in the first place. The woman can then help the little girl in her feel reassured and learn more realistically about the overall dynamics of the situation.

Once all the emotions and thoughts connected with the situation have been expressed, the woman may feel very peaceful. Integration would be taking place, and unless there are other linked incidents or elements from the situation, that had not been fully accessed and processed, then the woman would not be anymore troubled by the kind of disturbance which this incident had brought. Furthermore, she would probably feel a lot more happy and whole.

In such a case, it may be helpful to do some follow-up work, because in all likelihood she would have built up the habit of avoiding situations of confrontation where she could be doing anything of which others may disapprove. She could have been making herself 'smaller' in life than she needed to be. By 'visioning' and using her active imagination to encourage her how she really wants to be in life, new ideas and possibilities may open up for her. These need to be supported so she can open to more of her potential. Now that this part of her is integrated with the rest of her, she may be more open to trust - and in areas of what her father represented to her, she may feel more confident to express herself. Such changes can really make a permanent difference to a person; and this woman may then feel more in control of her life.

This example of Inner Child work is quite a simple one. Often the issues which are involved are more complex and can demand quite a lot of time and patience to resolve. I would like to present now a few case studies from my files bringing out different strands of the possibilities for Inner Child work.

Retrieving Lost Parts of Ourselves - The Case of Sarah

Sometimes when a child suffers a trauma, there can be splits in the personality to such an extent that part of the child may try to escape and leave the energy system of the child's body altogether - and not come back. When this happens, the person may feel a sense of void or emptiness around different parts of the body energetically. Then the qualities that were expressed by the part which has gone would no longer function for the person at all.

It is possible to enable these missing parts to be reunited with the person again, although it is not always easy. Spiritual help is needed. Also the person needs to be willing to be united with that part again. Once the part has returned then the experiences that it contains will be 'alive' again for the person. This can have its consequences, and it may be difficult for the person to face up to some of these experiences. But usually when a part does go missing, it takes chunks of memories with it. To illustrate this kind of work more fully I would like to share some selected aspects of my work with a woman I will call Sarah.

When I met Sarah, I was impressed by her positive, vibrant nature. She was a career woman and had been very successful with this. For the past ten years she had worked in the business world and she was near to the top in her field. Obviously intelligent and very creative she seemed to be someone able to achieve what she wanted. However, emotionally this was not the case. A series of personal crises had made her question her life and forced her to turn inward. She was wanting a change of direction in her life. As she examined her suffering and pain she could sense that some of it stemmed from her childhood.

Sarah sensed that there was a slightly incestuous situation from her childhood with her parents. Now she could not cope to be physically close to her father. She did not want him to look at her. Yet she also felt unable to refuse the excessive emotional demands which he placed upon her. The memories she had of her childhood were rather vague. But somehow she felt defeated by him. Her father had supported her academically and creatively but in other ways he had become too much for her.

During the course of our therapy work we decided to try and trace the source of these feelings of defeat as part of our work. As we delved into her childhood we uncovered experiences which had generated wounds for Sarah not only from her father but her mother as well. I tried to help her through these as best I could.

However, there was one experience which emerged that was particularly important and relevant.

In this scene she was young, and alone with her father and he was changing her clothes. However, he was changing her very slowly. Something was not right. She was becoming distressed 'by the way he was doing it'. He was coming closer to try to comfort her. He was nice really, so she couldn't complain. And if she did, her mother would get mad at her. She couldn't breathe properly and she felt trapped. The memory of what precisely happened felt blocked. And she was too young to run away.

Then she told me she felt helpless and had given in. The only way she could protect herself was for part of her to leave. That's what it felt like she had done. Part of her had left her body and gone to where it was safe.

Now, with all the earlier work we had done, I felt that Sarah could be ready to reclaim this part of her. I asked for Spiritual help for her to do this and I felt confident that this help would be forthcoming because Sarah was open to the Spiritual aspect of her being. So then she became aware of the energy of this part of her nearby.

Next she was able to dialogue with this part of her. The part told Sarah that Sarah had detached her from reality, but now she was the part that Sarah needed. Sarah was very sad that this part had been away so long, even though it had been safe. But she was afraid of what might happen if she let the part back in. She admitted that there would be no escape anymore then.

I waited for her decision. Finally she said 'yes' while acknowledging that she still felt very frightened. I asked for Spiritual help to support this.

There was a fusion of energies. Sarah felt vivid sensations. There was energy rushing down her legs to her feet. The central area and bottom half of her body was filled with energy. Sarah could feel that she had been given something back. It felt female to her - very female. She felt all the female parts of her coming alive. It was very happy, vibrant. She could not understand then what had made her so afraid. This female energy felt very beautiful. It gave her a feeling of being fertile with this sense of power and fearlessness. Suddenly, she had this incredible urge to have a child......And then she was sad.

Sarah was probably past the age of being able to have a child. Since she had been 19, she had been on the pill to prevent this. Now she realised how much she had been denying herself. There was regret as much as joy with this part returning to her.

We continued our therapy work. In the next session, there were experiences which the returned part wanted to bring forth.

In these memories she was younger and she was being physically beaten by her mother. This happened many times and then she was left on her own for long periods. Her mother thought this was for her own good. It was during these times that part of Sarah learnt to leave her body. She could float off and be free and then she wouldn't need to feel any pain.

90

I had to help Sarah now, bringing all her parts together, including the adult part to confront her mother rather than running away. From this Sarah became aware of her anger. She expressed this powerfully. Then later this led on to the memories with her father. He had touched her in her sexual area. Her rage at him for this was immense and she was able to let this out and let it go. Then she felt something more returning into place in her thighs - something that felt sacred to her - not for everybody, only for whom she chose. Then she was aware of white light and felt really good.

In our following session, Sarah met a Spiritual being within her. This was a woman, a woman of the Earth. This woman had come to help Sarah and guide her towards her new path. Sarah needed to learn healing, caring for people and the sacred Earth, teaching and using her male skills to help people learn and care for Nature again and learn respect. Sarah needed to learn Earth wisdom, the natural order of life, and try to bring peace.

Sarah could accept all this. It is what she had been seeking. Over the next day Sarah cried buckets of tears. There was obviously a lot of releasing completing itself. But then she felt happy. She was on her new path and it felt right, and good. The return of this lost part of her made her feel more fully herself.

Recovering Threads of Love - The Case of Isabel

Often in Inner Child work, the adult part needs to comfort and support, with love, the child within. This is usually needed to help release some pain or to find reconciliation of trust and openness. It is a process of learning how to attain inner harmony with those various parts of our Self. The key seems to be to help find bridges to link the energies of the different parts within us that are separated.

Occasionally though, it is the adult part more than the child part that needs the healing. Such was the case with Isabel whose story I will tell now.

The main reason Isabel sought Inner Child Therapy with me because of suffering she felt through loss of contact with her father. Now a woman in her late forties, Isabel had not had contact with her father from the time when she was four years old. Memories she had of time spent with her father when she was younger than this had long since been clouded over and suppressed.

Isabel's mother was very reluctant to talk about her father. Some relatives had information about him, so she could have tried to trace his address if she really wanted to do that. He may have been still alive. But she was very afraid. What if he didn't love her?

It was very important for Isabel to learn how her father felt towards her. Somewhere deep inside, her sense of self-worth and self-esteem were bound up in this. The little child within her knew how her father felt towards her. But the adult Isabel was not aware of what experiences her little girl Self had had. This is what she needed to know.

Isabel had been conceived out of an affair between her mother and father - her father being married to someone else. For the first three or four years of her life, periodically, Isabel had times where she met with her father. Her parents had loved each other. He had wanted a divorce from his wife so they could be together, but Isabel's mother had said 'no'. Eventually, her mother severed ties with him and told him to go away. After that Isabel did not see or hear anything more of him. Soon Isabel's mother married a man who became Isabel's stepfather. They started a family and had a number of children together. In this family set-up Isabel felt isolated and an outsider. Her relationship with her stepfather was particularly difficult. She felt that he abused her mentally, and physically she suffered frequent slaps and pushings - with occasional beatings.

Throughout her childhood years and right up to the time when she married, Isabel insisted upon using the surname 'Jones' which was the name of her father. It was clear where her loyalty lay. Her pride and dignity wanted to claim his identity as related to her own. She used the name of her father also, to defy her stepfather. As she grew up, Isabel developed qualities of independence and willfulness, strong masculine qualities which she felt she needed to maintain her sense of identity. But what was the cost?

She learnt how to be responsible and help others. There were younger children in her step-family. But who was there to help her? Her vulnerable self had to stay very hidden.

Isabel's strength increased to the extent where when she reached the age of sixteen, her stepfather came once to physically attack her and this time she confronted him. Her anger rose and she told him forcefully never to lay a hand on her again. He didn't. This was a relief. She felt safer after that, but she could not open herself emotionally to him.

With her real father, she continued to quietly love him. However, there were doubts and fears to make his image more and more distant in her mind. Even though her father had been sent away by her mother - although her mother did not explain this to Isabel fully while she was young - her father had not tried to make contact with her. There were times when Isabel had really wanted him to be there for her. She needed someone to defend her. But he had not come. How could a father leave his child? If he stayed away and never made contact did he love or care about her at all? These thoughts and feelings were too painful for Isabel to consider actively over an extended period of time. She had to bury many thoughts and memories of her father just to survive.

When she came to me for her therapy session, Isabel was ready and wanting to know more about her father, in spite of her fears. She knew that she would need to go into a very vulnerable place within her to contact her feelings about this. But she trusted me, and she trusted her inner consciousness to help and support her.

She was afraid that he may have rejected her. And if this was true she did not know how she would cope with that. But the timing felt right to explore this. I respected Isabel very much as a woman with a lot of inner strength. We decided to proceed.

In our session, I chose to use hypnosis. With this, I directed her consciousness to bring forth a memory of some important moment when she was with her father.

For a few moments there was silence. Then Isabel's face brightened up. She was accessing a memory. What follows is the experience that Isabel described.

'I'm indoors, walking. My father is there. He's stretching down from the waist to pick me up. I feel happiness. I'm laughing. I have on a white frock. There's a long hallway. I've walked down to him...He's looking down. I can see him....I'm looking into his eyes....His hair looks as if it is combed back....There's lots of laughter in his face....His sleeves are rolled up....

'I'm holding his ears....I like his ears....I feel as if I am playing with his ears....He laughs....He's happy to be with me....He seems so close.....He has a broad face.....He loves me.....He seems to be up very close, very close.....His hair is crinkly.

'He seems to be saying, singing a tune, a nursery rhyme....He's holding me. It's warm....He hasn't seen this dress before....He's touching it, flicking up the frill. He's looking down, touching the hem....I could feel his hair when I touched his ear....He has his hand clasped in mine....I don't want to let him go.'

Isabel becomes aware of another woman in the hallway. It's not her mother. Her father and this woman talk with each other. The woman is going to take little Isabel out for a walk. Then she sees her father kneeling in front of her.

'He's touching my cheek and hair....There's a penny in his trousers....He's playing....It's a game, finding the penny there....I found it....Now his hand is on my head....That's it....He's gone....All I look at is his trousers....He's gone....'

At the end of the session Isabel told me that she felt this was the last time that she met her father. There were tears but it was a tremendous relief for her. She felt much more at peace. Afterwards she was able to check with her mother that at about the age of four she did indeed have a white frock that she wore, as she had described in the experience. For Isabel, she was convinced that she had accessed a genuine memory. This was amazing and extremely healing for her because now she knew in all the different parts of her, that as a child her father did love her.

As a session of therapy, it was quite easy for me to support Isabel through this particular process. However, I know that for Isabel it required a huge step of courage. Although we also needed to do some inner child work around her relationship with her step-father and mother, this did not seem as important as the work we did to retrieve the memory of how her father loved her.

It was sad that Isabel had spent so much of her life separated from her father, but perhaps her Soul had its own reasons for putting her through this.

Some Thoughts About Our Parents

The birth of a child is a miracle. I remember with each of my own children, when I knew they were coming into our world how much excitement it generated in me. To participate in the co-creation of human life is a tremendous experience.

With an open heart, it can be appreciated as one of the fundamental experiences of our human existence. It cannot help but bring a deep and lasting bond to all who are involved with it. Potentially this is an experience of great joy and wonder. For the parents and ultimately the child too, it does bring responsibility. And it is an opportunity for great learning.

With Inner Child Therapy it is often the relationship between child and parent which is the focus for healing that is needed. Wounds can be formed through mistakes, difficult interactions or through parental absence as in the case of Isabel. Generally, our parents are not as perfect as we would like them to be.

It can be easy for us to blame our parents for our inadequacies and shortcomings. Because we are so connected to them, we can become very aware of their limitations, sometimes even more than our own!

Yet, when we become parents, the picture changes. We love our children and we struggle to do our best. We have to sacrifice a lot of our lives to be there for our children. When we are tired or stressed it is not always easy to be in a good temper. Quite often, we can hardly help ourselves from acting with our children in the way how our parents acted with us. Some behaviour traits continue to be passed along through the generations.

Our children though are not always angels either. Their behaviour and personality can be very challenging for us. It can be difficult for us to cope with them. However, when we know we are not being as devoted to our children as we feel they need from us, we can easily take on guilt and blame ourselves.

As parents, we don't want our children to blame us or think badly of us for our mistakes and shortcomings. Therefore, if we are honest and compassionate we cannot blame our parents either. We are all human beings learning and suffering together and sometimes on our own. We need to find our own identity and inner freedom so that we will not feel victims of family patterns, difficulties and wounds. But at the same time, for us to feel whole, we cannot ignore the heritage and love which binds us to our family.

Resolving pain and releasing suffering through therapy and meditation can be very helpful. Sometimes though, to actually meet with an important member of the family, to share open communication and love may be even more healing. It may feel very frightening to do this, especially if we have established very limited forms of interaction between us. So it means daring to go beyond this. However, with the support of friends or therapist or a group, this may be very rewarding. Of course in some situations direct communication may not be possible. For instance, a family member may be dead, or else the difficulties may just feel too insurmountable emotionally to get through. In these cases inner communication may be the only way.

Without communication though we become isolated and lonely. Then the suffering we feel and the suffering of those near to us will be greater.

In relationship to those with whom we are deeply bonded, we will feel most free inside when we can dare to be ourselves. While we wear masks or disguises to present only some aspects of our personality, we will not feel peace. We cannot really hide from anyone who truly loves us. On some level they will always perceive the truth of who we are.

Reuniting With a Shattered Family - The Story of Jane

My first meeting with Jane took place when she came to attend one of my Self-Hypnosis classes. I enjoyed Jane's presence in my class because she brought energy and vitality to the group. Jane was a social worker. She cared passionately about people who were oppressed, those from broken homes, the outcasts of society. Yet when I questioned Jane about herself, she became very timid and shy. Apparently many of the problems of those she worked to help were in herself as well. Somehow she had reached a critical point in her life where she knew that she needed help.

Inside, Jane was a mass of insecurity, with confusion about her identity. She tried to conceal this with her mind. Mentally she was strong, and she could defend herself well if she perceived any attacks were coming her way. However, on an emotional level, her feelings and body awareness were very fragile She was very afraid. It was difficult for her to trust anybody, or to let anyone come close to her, except strictly on her terms. There were some compulsive and irrational traits to her behaviour. One example of this was with shopping binges when she would spend on occasions far more money than she could afford. She wore her hair very short and I was not sure that she really accepted to be a woman. When I asked her about it, she was very unsure about what she wanted in life.

For some months Jane had been seeing a woman counsellor, patiently and slowly starting to address some of the issues coming from her childhood. Through working with this counsellor and what we were doing in my class, Jane started to become aware of the little girl inside her. This was the part of her that really needed help and the part of her who tended to be so afraid.

Jane was interested to see me for some individual work, but it took her a while to do this. She was gaining quite a lot from the support of her counsellor, and she did not want to intrude upon this. But she sensed that there were limits to how far she could go with her counsellor's style of guidance. Her counsellor acknowledged this as well. Jane was aware that coming to me would mean going more deeply into her problems. She needed to feel ready for this. So I was delighted when finally she made an appointment to see me for a therapy session.

At the outset of our session, I needed to gain a profile of Jane's life. It was quite painful for her to tell me this. As I had expected, Jane's early life had been full of suffering.

When Jane was conceived her mother and father were in an unhappy relationship. During the pregnancy Jane's mother was involved in a relationship with another man. It seemed that Jane was not wanted as a baby. Her mother wanted to leave her father and they really struggled to stay together.

For about eighteen months after Jane was born, Jane's mother remained with her, although almost leaving several times. Then came the separation. Jane's mother did not have the circumstances to be able to support Jane, and so left without her. Jane's father also did not feel able to be a full-time parent. So Jane was sent away from both her parents to live with her Aunty (her father's sister) and her husband.

Jane stayed with them until she was seven years old, after which her father had remarried and she went back to living with him. From the age of eighteen months onwards then Jane had no further contact with her mother. There was much residual hostility between Jane's father and mother. Jane's father told her that her mother was bad and did not want her. She was urged to believe that her mother had totally rejected her. This was very difficult for Jane.

Once, her grandparents tried to give Jane her mother's address. This was when Jane was quite small. Unfortunately Jane wrote down the address wrongly. Even worse then, her father found out and banned Jane from any further contact with her grandparents. She didn't see them again while they were still alive.

In another terrible twist to her story, while Jane lived with her Aunty, her Uncle repeatedly sexually abused her. She did not find support with her Aunty. This made Jane very afraid. She was very relieved to go to live with her father again.

Throughout her growing up years after this, her father was like a pillar for her. But he was not perfect. He had quite a possessive and demanding nature. When Jane was older, he threatened her that if she ever made contact with her mother then that would be the end of her relationship with him.

With this demand, Jane felt that she had no choice. Her relationship to her father was her lifeline. Without him, she felt she would have no family. Her relationship with her step-mother was antagonistic. He was the only one with whom she felt a sense of belonging.

By now, Jane felt almost completely convinced that her mother had utterly rejected her. This was a huge loss for Jane. There was only one tiny part of her that did not believe it, wanted to believe something else. But this part of her only had a very weak voice.

I feel that Jane must have a truly resilient Spirit to have survived all this. But now as she came for a session with me, she earnestly wanted to heal the divides and pain she carried inside her.

In this first session, it was the sexual abuse with her uncle that was the main issue that came to the fore. For the first time in her life, Jane was able to express some of the anger she had been holding in connection to her uncle. Her adult part helped the child part to find the strength to do this. This was a breakthrough for Jane. She had previously regarded anger as something to be avoided or forbidden. She had not realised that the expression of it could be anything other than destructive. For her now, this enabled her to feel she had the strength and power to be able to confront her Uncle. If she could confront him, she could make other changes in her life as well. This session helped Jane greatly to feel less afraid in her life.

Jane now felt very determined to sort out her life. With the patient support of her husband Patrick, with the help of friends and groups as well as working with me from time to time, Jane began more and more to tackle the important issues that tormented her inside. At the core though, of her inner suffering, was the relationship, or lack of it, that she shared with her mother.

Jane did not know how her mother felt towards her now. But she couldn't attempt to make contact because of the threat posed by her father. Besides, to establish contact with her mother may just serve to confirm the rejection she imagined her mother felt towards her. Jane continued to feel troubled by this though. Deep inside her psyche Jane sensed dark and terrible feelings were lurking in connection to her mother. More and more, she knew that she would have to face up to those feelings if ever she was going to find peace in her life. It took her some time, but eventually, she found the courage to approach me and ask for a session to explore this.

Because I felt that Jane was ready, I directed her consciousness to go straight to the source of the inner disturbances Jane felt towards her mother. Immediately, her consciousness opened so she felt she was in a dark place. As I questioned her it became apparent that this was a memory of being in her mother's womb. Her body started to react, shaking and trembling. In this state her own thoughts and the thoughts of her mother were almost merged together. I then asked her what the trembling in her body was wanting to say.

'I'm frightened....frightened....I've got to not be anything....'

She then became aware of a pain. She was wanting to feel nice but she couldn't do so. There was a numbness. I asked what this pain was wanting to say.

'I feel like I'm a pain...get rid of me....an object of pain....'

She repeated this as she heaved with emotion. She had picked up her mother's thoughts that it was painful for her mother to be carrying her. Jane did not want to be regarded as a pain by her mother. She became more and more emotional.

'I feel angry...I'm an excuse....'

I got Jane to breathe with all the emotion that was coming up. To help Jane find more a sense of her own power, I then asked what she wanted from her mother. It felt a relief for her to answer this.

'I want to be valued by you, not a pain mum.'

As she repeated this, she felt enormous energy movements in her, freeing inner constrictions.

'Have contact with me. Love me, don't hate me'

With this, Jane was able to express thoughts and feelings that had been bottled up inside her since before birth. It was a tremendous release. As she continued with this, suddenly she started coughing. Soon Jane coughed up a lot of mucus from inside. This seemed part of the process - another layer of the cleansing of her psyche. I urged her to continue to affirm what she really wanted until eventually she started to feel a wonderful peace. The inner resistance around her mother was gone. This session shifted a lot for Jane. When I saw her next, she told me some amazing news. She had taken the risk, she had been very bold and written a letter to her mother. She had not told her father yet. But her mother had written back an eleven page letter. The letter was so full and so open. Now they were planning to meet up.

They did meet and they have gone on meeting since then. Their first meeting was very joyful. They had so much to share, so much to catch up on. As they became more familiar with each other, they started even to play with each other, meeting on many different levels. Jane could recognise herself in her mother. Meanwhile her mother was extremely happy to be with Jane.

Jane's mother told her how she had attempted to gain access to Jane several times but was prevented by social services. Her heart was at peace now that she was reunited with Jane again. She told Jane that she was wanted as a baby. Also, she shared her own perspective to Jane about how difficult it had been to be with Jane's father. The two of them became very close, although Jane was not fooled into thinking her mother was perfect. The reunion though was certainly a blessing.

As a consequence of this, many changes occurred in Jane. She started growing her hair longer, becoming more feminine in her appearance. Jane took the step to begin working part-time instead of full time so she could have space to honour her own needs as well as the needs of others.

After a while, I asked her about her father. She had spoken to him at last, and he was understanding. Although it was difficult for him, he did manage to accept that Jane had made contact with her mother. As a consequence, her relationship with him was in her own words 'massively better'. She felt that he had let her go, for her to be an adult now, not just his little girl. Another miracle had occurred.

Jane felt that the universe had been supporting her process. What happened for her was right, and had taken place at the right time. She felt very happy about it all, and was grateful to have found her family. The little girl in her was happy too.

In the last contact I had with Jane, she was pregnant, about to give birth to a child of her own. She and her husband Patrick were joyful at this turn of events. I have a feeling that their child will be very well loved and looked after!

Chapter 7

Psychotherapy in Groups

There are many possibilities with groups how productive inner work can be accomplished. However, there is one method which I have used that I would like to share because I have found it to be very dynamic and effective, especially for Inner Child work and with past lives.

This method is a process of making symbolic external representations of inner states of awareness that people may be experiencing. From these external representations people may be able to act out what they are feeling inside and bring forth much productive releasing of energy.

To give a couple of examples of this, in a recent workshop, a man was recounting about his mother and how cruel she had been to him. He got to a point where he described how she used to punish him by placing him in isolation in a coal bunker and leaving him locked in there. As he started talking about this, his voice broke and it was obviously upsetting for him to recall this. However, as he was talking I sensed a 'deadness' around the energy of his body. From what I knew of his life, I sensed that there was still a part of him in that coal bunker. For much of his life he had felt helpless and isolated.

In order to take his process forward, we constructed a coal bunker in the room where we were working. We did it quite simply using cushions and blankets, materials that were malleable and could not hurt people or be easily damaged. Then with him in his coal bunker surrounded by blankets and cushions, the group came to lend assistance to keep the structure in place and lend some weight to it. To take the process further it was necessary for him to know on one side that we were there to support and encourage him. On the other side though we needed to bring out the dynamics of the situation and make it as real as we could. So by finding out what his mother said and did, I could act that out and 'play mother'. At first there was no reaction, but eventually he was stirred into action. He didn't want to be there any longer. Using our strength, we tried to prevent him from coming out of the 'coal bunker' so he would really need to connect with his own power to succeed. But he was very determined. By us giving way a little he was able to use his own force of determination to get out of there. This was extremely liberating for him. By speaking the words he wanted to say to his mother and scattering he cushions around the room, this helped complete the process. That psychic blockage from inside him was gone.

In another example from a workshop with a woman I will call Paula, when I led a meditation into an inner wound, she experienced a tightness around her throat as if she was being suffocated. There was much emotion and distress with this. In my first session with her I asked her to look up and see who was doing this. With much rapid eye movement, but with her eye lids closed, she told me it was a man in black.

From a later meditation this experience came to her again. However, now her awareness of it was more expanded. She was in a courtyard being hung.

Finally, she felt the courage to work with this with the whole group. We set up the scene of the courtyard. She realised she was a young man. I told her to close her eyes so she could connect more easily with her feelings. Then counting to 3, I put my hands gently around her neck to simulate the hanging. Straight away, her body went through all the dramatic motions of reliving this experience. For a long while, her body was shaking with fear, until finally it was inert. However, I knew there was more to it than this.

This young man had stolen a jewel. He was being hung on the orders of three authority figures dressed in black for this offence. We set up the scene for this. Three tall people from the group served this purpose. We did not have any black material so we used orange blankets instead. For Paula, this did not matter. They were still men dressed in black for her.

At first she was totally overawed by these men. She couldn't speak. So I helped to play out the voices and sentiments of these men. I said things like 'You stole the jewel. You deserve to be punished. You have to be hung.' While taunting her with this I tried to encourage her as this young man to speak his truth.

Eventually she could speak. She said 'I am one of the people'. She told them that they didn't care about the people. Paula became very emotional. When I asked her as this young man what he wanted, she said he wanted to be educated and helped so he could live a good life. These authorities didn't help at all.

Suddenly, the key to all of this dawned on me. For her as the young man, these authorities held all the power of what she wanted and needed in her life. She felt helpless before them. However, the more she spoke the more impassioned she became that they had no right to keep this from her.

I asked the strongest man who was 'playing' one of the authorities to hold a cushion. Then I told her that this represented the opportunity for him (the young man) to learn, to be educated and to live a decent life. The authority man held it to himself. Paula didn't hesitate. Her whole being became enraged and grabbed for that cushion. She was a small woman compared to him, but nothing could stop her from wrestling from his grasp the cushion and claiming it for herself. This was about claiming back her own power. When she could let go of the cushion she could feel this energy in herself. Afterwards she felt well satisfied. We could talk it through and the group were able to give their reflections as well. For Paula, this had been a big energy release.

This kind of process can be very helpful in a group. Often many people in the group can be actively involved in the process and it gives a strong outlet for energies that are moving about internally to be expressed. However, much sensitivity is needed to find the right moment to act, to home in on the vulnerable place within that needs attention and also to support the person with love to succeed and bring out what is needed. When I am doing this process with people I like to check at each step that they agree to it and that it is what they choose as well.

Chapter 8

Enlightened Societies From the Past

History through Past Life Regression

Past life regression can have other applications besides helping therapeutically to clear personal psychic, emotional and mental blockages from within. For instance, it can also be a useful tool with which to study history.

Archaeologists and historians have tried to piece together what life must have been like for people at different times. However, through Past Life Regression, people can have an experience of what it was like living in various past conditions. Usually, information coming through regression will correlate very accurately with what is known of different historical periods from other sources.

Of course, a lot of regressions may be uninteresting from the angle of historical study because of the ordinariness of lives which are uncovered. Often there will be an insight, emotional release or an understanding that is important for the person to assimilate. In this context, historical details may not be relevant for the person to experience. Nor may such information even be forthcoming. So it is only in some past life regressions where exploration of historical data is appropriate and possible.

The most commonly held view of history is that our humanity has gradually evolved from a very primitive, humanoid existence. From Stone age hunting and gathering, humanity has made gradual progress through discoveries, developing more sophistication, learning and organisation. Then in our present age, with scientific advancement and technology, we know more

107

and can do more than ever before. It is a view which assumes a continuing ascent in our progress as a humanity, where our life as a collective group has got better and better with time. Achievements such as rockets to the moon, computers, cars, television, medical advances and ways in which we can manipulate our environment to suit our needs are all taken as signs of our continuing evolution.

There is a shadow side though. Environmental destruction, widespread poverty, war and inter-community strife, mean that there is a lot of unnecessary suffering in our world. The fact that many people feel lonely, unhappy and alienated in our materialistic culture are indicators that all is not yet in balance in our modern society. Yet, many feel that these conditions are a necessary price for progress.

In my own personal view, I value the achievement of happiness and peace more highly than that concerning science and technology. From this perspective, I am not sure especially with our western society, how far we have advanced.

Past life regression lets people experience their inner life as a personality from particular historical settings. Studying the context of these past lives, it is clear there have been many terrible situations from the past where people could be forced into great suffering. However, there are also indications of communities and societies at different time periods where people could experience a much more satisfying, peaceful and rich inner life than a lot of people experience today.

From a therapist angle, sometimes people may be given a past life to experience that is inwardly rich and happy as a means to give strength and motivation to help them face the struggles and difficulties of their present life in our modern age.

Anthropologists and other interested people studying the ways of more 'primitive' people like the Native American Indians or the Australian Aborigines for instance, have begun to realise what a rich inner world some of these peoples inhabit. They believe the Earth to be sacred and that animals, places, stones and ceremonies are also sacred. This respect for life around them enables them to appreciate their relationship with all the elements of their existence. For them, the world is Spiritually alive and interconnected. Some of these people seem to know a lot more about reality than we do. Yet, they have an outwardly simple life - unlike us, leaving very little signs for us to know the details of their civilisation or markings that could be passed on through history.

I have noticed with past life regressions which I have guided, that very often when people return to lives with cultures of people living in harmony with their environment, such as the Native American Indians, then these lives tend to be very happy and peaceful. Of course, these people have also had their wars and power struggles. Human life cannot be perfect!

Perhaps there could be a correlation though where Spiritual inner richness for a community may connect with an outwardly simple life for its people.

Civilisations which have concentrated their attention on conquering others with their large armies, or having ostentatious expressions of architecture and outer riches may actually have been civilisations suffering an inner decline, where the inner life of the people was becoming more limited and poor. The Roman civilisation could be an example of this.

Some of the inwardly richest and most worthwhile cultures and civilisations from our past may have been lost without our being able to appreciate their existence because they left so very little outward traces of what their life was like.

Past life regression can help with this, because people may experience living in an epoch and a culture which is virtually unknown to our historians. This can help bring forth much valuable knowledge and information.

Initiation

From witnessing numerous regressions to vastly different cultural backgrounds and historical epochs, I feel that those communities where life has tended to be happiest were ones where Spiritual values were at the core of that society. The expression of these Spiritual values could range from aesthetic and studious communities like the Tibetans, Indians or monastic life in general to more Earthly orientated communities like the Native Americans or the Celts, and many others as well. The Spiritual leadership of these communities needed much awareness to support the inner well-being and harmony of the people. It could be the shaman, the priests or the priestesses who had the role. Their knowledge was fundamental to the successful functioning of the society in which they lived. They were then intermediaries between the Spiritual worlds and life on Earth for the people in that particular community. It could be a large responsibility.

People who had this responsibility needed to learn about the inner mysteries of life and the life of Spirit. This could be a training lasting many years. When it was done well, this could prepare a person to take on the task of Spiritual leadership of the community. Tests and aspects of the training that would determine if a person was fit for this particular role were called Initiation.

Many communities in the past have had Rites of Initiation. Sometimes these would be specific initiations for everybody - like rites to mark the passage from boyhood to manhood, or girlhood to womanhood. However the more important Rites of Initiation for Spiritual learning were usually for the selected few.

These Initiation Rites would help people to become more embedded and committed to the particular cultural patterns of that community. However, the main purpose of the Initiation Rites were to open up perception psychically and learn how to use that perception and the powers that went with it wisely. There would be teachers and wise elders within the community to help guide this process. Then those with opened perception within the community would be respected above all others and would be needed to help guide the Spiritual life of the community. There was a moral aspect to this too. People in this privileged position were expected to dedicate themselves to serving the needs of the community and to respect the powers of Spirit. While this happened, the life of the community would generally proceed in harmony and peace. However, these powers could also be corrupted and used for selfish ends. When this took place, the perceptual life of the community would inevitably go into decline. People may then be taken up more trying to solve disputes, power struggles and wars.

When people were opened in their perception to the living Spirit of life around them, they could gain energy from these sources. There may be places of power where the energy forces for those people were very strong - sacred places like for example a grove of trees, where perhaps people could go for particular reasons at certain times.

Ceremonies could be arranged and used to invoke the power of Spirit to help people in their lives. When people were inspired by this it could add greater depth and meaning to their collective existence. The belief in the reality of Spirit would also help these forces to touch and affect people's lives more fully. This would help people's sense of belonging with each other and the sense of being connected to a greater whole to which they were contributing.

Those who had successfully achieved Initiation could be called upon to serve in many ways. They would be in charge of keeping the balance, guarding and protecting the inner well-being of their community. But often they could be called upon to make practical and political decisions on behalf of the community as well. When their time was nearly over, they would need to pass their knowledge on, so the well-being of the community could continue. They had to be dedicated in service to their task. It could be quite a lonely and solitary position. This may also involve for them to sacrifice some aspects of ordinary human life so they could fulfil their duties. It was not an easy path for people to undertake. There was also a strong danger of corruption if Initiates decided to act for wishes of personal gain rather than coming from the heart and acting for what was right and true. There had to be a lot of care to protect the life of Initiates, but even more to protect the Spirit of their teachings.

Through mistakes and corruption though, it was not always possible. Therefore, many happy and peaceful communities have declined and ultimately perished because of this.

Legendary Civilisations

Many people wonder if there may have been hidden golden ages in our past as a humanity, times of achievement and peaks of earlier civilisation which may have been lost to us.

Much has been written with speculations of fabled places like Atlantis or the lost continent of Mu in the Pacific Ocean. Many people dismiss these suggestions. However, experiences from numerous Past Life regression give indications that these places did actually exist.

It is possible with regression, once people have started experiencing their past lives, to ask questions to their inner psyche, about when they began their cycle of lives on Earth. My research to these kinds of questions, has yielded quite interesting results.

Most people with whom I have worked in this way, seem to have started their cycle of lives on Earth in the time period since known historical events have taken place. However, there are some who have indicated that they have memories of lifetimes from before then. With some of these, when I was able to investigate the lifetimes concerned, people have recounted lifetimes in tribal settings. With our present knowledge of history, this is what I would have expected.

But there are also regression experiences I have witnessed of lifetimes in seemingly very remote times on Earth, that defy conventional views of history. These experiences speak of more advanced cultures and civilisations, where people's own perception appears to have been very different from our own. Atlantis and Mu seem to be the names of two of these civilisations. There is enough consistency in the "memories" of these ancient civilisations for me to believe that there is a shared knowledge of these places existing in the inner psyche of a large number of people in our present population.

For a long time, I have been interested in Atlantis. I have wondered, assuming that such a place existed, what is must have been like to live there. From stories and books I have come across, it is often spoken of in quite a glamourous way. But from what my clients have shared with me, it was not necessarily such a pleasant place to be at all.

It has not been possible for me to gather a comprehensive view of life on Atlantis over the course of its history. I will try to explain some of the reasons for this. But I will also share some details of what I have learnt.

Some of my clients, who have been given indications of lives on Atlantis, have been shown or told inwardly that it would not be appropriate or possible for them to access these experiences.

Usually, the lifetimes from Atlantis that could be consciously recounted have been more 'problem' lives. These are experiences where there are unresolved traumas or difficulties which are affecting the person now. So I have had to help these clients using methods which I have outlined in earlier chapters.

However, this has meant that I have been lacking information about what life was like in Atlantis when things were going well, when much was in harmony, and people were happy. Unfortunately, people do not usually access these experiences of Atlantis.

A bigger problem I have had is connected with how people seem to have perceived their life differently then to how we do now. The effect of this has been that when people try to channel experiences from their Atlantean lifetimes, it is often difficult for their minds - the way how our minds are structured and organised in our present time - for these experiences to fit. People often struggle to conceive and communicate what they were experiencing from these lifetimes.

In some cases, people have been aware that their psychic awareness was much greater in those Atlantean times. Our minds seem much more limited now. But perhaps our thinking is more advanced than theirs.

From my research, people were very sensitive to natural energies then. Stones and the Earth itself, felt to be alive. People felt that they could affect changes in the world around them, by using their Will, and aligning themselves with certain sources of energy. Crystals were used to amplify energy and people could use crystals to exert more power in what they wanted. Struggles that people had with each other were usually more of a psychic warfare than using physical weapons. And people did struggle with each other then, as they do now, for power.

Materially, people seemed to live quite simple lives, in stone or wooden dwellings. Their food came through basic agricultural methods. But this did not seem so important to them. It was with a psychic awareness that they felt their passion.

Once, one of my clients accessed an Atlantean life where she was a man. In this lifetime, this man became obsessed with power. He worked for another man who was generating power from a huge crystal. This power was like an intoxicating drug, making them feel more and more mighty, and like God. Somehow, they drained energy from the people and the land around them, to maintain this feeling of power. By the end of this lifetime, a vast area of land around the physical site of these manipulations had become like a desert. When this man realised what he had done, he felt utter despair. He also felt used by the man for whom he worked. This Soul then spent many lifetimes as a victim, trying to work off what he had done. In her present lifetime, this woman has suffered much from feelings of unworthiness. Now, she is committed to trying to help raise awareness about the needs of the environment.

According to my clients' experiences, there were temples of Healing in Atlantis. People could be very devoted Spiritually. However, towards the end times, this became less prevalent. As time went on, people seemed to become more and more separated in their actions, from the needs of the whole. Some tried to prevent and correct this. But, those efforts were in vain. Some form of major Earth disaster finished the civilisation of Atlantis very suddenly. Whatever were the actual causes of this catastrophe, people there believed that their own collective psychic actions had contributed to the destruction. It was an enormous shock for everyone involved to realise this.

During one of my own regressions, I felt myself to be living in Atlantis near the time of its destruction. When this happened, I felt a huge sense of loss and despair in my mind, with the sad thought that 'the people wouldn't listen' I could hardly imagine how such an advanced civilisation existing with so much potential for good, could end up so corrupt and sink beneath the waves.

Other high civilisations have also fallen due to people's greed and capacity to put self-interest before the needs of the whole. When we have destroyed what is beautiful we suffer accordingly. It has not always been easy though for humans to put the needs of the whole before their own personal desires. The choice is ours, and the struggle about that continues to be with us today. The legendary civilisation of Mu also ultimately fell like Atlantis. Indications from regression reveal that this place may have been the original Spiritual paradise for people on Earth, an important seed place for the beginnings of our humanity and the cradle for religion and Spiritual worship. It appears that the Mu civilisation extended back into very ancient times. People's way of perceiving was very different there too. People could experience through symbols and collective worship.

Unfortunately, this civilisation also ultimately degenerated. Through selfishness and abuses by using free will, people lost more and more contact with Spiritual sources. People started mis-guidedly offering sacrifices as a means to attain Spiritual rewards. Then corruption set in. Ultimately, due to Earth changes, this continent too, perished.

The Struggle to Maintain Enlightened Societies

Through the ages, it seems that there have been many attempts in different cultures by Spiritually inspired teachers and groups to create and establish a more Spiritually based society. Indeed, from very ancient times, we may have had this. However, the forces in us that want to destroy have not allowed these kinds of societies to endure. From the ashes of high civilisations that have fallen, new ones have emerged to take their place.

It may be part of our human Soul journey to learn to adapt to experience all kinds of conditions. Life on Earth is full of change and movement. It is the challenge of living as a human being to accept change including the processes of formation and creation, maintaining and developing as well as letting go and the ending of that which has served its purpose. It is often our attachment to that which we do not want to change which can bring the greatest suffering, because those attachments are avoiding what is true.

We may wonder then if life on Earth has an infinite capacity to renew itself - that the Earth is like a playground to us and we can do what we wish while we are here. Somehow, I doubt that this is true. The Earth is a finite physical organism. There is a very delicate state of balance which allows us to live our lives here. Once this balance is disturbed too much, life on this planet could be ended very easily.

I believe that we as a collective humanity have a choice. We can either learn to live in peace or eventually we may destroy life on this planet. That would be very sad, but would also be our own doing. I believe that the only way we can live in peace is for societies to function within Spiritual principles where we as individuals can allow ourselves to be guided and inspired by Spirit. Some societies from our past have managed to do this. Hopefully, we in our modern age can learn to do this too.

In one life which I have experienced through regression, I found myself in Ancient Greece at a time before recorded History, possibly around 2000 BC. I was helping to serve and administer one of the temples there. People around me lived simple lives which were connected very much with the Earth. It was a gentle and peaceful society where the Temples were central to the culture of the people.

I felt that I could communicate by Telepathy with my friends and I had a rich inner life. However, that life was ended when warriors from the east came and destroyed the temples, and with it they destroyed a delicate and nurturing culture that had been patiently built up over a period of hundreds of years. The warriors did not understand the subtleties and powers of the Temple life, and so they exerted their power over this Spiritual culture by destroying it.

It was very difficult for me to leave that life. I loved the land and I loved the people and I felt deeply attached to it all. Inside, I felt bitterness about what had happened.

The experience of this life made me realise that the precious resources and beauty of the Earth have no real defence when people set their minds upon the destruction of it, perhaps to achieve some selfish goal. In this case, those warriors from the East had no active Spiritual perception. They did not understand this. They had strong instincts for survival, to fight and conquer and they chose to use these instincts ruthlessly, to achieve their goal.

There are many examples, both from our modern age and throughout history of peaceful societies being threatened and overrun by the power of might, where the value of wisdom and love has been ignored. From recent times examples may include Tibet, South American Indians, the Native American Indians and Australian Aborigines. The list could go on. Some people and governments would argue that the only way for such peaceful societies to be maintained would be to protect them and have them defended by huge armies and weapons. Such defences though are based primarily on a premise of fear. Where fear predominates, there is no opening for love and Spiritual inspiration. Fear generated enemies and isolation. The answer seems more connected with a need to trust.

Although it is very sad, it is apparent to me that when 'enlightened' peaceful cultures and ways of life have been destroyed, not all is necessarily lost. An impressive case to illustrate this would be the story of Jesus Christ. Jesus came to the Earth as a great Spiritual Master, teaching about love and peace. He gained followers and helped many people. Yet, through ignorance and intolerance, he was persecuted and finally killed. Jesus, himself, felt there was nothing he could do but go along with this.

From one or two regressions I have witnessed of people who lived at this time, the sense of loss at his Death was appaling. Yet, there was also then a great release of Spiritual energy. People who opened their hearts to Jesus were inspired by the love of the living presence of Jesus in Spirit. This process has continued to unfold, and through the centuries, millions of people have been inspired and helped by the living presence of Jesus in Spirit.

There have been many corruptions in the way that Christianity has been institutionalised. For instance, from the regression of Edith to her life as Antonia, it is difficult to imagine Jesus acting with the same degree of intolerance and violence towards people practising healing with herbs and wanting to help people, as representatives of the Church did in Antonia's day. However, I do not feel that this detracts from the fact that the true living inner presence of Jesus has acted as force for much good in people's lives.

So the struggle goes on. Many people in today's world seem to act mainly from self-interest with little particular concern about the consequences of their actions. But it does matter. From the principles of reincarnation, we are obliged to face the consequences of our own actions. That is how we learn. As a collective group, our future life as a Humanity on Earth will affect us, because we will be called upon to experience it. We are co-creating that future now.

I believe that we are not alone with this though. Spiritual love, help and guidance are there for us, if only we can reach out for it, and learn how to ask for that help, and make the choice to do so.

I do not think that this is a perverse trick from God so we will destroy ourselves and suffer Hell. I feel that our lives on Earth are an opportunity for us individually and collectively to attain liberation and love.

As far as our past is concerned, we can learn both from our successes and the mistakes that we have made.

Case Studies

To conclude this chapter, I will share two case studies of regression to peaceful and more 'enlightened 'societies from the past, as illustrations of how helpful these experiences can be, and what they tell us of our history.

In the first case, Lucy experiences a past life as a Native American Indian. This is a simple story without elaborate detail of the kind of life she lived. Yet for Lucy this regression helped tremendously. From a life that had become very restricted and claustrophobic for Lucy, this experience inspired her, made her realise she was more than who she thought she was, and gave her motivation to create a better life for herself.

With Alice in the second case study, I relate about two lives she recalled having lived in Ancient Mu. The first of these lives is interesting because there is a sense of it having taken place long, long ago. But also, Alice's emotional perception of the Spiritual nature of this experience was tremendous. Recalling that life was like ecstasy for Alice. It was so inwardly rich for her that she could hardly cope with being Alice again when it was all over. It was as though the effect of living this life on Earth had affected her so profoundly, that each time she had been born again since then she has wanted to recapture the quality of that first experience - without success. It was intoxicating for her! So by remembering the experience through regression, she could realise that it was not lost for her. She wanted so much to be back there again - and I needed to help her come to terms with this. But then, as she integrated this experience, it brought her much peace.

There was a second life on Mu which Alice experienced. This one seemed to come from much later in Mu's history. There is a theme of disillusionment and corruption with this particular story. However, Alice could share more details about her life in this experience than the first one and it is apparent that even though her own consciousness was now in a much more limited frame than in earlier Mu life, it is still very much more open than how she could experience life today as Alice. After this regression Alice felt a similar sense of wanting to go back there, though not as strongly as in the first life.

Lucy

I had only recently started my work as a therapist when Lucy came to see me as a client. Still trying to find my way and feel secure in this work, I felt a little nervous about how I may be able to best help her.

As she sat down with me, I felt Lucy to be sensitive but also shy and very unsure about herself. As I asked her questions about her life, she reported to me a variety of problems from which she was suffering.

A few years previously, a series of very difficult situations had befallen her. Within a short period of time she had a fallopian tube operation, been in hospital with a collapsed lung, discovered that her husband had been having an affair, and her dogs, who were her most precious companions, had been attacked and injured badly. Shaken by these events Lucy had more and more isolated herself, spending increasing amounts of time at home on her own, with only her dogs to keep her company. Twelve months later she had been diagnosed as having a thyroid gland disorder which need treatment and medication.

By the time she came to see me, she was continually depressed, very mistrustful of people and fearful of bad things that would happen in her life. Besides her dogs, there was very little activity in her life that fulfilled her.

When Lucy came to me for her second session, she related to me how a few days earlier, while she was driving, the car in front of her had run over a cat. The driver proceeded to ignore what had happened, and leaving the poor animal in its death throes, drove off. Lucy desperately wanted to help. But there was nothing she could do. The cat died before her eyes.

Lucy was very shocked by this. She had a deep love of animals, and this accident to the cat prompted her to fear for her own dogs. One of them was getting older anyway. What if her dogs would be killed in a similar way? How could she cope? The thoughts of this sent Lucy into a deep feeling of depression. Besides me, there was no one with whom she could really talk about this.

We began our therapy with hypnosis. She was a good subject. I suggested for her to recall the moment when she first saw the cat being run over. In her distress Lucy felt anxiety about this most strongly at the front of her head. It was like a band. Gently I encouraged her to move her consciousness inside that anxiety. For a while when she did this, she perceived nothing. It was just dark Then she saw a pile of sticks, She did not think much of this and I could have easily ignored it. But something in me told me to pursue it.

I asked her to focus her attention upon these sticks and tell me more about them. Gradually she became aware that these sticks were arranged in a pile for a fire. Then she saw that the fire was burning. She was tending to the fire.

My intuition told me she was perceiving a memory, possibly a past life. I did not say this to her. Instead I directed her to notice her own body, what she had on her feet and the clothes that she was wearing. Her clothes were skins and she wore simple sandals on her feet. She could see that her skin was a darker colour than her present day skin. Very soon it was obvious to her that she was experiencing herself as a native American Indian woman.

For Lucy, this was astonishing. It was very unexpected. At first, she could not accept it. We had not talked about reincarnation or the possibility of past lives. This was a total surprise for her.

In the beginning she reacted by flipping out of the past life experience and into present childhood images instead. At least this was familiar to her. However, with some determination I kept suggesting for her to return to the past life until she was able to settle in it.

Once she was able to do this the story of the life emerged very easily. It was a very happy life. She was a member of a semi-nomadic tribe. Through marriage, she had come to live with another tribe than the tribe of her birth. But she accepted this. She lived very much according to the way of her tribe and felt well integrated with this. With other members of her tribe she felt harmony. With animals, the Earth and life itself she felt at one. The main qualities she felt with this simple life were peace, freedom and acceptance. There was a sense that all life had its purpose, that she could be in harmony and live her life the way she knew was right, and that all was very well. She could breathe this in.

During this life, she encountered Death many times. Her husband whom she loved had died when he was still quite young. Other members of the tribe and her family also died at different stages. However, Death had its place in the tribal life. She could grieve for those she loved who had died. But this did not stop her living her own life to the full. She had her part and her tasks to do.

Physically, for her tribe, it was not an easy existence. Winters could be long, cold and harsh. When conditions became adverse they needed to move their home. However, for Lucy as this Indian woman, she felt the Earth and the Spirit of Nature around her enabling her and her tribe to live the life that they needed to live.

When she grew old, and she was not fit enough to travel anymore, she was able to leave the tribe then and die alone. This was something she could experience with dignity, acceptance and gratitude, knowing it was the end of a life well lived.

There was nothing to fear in Death. She could experience leaving her body quite effortlessly and going up into Spirit. All the events from this life, including her death, could be accepted as part of a greater purpose and as such, could be acknowledged with thanks.

Reflecting on this life from the Spirit side, she felt it to be one showing her Truth and Knowledge. Lucy could now sense a part of her running and laughing now and telling the other part of her to 'come on'.

Coming out of the trance state, Lucy was visibly moved by what she had experienced. We talked about past lives. I discovered that Lucy did actually believe in reincarnation. She seemed happy though. A positive experience like this may have been just what she needed.

I was very interested to learn afterwards what a huge impact this session had upon Lucy's life. Immediately Lucy noticed that she had more confidence and her depression had lifted. Soon she found a job for herself as a receptionist working in a veterinarian surgery. Now she could be at the front line of caring for animals. It was the perfect job for her. Twelve months later she had a medical check up and her thyroid glands were found to be functioning normally again. Her life had become more outgoing and changed significantly.

In this case, reconnecting with this inspiring past life for Lucy helped her to find values, trust and positive belief in life which she had lost. In recovering this and affirming it, this helped to restore a healthy perspective to her life, so she could express more her creative energy and be more fully herself. The wise and loving inner self of Lucy knew what she needed to experience for her to be well and find health again.

Alice

One of the most moving accounts of the apparent loss of 'paradise' on Earth in Ancient times has come to me through regression work I have witnessed with Alice.

Now, Alice came to me suffering from depression - guilt and anxieties within her making it very difficult for her to feel able to cope with life. There was an atmosphere of melancholy around her. Yet, on the surface her life appeared fine. She had a loving husband and family, a satisfying job which she enjoyed. To me, she was a warm, tender and caring woman and I am sure that there were many in her life who loved and appreciated her, benefiting from her gifts. But she was not happy. This unhappiness extended back to the earliest stages of her life. She found it hard to stand up and express herself to people who threatened her. A bereavement in her early adult life was a blow from which she had never fully recovered, although in appearance she seemed to manage satisfactorily in most situations.

As my work with Alice progressed, a theme about 'the loss of something precious' emerged as a key issue where huge quantities of emotions and feelings were locked up inside of her. There were instances of this theme from circumstances in her present life, like with the bereavement she had suffered, but the core of it seemed to go into an experience that went deeper. More and more Alice trusted the work we were doing. It was helping her. However, she knew that we needed to address this fundamental issue if we were going to make a substantial difference for her. Eventually, even though she felt afraid, she found the courage to say 'yes' to allow her consciousness to go to the root of this problem.

It was then by directing her consciousness to this goal that what emerged were the memories of two very ancient lives from Mu.

Now, Alice did not know anything about Mu before we started these regressions together. But she sensed clearly that these were memories from long, long ago, thousands of years before our recorded history of humanity. We had to explore and investigate different possibilities before we could decide that the experiences actually came from lives on Mu. But when I mentioned Mu for the first time while she was in trance, it caused such a strong emotional reaction in Alice, that she knew that this was where these lives came from, and in my intuition, I knew it as well.

Although later we also did regressions to several other past lives on Earth besides the ones to Mu, it was these particular regressions to Mu that mattered most for her. Alice described these experiences of her memories living in Mu as being 'more real than anything' she had experienced. She had no doubt these were true memories from her past on Earth. Because these memories touched her so deeply, it took many months of counselling and processing for her to come to terms with their contents.

It was unusual for me to find someone who had previous lives extending as far back as Mu. Many people's soul journeys on Earth appeared to start from much more recent times. Certainly then Alice was an 'Old soul'! My intuition suggested to me that the reason Alice may have not already completed her cycle of lives on Earth could be due to wounds connected to these ancient lives on Mu - experiences which until now, she had not been able to resolve.

To enter the experience of the first Mu life, Alice had to go on a symbolic inner journey. She experienced herself going down through some underground caverns. As she proceeded, there were people around and it felt dangerous. She was not sure if she was allowed to come here. It felt as if there were hostile forces around her, but she had to keep going to find something. Finally then, she entered a room and found a box which felt to be made of living wood, something very good and precious which she had known before. Then she felt very frightened and uncertain before opening the box. With great outpourings of emotion she felt very strongly that what was in the box was hers.

What she found in the box was a stone, something very valuable, given to her for her wisdom. Experiencing this stone filled her with joy.

Then immediately, she felt herself to be in this ancient life. She was wearing long, blue robes. Her work was taking place in a stone building. The nature of her work was to help the sick. She kept repeating how much she felt that this was her place. It was Spiritual. There was worshipping of the Light, the source of life.

She was one of a group who worked together. Everything had its sense of order and its right place. She was doing what she felt she had to do, but loving it. The way she was helping people seemed to be through forms of Spiritual Healing.

Watching Alice's body while she was going through this, her body was totally involved, with huge sighs and eruptions of emotions. This was a tremendous experience for her.

There did not seem to be any disharmony in this life, except that she did not want it to end. She wanted to stay and continue her work. She could hardly bear to be wrenched away from 'her place' through Death. But she could just lay down and die in the appointed place, as she had done before! There was no fear.

The descriptive details of this life were sparse but the emotional involvement from witnessing it was very strong. Alice did not want to come back into her present life body from this. She felt her body as Alice horribly restricted and full of pain that she did not want. What she wanted was to be doing her work in Mu. Alice felt very distressed by this. By finishing that life, she felt that she had lost something very beautiful. It was as though she had left part of her Soul behind in that life. She never willingly left it. There was this air of hopelessness around Alice now as we sat together and talked.

I felt astonished by the passion of Alice's response. She must have felt utterly dedicated and at peace with her work in that life. She did not want to be separated from those people with whom she was working, or the place. It was incredibly important to her. The experience of it went beyond words.

I tried to help her. In talks afterwards, I reassured her that this life was no longer lost to her. It was still alive in her Soul. In accessing it, and in particular by making contact with the stone she could begin to integrate those experiences more now. They no longer needed to be totally separated from her. It seemed even that accessing this life was helping her to unlock an entrance to the Spiritual source within her, helping her to retrieve this aspect of her Soul.

126

For days and weeks, Alice continued to be preoccupied with this. Gradually though the upset diminished, and there were tangible benefits for her too. For ages, Alice had been having difficulty sleeping. Then after this session, she was sleeping deeper and longer than she felt she had done for ages.

Finally she was ready for her next session. In this one, she went to another life in Mu. However, this one seemed much later than the first, although still very ancient.

From this life, the Spiritual energies did not appear so strong anymore. But in the description Alice gave as she experienced it, her perceptions still seemed so much more alive and magical than what we are able to experience today.

Again Alice conveyed what happened to her with full involvement from her emotions. She spoke of a music in her awareness, like heavenly sounds that were with her all the time, especially when she turned her attention to Spirit. There was an energy flowing through her, an energy of joy, through being in harmony with her environment. She could feel and sense the living force of stones, holy water that nourished her and the power of the sea. As part of a group of women who worshiped the source together, there was a deep sisterly Spiritual bond. There was a cross which was a very important symbol for her worship - it was a pre-Christian cross.

Once again, as in the previous life, Alice's soul lived as a woman. But this life was not so straightforward. As this woman, she sensed dim memories of her former life, and the desire in her was very strong to create a dedication of service to the Source in the beautiful way that she had done before. However, this time the conditions were not right for her to do this in the same way. Her Soul urge this time was to have a husband and children and partake fully in normal Earthly life.

This knowledge of her Soul purpose and the longing to live as she did in her previous life caused a huge conflict in her. She did not know how to resolve it.

With her, she carried a stone which she had acquired from a secret place. This stone helped her link with the former life and the stone of wisdom that she had been given then. It was as if this former life had had a Spiritually infatuating effect upon Alice's soul. She could not let it go. Unfortunately, the outcome of this conflict within her was ultimately extremely tragic and brought much suffering.

In the next sessions we explored the latter stages of this life. As a young woman, Alice in that lifetime wanted to work in a Temple. But then she made the mistake of becoming sexually involved with the male High Priest. Perhaps subconsciously she felt that she could combine her wish for a Spiritual life with her Soul urge to have a family in this way.

But the priest was rather selfish, proud and ambitious in the position that he held. At first, she felt it to be wonderful in the nature of the union she experienced with him. All the world seemed to revolve around their togetherness. However, after she became pregnant and had a child, he rejected her.

In a totally shocking move, he had the child killed because it threatened his position. When she learnt of this, she became so enraged that she attacked him physically with a rock at his throat. This made matters much worse. Hatred flared between them. For this, he had her publicly sexually humiliated and killed in sacrifice for her crime.

Going through this death and humiliation was extremely harrowing for Alice. As this life had gone wrong, her perception of the heavenly music, the awareness of the living forces around her dissolved. She lost her connection with it. This caused overwhelming feelings of despair. But with the guilt she carried in the way events had unfolded she felt that this outcome was what she deserved.

In some ways her problems were caused by her attachment to the earlier life. She suffered through her emotional reactions, feeling shame and despair as a result, blaming herself for everything.

Going through the experience of these two lives was ultimately a liberation for Alice. She needed time and counselling to come to terms with it all - time to accept her weaknesses and mistakes from this past, but also honouring that this was the past and now it was all over. She knew that she had not lost the experience of that first Mu life. It was still there in her consciousness. She could cherish it, but she needed to let it go.

Later, Alice felt to have become much stronger in herself and at peace for having gone through these experiences.

The question remains about whether 'Mu' and these 'memories' ever really actually happened - whether this ancient lost civilisation did actually exist. It is not easy to answer such questions conclusively. For Alice though, speaking with her recently, three years after these Mu regressions, she volunteered to me and repeated what she had said earlier that she still feels these experiences to be as real and true to her as anything she remembers from her present life. For her there is no doubt. For me, I know also that when she was going through these Mu lives, it involved every fibre of her being.

Chapter 9
Future Lives

Introduction

As well as regressing into the Past where we can experience past lives we have lived, our inner awareness can also project itself forward into the future. These future visions will reveal themselves in a similar fashion to past lives, and the emotional experience of them can feel very real. However, such visions often are not quite as fully formed or distinct in all their details as past lives can be - like any plan which is still waiting to be manifested.

In some cases I have found this future journeying to be therapeutically useful. I do not believe that these experiences are giving a preview of exactly how the future is going to be. Because we have free will, individually and collectively, the future is shifting and changing all the time. How the future unfolds for us is full of possibilities. But the reality of what will happen to us depends upon the choices that we make. This cannot be accurately predicted because we do have freedom to decide. Still, there can be the outline of people we are drawn to meet, circumstances we need to face, challenges we need to endure. As souls, we do make plans for what we want to go through in life. But it is up to us how far we stick to that plan. Our personality Self does not always co-operate with our Soul or Inner Self in how we live our lives.

What future lives can present then, is a vision of how the soul of the person wants to unfold - what next lessons it wants to learn, and some aspects of the potential of what a person may be wishing and needing to express. With this can come a projection of how our soul experiences our Humanity and Universe to be unfolding as well. By being given a revelation of what we envision of our future, this may help us to become more fully aware of our deep inner goals. Integrating and assimilating these experiences into our being can help us reach these goals more easily.

A Small Group Future Life Session

One evening I invited some members of my Healing group for a session to explore one of their future lives. We talked a little about this to begin. Then I led them into a light state of trance and asked their consciousnesses to journey forward to the next life experience or task once their present life was over. I was careful not to presume that this would be another life on Earth, so as to allow the space for different possibilities to emerge, even if this meant that they would experience themselves in a heaven world with the angels! As we reflected on the experiences that came to each person afterwards, the results were very interesting.

Judith experienced herself as being very heavy. She was looking at a beautiful sunset. She became aware that she was a very large man. As this man, she was painting the sunset. She was travelling upon an oval transportation vehicle which seemed to be shooting towards the sunset. As this was happening she sensed the understanding come to her that as a Soul she wants to be dominant. As this man, she could be very powerful and dominant, but also creative and artistic. Being this man, she could quite easily express the true nature of how she wanted to be.

Judith felt quite shocked by this vision. It was not what she had expected. She realised as far as her present life was concerned, that she couldn't achieve all the things that she wanted to do. She reflected about the many ideas and wishes that she had. Sometimes she would feel frustrated about the limitations in her life.

As she gazed into this future Judith could tell that the stronger vehicle of being this man would help her to express her Soul more fully.

She could see some of the beautiful pictures she was making as this man. The colours were so strong. The message seemed to be urging her to be patient, and perhaps suggesting that for her to incorporate some artistic activities into her life now would be fulfiling.

While he was settling himself into the meditation, Reg suddenly felt himself to be shooting through the window. The next impression that came to him was that he was a prisoner in the desert. He was being dragged somewhere. Heat from the sun was burning down upon him, offering no protection. Reg could feel this heat searing against his cheek.

Somehow in this future life, he had been captured and was being forced to walk. It seemed to be military people who had captured him. His main impression was of the sun, powerfully reflecting in his eyes, glaring the whole time.

As the events of the life moved on, there was a dramatic change. Suddenly there was a sandstorm, bodies all over the place, sand covering them.

In this life, Reg sensed that he would be a young man who had learnt how to survive. The life seemed far in the distant future. Reg felt that though he may have to suffer humiliation, torture and hardship, he had so much knowledge and Spiritual feelings inside himself, that whatever he had to bear, he could come through it.

With Reg needing to endure and help others and face considerable hardship in his present life, this vision brought strength and the message for him to learn the ways of Spirit.

For Marjorie, she experienced herself in the midst of a battle, a future war. She felt as though she was looking at it, rather than being 'fully there'. There seemed to be energy lines shooting about. It was some kind of raid.

While this was happening people were walking slowly towards a very tall building. This building had a very large dome and offered people protection. Once people entered this building, the feelings came that nothing could harm them.

Marjorie felt herself to be a young girl, having two people, her parents reassuring her. She felt very safe with them. They were used to this kind of situation. The battle must have been going on for some time. With people who were more afraid, there was a man laying hands on people, calming them down, so everyone was feeling peaceful.

Marjorie was given the information that this was a preview of a life where there would be arguments and wars from another planet that had come closer to Earth. She felt that these battles were coming at the end of a thousand years of relative peace on Earth. The weapons of attack being used were energies quite different from what we know now.

Marjorie felt that in this life, she would learn about healing and helping people, learning about this new energy which was much stronger than electricity and nuclear power. She would begin to study at 15 or 16 and become a scholar. She would work and help in this way.

In her present life, Marjorie had been keen and eager to learn and help, but in restricted circumstances, not so easily able to do so. Perhaps this future life would give her more opportunity to do this.

Chris had a very different kind of experience. Instead of being a person on Earth, she felt herself to be a 'light being'. She had no body as such, except for light. With this she could feel a sensation of pulsing.

She was one of many light beings joining together often in clusters, sometimes becoming very intense light, which felt all embracing.

The purpose of her existence seemed to be to generate 'love'. With other light beings, she had a connection to the Earth. She would be there when candles were lit. She could go to individuals or groups when they lit a candle for guidance or in prayer. As people would light a candle in the hope that something would happen, she would be there, often with others, trying to energise the atmosphere so they could really change things. She sensed that this was a two-way thing, so that the more that people on Earth believed in guidance and sought for it, the more powerful the light Spirits could be in being able to help. Although working on the Earth, she felt she had to go back to the other planet (her Spiritual home) frequently, to be with the other lights.

For Chris, this experience was inspiring her towards more Spiritual work, and she was very happy with this.

Jill also felt herself not to be on Earth, but in a Spiritual world connected to Earth. She felt this place to have an intensity about it - something very vibrant and colourful.

At first she was aware of a building which seemed iridescent, a place where souls come to rest when they'd passed over. She then felt that her main work was with Spiritual Rescue work. So, with Souls who had become lost or Earthbound, or confused, she would help them to make a safe transition to the Light or Spirit. Usually, she would work as a team with others. She would then help to bring these souls to the building where they could rest. Then they would receive care until they were ready to move on.

It seemed important in her work for people on Earth to request help so she would more easily be able to reach those distressed or lost Souls needing help. She would communicate with thought with these Souls to try and convince them to move on.

As a group, they were organised together, and received teaching from more advanced Spirits to learn techniques how they could help better. She was learning all the time and she would share together with the others. She felt she would be enjoying this work very much, finding it interesting and demanding. Jill felt it to be a marvellous place to learn, with incredible singing, music and art - very creative. Like Chris, this experience was very inspirational for Jill, urging her to want to learn more about Spirit and Spiritual life.

From this session it seemed that everyone in the group gained an experience that was worthwhile. The variety of the experiences spoke of a future with many creative possibilities. We may as well be unfolding towards future lives on Earth as existences in Spiritual realms on other dimensions away from the physical life on Earth. At the end of this evening, I was left feeling a sense of awe about the great mystery that is life.

Part 2

Healing and Channelling

Chapter 10

Marjorie

Marjorie is much older than me. She is disabled and has a very different background to me, having come from an acting family and living in England all her life. Yet meeting Marjorie and working with her has significantly changed the course of my life. Through Marjorie, the focus of my work has shifted tremendously to directions which I had not foreseen. I feel very enriched and happy about what has happened. For Marjorie too, her working together with me has led to a co-operation which has opened many happy possibilities for her life that she previously would not have thought conceivable to her. It is hard for me to believe that this meeting has occurred by chance. Far more likely, I feel, hidden forces have operated behind the scenes to bring us together as a web of destiny where we could help with something bigger than ourselves. Like parts of a jigsaw though, we have needed contact with each other for this to happen.

I will try to explain how the significance of our meeting unfolded. Marjorie's best friend Ruth introduced me to her. Ruth was attending one of my Self-Hypnosis classes. She requested that I come out and visit her friend, who was wanting my help. I was told that this person, Marjorie, was not in a position to come to me. I phoned and made an appointment.

It was very easy for me to find Marjorie's place because she lived only a short five minute walk away from my home. When I came into the room where she was sitting, I was met by a very frail, thin woman in her late fifties. Her spine was bent over and she could hardly move some parts of her body without grimacing with pain. Marjorie had been crippled by Rheumatoid Arthritis.

For ten years or more, her body had rapidly degenerated. She had had a hip replacement and a knee replacement operation. Now, she was awaiting the go ahead to have three further operations, for her elbow, a shoulder and to remove a large deformity that was situated on top of her right hand. There was hardly anywhere in her body where deformed joints and ligaments were not causing her pain and discomfort. Doctors had given her steroids, tranquillisers and other medication to try and stabilise her condition. But nothing was able to prevent the relentless deterioration of the functioning of her body.

By now, she had become nearly bed-ridden. She had a special chair where she could sit in her lounge. But even for her to walk a short distance was a major undertaking. She had a battery chair which enabled her to get out and about in the summer months. But she was not optimistic about how long she'd be able to continue using that. Besides, it was now nearly Autumn and Marjorie could only see ahead a long, wet, cold winter. The winter months were always the ones where Marjorie felt the most pain and discomfort, when the Arthritis would tend to flare up, and she couldn't get out. Her anger and frustration at this just seemed to make the Arthritis worse.

There were parts of Marjorie that wanted to give up. Less and less could she do the things she liked doing. What was there to live for? Even eating a meal was becoming more and more formidable as a task. Her painful elbow and diminished grip made this very difficult. The thought of having to be fed felt so humiliating to Marjorie that she did not think she could cope with it. As far as family were concerned, Marjorie's mother and father were dead, she had no children - although she loved children. Her beloved sister, Joan, had died tragically some years earlier after suffering from Alzheimer's disease. Her brother, Charles, lived on the other side of the country, and they only met up usually once a year.

One person though, mattered. This was Marjorie's devoted husband Reg. Through all her illness, Reg had attended to Marjorie's every need, helping her as best he could. Having sacrificed many of his own interests, Reg now lived to look after

Marjorie. They were close - too close in some ways. Sometimes they needed more space from each other, and they would feed off each other's mood. So, if Marjorie was depressed or irritable, Reg would be the first in the firing line. He did not acknowledge his emotions nearly as easily as her but he continued to dedicate himself to looking after her. They loved each other. Marjorie was really only able to continue coping with her life through the attentions which Reg gave to her.

The only two interests in which Marjorie could engage were reading and watching television. She was a social person. However, through the winter months especially, hardly anyone besides Ruth ever came to visit. She felt lonely. I did not envy the type of life she had to live.

As we talked Marjorie admitted to me that I represented a last hope to her. She had heard from Ruth about the Past Life Regression work which I did. Marjorie wondered if this might help her Arthritis. I could tell that Marjorie was crying out for contact, and some new interest as much as wanting help with her Arthritis. In many ways, she had given up hope that anything could help with her condition.

I continued to question Marjorie about different aspects of her life and I discovered that she was a more interesting character than I first realised. She had come from a theatre background. Her grandmother had been a Medium. She had a wide ranging interest in many facets of life.

While I looked in her eyes I would sometimes see her sadness and despair. But occasionally when there was something of interest to her, her eyes would twinkle. Within that twinkling I felt there was passion and a zest for living and experiencing lots of things - a zest for living that was now seriously frustrated. Also, I enjoyed her sense of humour. There were times when Marjorie showed the capacity to view life from far more than just her own perspective. This wasn't always so when she was feeling depressed. Although I did not feel very hopeful that I could ultimately be of any help to Marjorie, I liked her and I wanted to help her if I could.

Marjorie's past lives

As I brought my focus to doing past life work, I was surprised and delighted to find that Marjorie was a good subject for inner exploration. She was very interested in the subject of Past Lives and she was very open to suggestion. It was possible for Marjorie to go into a quite deep state of trance. Soon she was involved with accessing the first of many past lives that we explored.

I wondered what kind of psychological experience could be the source of Marjorie's debilitating condition. In her present life, the onset of Arthritis had followed menopause. There was some coincidence with the illness of her sister, and Marjorie suffered a lot about this. However, I did not think that this could have been responsible on its own for the illness. Marjorie's life had been quite happy in most respects up until the time when the Arthritis took hold. She had suffered through not having children. So, as I considered whether the experience of a past life was intruding and influencing the onset of her present illness, I felt that I must look for instances of repressed suffering where perhaps what had been suppressed from the past was now manifesting physically in her body. If I could help her to release this suffering, then perhaps I could halt her illness from progressing further. At the back of my mind, although this approach was the way how I was used to working, I was not sure how well it would help Marjorie.

At the outset, Marjorie could enter into the past lives and experience vividly and emotionally their stories. However, it took a while until Marjorie could gain an inner acceptance to allow the direct accessing of incidents of trauma and repressed suffering. Within a few sessions though she was doing this and I tried to help her through these as best I could.

In the first life, Marjorie was Laura, a Victorian teacher. We discovered after a few sessions that Laura had been raped as a teenager, but had hidden the knowledge of this and the distress it caused from all around her. Consequently, her life had become quite barren and empty by the end of it, with no close relationships. Going through the rape experience a number of times to help release the pain and beliefs that she took on as a result of this, she realised that she should have stood up to tell people about what happened. I helped her reclaim her power so that inwardly she could do this now. But I noticed that the effect of this therapy made little significant impact upon her Arthritis.

I tried similar approaches with other lives, where repressed suffering was to some extent a theme. They were varied lives and some were very engrossing. Marjorie was interested in the drama of them.

In one life she was Naomi, a Jewish woman having to flee from Russia, with soldiers chasing her family and community through desperate situations until she was able to emigrate to America. From another life, Marjorie was Alice, a young teenager aged 15, living in poverty and hardship with her family, dreaming of the bright lights, wanting to be part of a theatre that performed shows nearby, but feeling somewhere inside that it would be beyond her reach. Alice then got ill and died. In a further life, she was ìboyî, a young beggar boy who was set upon by a group of other boys and then thrown over a bridge to die. Then, in a more pleasant life, apart from the death, Marjorie experienced herself as a young Native American Indian brave, living as part of a tribe, enjoying his life, planning to marry a girl from his tribe. This life ended when suddenly his tribe was attacked by another group of Indians. He was killed by fire, and Marjorie could feel this most painfully.

The Spiritual Realms

Marjorie's consciousness in our sessions tended to go to the more Spiritual realms. I often tried to pull her back from this because I wanted for her to go through the experiences of suffering from the past lives and work them through. However, after a while, when I noticed no improvement in Marjorie's physical condition, my determination weakened and I wondered if by encouraging Marjorie's consciousness to go in the direction where her inner Self wanted to go, she may find benefit in that way. This proved to be so.

Very often when people regress to a past life and go through the death from that life, the person will experience their consciousness leaving the body and floating upwards, usually to a realm of light and peace. For Marjorie, with these facets of her journeying, she found the experience of being in the Spiritual realm to be immensely satisfying, peaceful and deeply nourishing for her. She wanted to stay there. Very easily, she could distinguish the forms of other Spiritual beings, of Spiritual landscapes and buildings. Also, she was able to communicate by thought with other Spiritual beings who were there. Among the Spiritual beings she met were teachers who were telling her and showing her different aspects of Spiritual life. At first, I found this rather incredible, but I respected that for Marjorie it was very real.

Marjorie enjoyed being in the Spiritual realm because she felt harmony, kindness and love there. But additionally she felt charged with energy just by being in this place. Bringing her consciousness back to her body in her sitting room with Reg and I felt disappointing and much duller by comparison.

Initially, I speculated if these experiences in the Spiritual realm were a form of escapism for Marjorie. I could understand her desire not to suffer anymore and I thought that maybe these experiences were an inner projection coming as a manifestation of those wishes. More important I felt, was for her to face the suffering from her past lives and to confront the necessary situations from these. However, in spite of my struggles to direct her consciousness to her past life memories, she continued to find herself going to the Spiritual realms.

In the session where Marjorie first experienced herself as Laura being raped, this started with her enjoying the peace, love and well-being of the Spiritual realm. It was as if the peace and calm from these Higher planes helped give her strength to face the horrifying ordeal of Laura's rape scene.

I began slowly to realise that for Marjorie, she had experienced a lot of suffering in her life. She did not need more. Piling onto her consciousness more and more memories of past life destruction, loss and despair may really just be adding to her woes now - not helping. By leading her to the Spiritual realms, Marjorie's consciousness was actually protecting her and bringing her experiences to nourish her as a balance to her suffering. It became clear that for Marjorie to have a place in her consciousness where she could go and not be suffering, where she could truly relax and be happy - this was far more valuable than anything which the past lives could offer.

Meeting Marjorie's Spiritual Guide

As I accepted this and encouraged Marjorie more to explore the Spiritual realms, she met some very kind Spirit people. One was a lady who said that she was a 'deliverer', helping people to make the transition from Death into the Spiritual realm. Once, Marjorie went to a nursery where Spirit babies and children were looked after. On another occasion she sensed that she could see her mother, who had died many years before. As Marjorie's concentration wavered she seemed to flitter from one place to another. Gradually, she learned how to stabilise her attention to stay in one particular place.

One large building attracted Marjorie's attention more than anything else. Inside, this building seemed to open up in a multidimensional way and contain an abundant space. This building felt very peaceful and appeared to be as a Healing Hall or Spiritual Hospital. Marjorie felt that here there were many people from Earth and Spirit people receiving help and treatment. Spirit Doctors and healers worked to assist people with their needs. This place was very restful to Marjorie. We were both fascinated by what she was able to witness and relate to me. However, it was only on Marjorie's second visit to these Healing Halls that it occurred to me that of course, Marjorie needed help too. So I asked through Marjorie if there was anyone there who may be able to help her with her Arthritis.

At this invitation, a Spiritual being approached. He appeared as an older distinguished man, with a kindly face and white hair, dressed with robes in an outfit like a Roman Toga.

Dagmar

Linda Pope.

This Spirit man began to talk with Marjorie about her Arthritis. He spoke with authority and told Marjorie that she needed to learn to relax. When she got angry, this stirred up the poison in her system and tended to aggravate her condition. To my surprise, he reassured Marjorie that her Arthritis would not last forever. Then he told Marjorie that she was in the presence of someone who had healing power. Since there was only Reg and myself in the room with Marjorie, I asked this Spirit man to indicate who he was talking about. He said to me that I had the ability to channel healing through the laying on of hands. He suggested that I could try this with Marjorie if I wished.

This revelation astonished me. For years I had built up my sense of identity with my work as a therapist, not as a healer. However, I had done some healing in the past, having trained with the Reiki system of healing. But I had disregarded this as having no great relevance or importance for my life. What this Spirit man said though intrigued me. I felt I had to try it. He suggested that by the laying on of hands and opening to be a channel, this could help Marjorie to relax. In addition, he told me that I could heal others too, besides Marjorie. To help me, he stated that pain need not be suffered if people knew the power of love.

Asking for his name, the Spirit man told me that he was called 'Sojah' (pronounced as we would say 'Sawyer'). For a long time he had been waiting to make contact with Marjorie. He said that he was Marjorie's Spiritual guide. With this he smiled, and Marjorie felt waves of love coming from Sojah to her.

Doubts and Questions
At the end of this session, Marjorie and I needed to talk. Somehow, I felt that Sojah's appearance and the thoughts he had spoken as a challenge to me. Although I had read some books on the subject of Spiritual guides, met a few people who claimed to have a Spiritual guide and been to the Spiritualist Church a few times as part of my explorations, the concept of a person having a Spiritual guide still felt almost foreign to me. It was outside the circle of my experience. In the past, I had been quite sceptical

about the claims made by people in this direction. I did not share all this with Marjorie, but listened instead to her feelings about what had happened.

Marjorie felt quite bewildered. The experience of meeting Sojah had been intense and real for her. There had been strong feelings and emotions, thoughts coming to her as well as the images she could see of Sojah.

For many years she had felt there was someone in Spirit looking after her, without knowing who it was. She recounted to me a story of an incident which had happened to her many years earlier. Once she had been preparing for herself a foam bath. When it was almost ready, she needed to slip out of the bathroom for a moment. While she did this, something must have disturbed a glass bottle resting above the bath. It fell down into the bath, breaking into dangerous pieces on the way. With the broken glass beneath the foam, Marjorie was completely unaware of what had happened. She was about to step into the bath when she heard a voice shouting in her head, warning her not to get in. Marjorie considers that this warning saved her life. Had she not heeded it, then upon easing into the bath, she could have been cut to pieces.

However, even after sharing this story with me, Marjorie and I continued to have our doubts. Could 'Sojah' be merely a wish--filled projection coming from Marjorie's subconscious mind? Were these visions just coming from her vivid imagination so that she was in effect making it all up? Or were these experiences as true as they seemed to be?

Dagmar

In our next journey, Marjorie again went on an inner journey to the Healing Halls. This time she felt herself to be directed to a single room, within the building where she could receive treatment. As she entered this room, Sojah was there and another Spiritual being who had the appearance of being female. This Spiritual being gave her name as Dagmar. To Marjorie, she appeared wearing a white coat. She had a slim figure with dark

146

wavy hair and slightly tanned, beautiful smiling face. Dagmar told us that she was connected with me and she was wanting to help me with healing as my Healing guide. Like Sojah, she too had been waiting for a long time to make contact. Now she had been given permission by Sojah to make contact with me through Marjorie.

I asked Sojah about the way he and Dagmar appeared to Marjorie. Were there really male and female Spirits? Sojah told us that in the Spiritual realms, they communicated through the power of thought. By thought, they could create a form for themselves of how they would appear to others that they chose themselves. Thus, Sojah appeared the way he did to Marjorie because that was the way he wanted to appear to Marjorie. He could change his form if he wished but he would not do so because it may startle Marjorie. There were no male or female Spirits as such on the Spiritual planes.

Dagmar wanted to teach me some fundamentals about healing. Marjorie would receive energy and help while she was in the Healing Halls. However, Dagmar told me that she could also channel healing energy through my hands to Marjorie's body on Earth. Dagmar told me that the most important ingredients for me to practice Spiritual Healing were for me to care for Marjorie, wanting to help her and then open myself as a channel asking for the Spiritual energies to come through me. I needed to open my heart with love and then the healing channels would flow. Dagmar told me that if I trained myself to listen, she may be able to tell me where to place my hands to help in the best way.

Afterwards we experimented with this. I placed my hands in different places around Marjorie's body. At first I felt rather awkward doing this and I felt self-conscious wondering what would happen. In particular places though, Marjorie felt strong sensations of heat and other vibrations. She liked having the healing because it made her feel relaxed. I felt quite surprised that it seemed to be working.

In the following sessions we continued our healing experiments. The results were encouraging. Marjorie did experience relief from pain, and peace. The warmth from the healing seemed to give her energy. Strangely I noticed that I also felt more peaceful when I was doing the healing for Marjorie.

Then Dagmar, speaking through Marjorie asked me an important question. She asked me if I wanted to be a healer? Although this question came in the midst of other discussion, I knew that the way I answered this question would have many consequences. I sensed that she needed my conscious co-operation for her to be able to develop her work with me. But there was more to it than that. I felt that she was asking me if I could dedicate my life to healing. If I said 'yes' I did not know how my life might change. However, as I listened in my heart, there was no other answer. I could only say 'yes'. I wanted to be a healer. Dagmar was pleased.

Soon afterwards, Sojah and Dagmar made a promise to us. Dagmar referred to the ugly deformity on Marjorie's right hand. This lump of mangled tissue was as large as a golf ball. Marjorie's consultant Doctor had indicated to her that the only means for her to remove this lump would be by surgery. The promise they made was that if I concentrated and focused my attention upon this lump regularly as part of my healing with Marjorie, then within a few months it would disappear.

I greeted this promise with disbelief. Such a task seemed impossible. Yet Dagmar and Sojah told us that we could regard this experiment as a kind of test and that for them it would act as a demonstration of the power and reality of Spirit.

We decided to participate in the experiment. When I came to see Marjorie I gave this lump the regular attention and healing that had been requested. Amazingly the lump did start to grow smaller. Dagmar encouraged me also to use 'Absent Healing'. She asked that each day I could ask in my private moments for Marjorie to receive help and healing, and imagine this happening. This would help them and enable Dagmar to work further with Marjorie even when I was not present.

As we went on, each week seemed to bring progress. Then before the agreed time had elapsed the lump on Marjorie's hand had indeed disappeared. There was no trace of it left. Not only that, Marjorie was experiencing pain relief and improvements in other aspects of her condition as well.

The Path Unfolds

The faith which Marjorie, Reg and I had in Spirit started to grow. And yet, this was only the very beginning, Dagmar continued to help me with healing. I began to feel more confidence, trusting that the energy would come through my hands, to help Marjorie when I asked for it. When Marjorie was finally called upon to have an operation to insert an artificial joint into her elbow, she felt she had recovered enough mobility in this joint through healing, that she decided to refuse.

In the meantime, Sojah wanted to teach. He wanted to explain about many facets of Spiritual life, about the inner meaning of our lives on Earth. We found his gentle and considered teachings to be very interesting and helpful. However, it became apparent that Sojah was not wanting to teach only us. He was wanting to reach out and teach many people. Likewise, Dagmar was wanting me to extend my healing work far beyond just working with Marjorie.

We were told that in time, we would start a healing group, hold workshops, conduct Public healing sessions, build up our Spiritual capacities and help others to do the same. Sojah and Dagmar had plans for us. But we also needed to be patient to let things unfold gradually so we could cope with it. At this very early stage, we could hardly imagine that all these things would come to pass. But deep inside ourselves we felt excited, because it was what we wanted too.

For many years, Marjorie had a secret wish to be involved in some form of healing work. She was a fan of the famous Spiritual Healer, the late Harry Edwards. When Marjorie and Reg came from Hove in southern England to live in Morecambe, Marjorie

Sojah

Linda Pope.

sensed that there was some hidden reason why they had to come. After her sister died, Marjorie no longer had any notion of what that reason could be. She felt lonely and isolated and the climate around Morecambe was not helpful to her Arthritis at all. Now, she believes definitely that the reason she came to Morecambe was to meet me and for us to work together.

Through our work, Marjorie has found renewed purpose in her life. In channelling Sojah, she has been offering help and guidance to many people in need. Sojah has suggested to Marjorie that her Soul actually chose for her to contract Arthritis as part of her learning in life and also to help in preparation to become a channel for him in later life.

For me, meeting Marjorie has helped my life unfold in ways I could not have expected. She has been a gateway for me to start learning about Spirit and Spiritual life. It has been a mutual learning process, and not without its dramas and upsets along the way. But then, life can have many unexpected twists and turns.

Chapter 11

About Sojah and Spiritual Guides

Through the years I have had many channelling sessions with Sojah speaking through Marjorie - sessions with me privately, with our Healing group and also with larger groups of people in workshops. I have asked Sojah to tell a little about himself and what it is to be a Spiritual guide. Here are some of the answers he has given.

Sojah's History

'I have lived many, many lives and so many times that many of them have almost been wiped from my mind. In one life, I was responsible for the death of many people and this was paid for in many lives to come. I was happy in the Roman times. This may sound strange because things were not good. There were many battles, much destruction and cruelty. I can tell you I was not part of this. I belonged to a farming estate and I was very much in love and shared much happiness in this lifetime which is the reason now I like to appear relaxed and in the clothes I wore then.

'But I have been a long time in Spirit and I have had much to learn. I decided the last time that I would not be reborn. I did by then have a choice. I could choose to be reborn and do a lot of work on Earth or I could work on this side. And this is what I did. I learnt, I taught, I helped and finally became one of the young Masters, although I have said, there are many above me.

'When it was time for Marjorie to be born again, it was decided that perhaps I would be the best one to help her. This is also something to do with a past life - that I knew of Marjorie as a tiny

baby but then no more because she did not live very long. So together we decided.

'I helped Marjorie choose most of her life and plan this out. She took one or two wrong paths in the beginning and this drove us further apart. But gradually, we became closer to one another and she began to realise I was there. We planned an illness that would prevent Marjorie from doing certain things. Also, in meeting Reg, it was part of his Karma to be with her.

'I am at the moment Marjorie's guide but because we have found this way of communicating, I wish to spread the love and light that we know on this side. I have reached the stage where I now dwell on the seventh plane. I do an awful lot of work besides being with Marjorie and I have friends in upper planes that can come down to me and take me on marvellous journeys to even higher realms. These I cannot go to until I have lived Marjorie's life through with her. Then, sadly, we will say good bye and I will move higher. But there is a lot more work to do yet'.

Sojah's Life and Work in Spirit Now

'I can honestly say my life is endless, because on our side it is just that. We have a lot of sad Souls come over needing help and protection. We have a lot of weary Souls, disbelieving Souls in the lower realms, who we also wish to help. And part of my job is trying to help them rise to Higher planes, see how they went wrong or help them if they are willing to admit mistakes, and finally go through the cleansing process so that they can move upwards. This is not always easy. But it is one of the jobs I have chosen.

'Another is a teaching job where I have a lot of younger souls, although when I say younger I mean the span they have spent over here. No one is of any age. They chose the age they wish to be. But let's say young Spirits who have not been over as long as I, and who wish to learn my work which perhaps I should really say is Soul saving. I concentrate mainly on this. I am not a healer in the sense of healing physically through someone on Earth. I am more of a Spiritual teacher trying to help lost Souls and unhappy Souls.

'You see, one is exactly the same when they step through the Door, and this is what Death is like. It is merely a step through a door and into the next dimension. And although the physical body is left behind the mind is exactly as it was before. You do not miraculously change the minute you reach us. And there may be still much you have to learn. You have to be comforted, you have to be reassured, and in a lot of cases, cleansed. So, I do this kind of work mainly. You could call me a Soul saver if you wish because that is my main purpose on this side, and teaching other Spiritual beings who wish to be the same.

'I do join in many Circles as the one you have on your evening. We do join in with people who wish to see the light and wish to care. But I do not speak through anyone but Marjorie.'

Sojah's Work With Marjorie

'My work with Marjorie was planned. I say that the next century is going to be much more advanced Spiritual-wise. We are coming to the end of this century soon. The next century will spread far more widely the teaching of Spirit, not necessarily in the Church, but in classes and groups which will come together. There will be far more people interested in this. There are people who care, who wish to help, who wish to reassure. They do not know how to do this. The Church has failed them in some way, or the particular denomination to which they belonged. They are looking for a new way.

'A new era, a new century - I hope will bring more sharing, caring and getting together. The time has come. We are working hard on this side and reaching out to anyone who can hear us and help us with this work. That is why we are so pleased to have made contact with you and Marjorie and also your group, because we feel we are reaching some of the people, if not all of them'

Sojah has suggested many times that our humanity through selfishness and greed over the centuries has largely lost contact with the Spiritual sources of our Being. Now, a huge effort is being made by the Spiritual Community to help restore conscious contact for people on Earth with the Spiritual realm, hopefully before it is too late. Sojah wants to help through Marjorie by teaching about Spiritual life and reaching out to as many people as he can. He wants to help enable conditions to be created through caring, love and knowledge whereby this reconciliation between people on Earth and the Spiritual worlds can be achieved. He has told us that there are many on the Spiritual side working towards this aim.

What is a Spiritual guide?

'A Spiritual guide is someone who decides that they will stay close to someone who wishes to be born, and it is exactly what it says - a guide to guide them through their life. Usually, the one who is about to be born has been born before and therefore understands. But there are new Spiritual beings that are born for the first time. These usually do not achieve a lot in their first life time. They have a guide to help them. But it is like sending a child to a nursery school. They learn the basic needs so they are ready to move up to a higher learning school later. And this is what happens with lives.

'Each life you have learnt. Each life you take a step up. Your guides are chosen at the particular time for a lifetime that they know they will be of best help to you. I myself decided to be with Marjorie because she wished at some part in her life to help Spiritual-wise, healing and channelling as we are now. We worked a lot on this and she remembered much and then of course, like most people being reborn, forgot. However, we are now on the right road.

'Not every guide wishes to do what I am doing. Not every guide is heard at all. Guides can spend the whole lifetime by the side of the person they want to help. People may feel their guide's presence. They may call it intuition. But somehow they know and at the end of that life span when they meet, they realise that they have been together and have been having help.

155

'Of course, it can go wrong. You can arrange a lifetime. The guide can also promise to dedicate himself to that particular life. And then things can go sadly wrong. The one you are looking after will not listen, will go astray, will perhaps lose all sense of what he or she was supposed to do. You've often heard someone perhaps say 'they have no conscience at all'. What they are saying is that they've completely blocked off their Inner Self, their Higher Psyche, and their guide. And it is almost impossible to reach them. Sometimes someone is sent that they can meet in the future. This may bring them back on the right path. But this is complicated and not always possible. It just depends what the person has chosen.

'Some have chosen very ordinary lives, especially those who have not lived many lives. Therefore they do live and they do die not having achieved anything, but not having gained much either. This is just a life span. And of course, they will come back again with another guide later.'

The Purpose of Spiritual Guides

'Without a Spiritual guide, life would be devastating. People may not be aware that we are here, but we are. Earth life/physical life is very, very hard. One, we hope has a lot of happiness. But it is always hard, because lessons are not learnt through happiness, but through hardship and struggle. It would be very, very cruel to send someone to your world without at least somebody standing by to help if they can. This is the way it is planned. It is God's law. No-one is completely alone. Sometimes one thinks they are alone and spends their whole life thinking they are, and although we have tried, there is nothing we can do about this, if they reject us. But believe me, a Spiritual guide is there because as I say, it is a poor way to have to learn, but the only way. And therefore, each person's guide is there to try and help, if you will listen.

Making Contact With Our Spiritual Guide

'Many have, and many are still doing, and have done through the centuries. It just depends on where you live and who you live with, *whether the people around you accept it, whether people ridicule you and talk you out of listening. It's all part of the plan. But really, it's very simple, if you will just sit quietly and ask, and sift through the mind all the words which are coming. It is quite easy really, like talking to someone in the same room as yourself. It may not seem like that to you. But it is. And this is what we are trying to do now, proving this - helping more and more people to believe we are here and helping them. At the same time, we are trying to spread love and goodness. That is our aim. We do not wish for people to be unhappy, and if they find help and reassurance, they then will try and help someone else and so it becomes wider and wider, and this is what we try to do.*

'Trust is the main object. It is very hard to do that; it is very hard to say 'this is so' when you disbelieve. So don't stop trying or helping anyone else who wishes to learn. It is very difficult sometimes because some want to reach their guides so desperately, they do try to make up things and they blot out the real Spiritual being. Even Marjorie in the past has known that I was around, did not know what to call me, invented something, invented names but all the time she did not feel that this was right. So she would ridicule it or leave it alone, and go on her way. But when I came and spoke my name, she knew at once that this was right and all the other names had been a figment of her imagination.'

Marjorie's Relationship With Sojah

Marjorie has been through many stages in developing her relationship with Sojah. At first, she could only reach him using hypnosis with my help. She would find her consciousness rising out of her body. One place where she would go very often was a meadow with beautiful flowers. This meadow had an aura of peace and nourishing tranquillity that gave Marjorie a lot. Sometimes Marjorie would be aware of Sojah's presence immediately when she arrived at the meadow. On other occasions Sojah and Dagmar would appear to Marjorie first as lights and then become the forms of Spiritual beings as she knew them. Each session was different. There were times when Sojah would let Marjorie travel and he would show her interesting Halls and places where she

157

could learn and pass on information to me. Other Spiritual beings would come and join in sometimes and occasionally be part of our conversations.

The contact for Marjorie with Sojah, was delicate. If Marjorie wavered in her concentration or if she got distracted in some way, she could easily find herself somewhere else feeling lost or disorientated. When this happened I would encourage Marjorie to re-establish the link with Sojah by calling his name. Usually this worked. Otherwise we needed to finish the session and bring Marjorie back into her body. Sojah explained that this process was like tuning a radio set. Each person had a unique frequency of contact with which he or she could contact one's Spiritual guide. It was work on both sides to clear this pathway and make the connection possible.

For a long time Marjorie tended to have periods of doubt and scepticism. She would consider whether Sojah was merely a product of her sub-conscious mind. She needed to find ways to test this.

Gradually Marjorie found that she was able to have contact with Sojah privately without me. She tried to challenge Sojah, to find out more if he was real. So she would ask questions to him - questions which she thought she could not possibly answer herself. Then usually after a pause, answers would come. Perhaps after some minutes, thoughts would come streaming into her mind. As she analysed them, Marjorie realised that these were answers to her questions. Marjorie often felt very surprised but also satisfied by the answers that were given. This helped to build up her faith that Sojah really was a Spiritual being independent of herself.

Learning Channelling Skills

Learning to be a clear and open Channel for Sojah to speak through her was a training in itself for Marjorie. A couple of times in our earlier sessions Sojah complained to Marjorie that she was answering questions from her own knowledge rather than letting him speak through her. Sojah insisted that she needed to learn to keep her own thought aside while he was channelling. Marjorie did manage to learn this very well. However, she did not wish to be pushed totally out of the way. Marjorie felt responsible for what was being channelled. She found she could withhold from speaking information if she wished. Thus she retained some degree of control over the process. This was important and it felt right that she should have the capacity to do this - even though it could be frustrating for Sojah sometimes when he wanted to communicate something and Marjorie refused to say it.

Marjorie grew to trust and respect Sojah very deeply. She realised that there was a lot of love and wisdom which Sojah had to offer people. Others were helped by what he told them. Encouraging feedback which Marjorie received from people helped to affirm this. It gave Marjorie joy that she could be an instrument to help other people. The suffering of her illness had reduced Marjorie's hopes and expectations of life tremendously. She did not seek any self-glorification as a result of Sojah. But it gave her feelings of peace and hope to know that he was there.

One of the most interesting aspects of the Channelling process was the discovery that they on the Spiritual side were also learning. They did not know everything. Sometimes they would also make mistakes.

An example of this happened once when I was channelling healing to the knuckles of Marjorie's hand while Marjorie was channelling Dagmar at the same time. Marjorie was feeling heat and tingling from where I was working. Suddenly, she felt a sharp pain in one of her knuckles. There was almost an audible crack. Immediately, Dagmar spoke through Marjorie to admit a mistake. She told us that she had been channelling energy through my hands to try to clear some crystals that had accumulated in this particular joint. Then, at this moment, she had sent too much energy through all at once. This had caused the pain and crack. However, the pain very soon cleared and Marjorie's hand felt quite a bit better afterwards.

On another occasion, Sojah, Dagmar and my Spiritual guide, Sebastian, were all so eager to communicate all at once through Marjorie to me, that Marjorie became very confused. It felt like a pressure to her and eventually we had to end the session prematurely because Marjorie could not cope. Sojah explained to us that they on the Spiritual side also had to train to learn Channelling skills, so as to be able to channel communication and energies in a supportive way. They were learning too.

However, these kinds of confusing situations were quite exceptional. Overall, Marjorie felt herself to be guided gently and sensitively by Sojah. He has become for her like a very close friend - someone who is kind and loving, often with helpful advice, almost like a fatherly figure at times, but in a relationship that suits Marjorie.

After a while with channelling, Marjorie found that she did not need to leave her body anymore to go to Sojah. He could come to her. All she would need to do was to close her eyes and relax. Marjorie did not even need formal hypnosis anymore. Sojah then described the process whereby she would let him channel through her as 'overshadowing' her. He also assured Marjorie that while he and others were channelling through her, he would act as a guardian and protector, so that her body would be looked after, and other external entities would not be able to interfere.

Often Marjorie, would spontaneously enter quite a deep state of trance while she was channelling. She would remember hardly anything of the session afterwards. As a result of this, we would tape our sessions with Sojah.

Marjorie's Period of Crisis

There has been one main focal point of crisis for Marjorie in her relationship with Sojah in the time since I met her. This happened as a result of an accident which Marjorie had. Sometimes, Marjorie feels very angry and frustrated with the limitations that her illness places upon her. She knows she needs to learn patience, but this is not always easy for her.

On one occasion when she was feeling angry, Marjorie went into the bathroom without her usual support. There she slipped and fell. From this fall, she injured her back and broke a bone in her foot. With her very fragile physical constitution, the consequence of this was that she was left bedridden and in constant pain for months.

Marjorie wanted to give up. She had had enough. She even thought about ending her own life. Marjorie could not understand why she needed to suffer so much. Just when she seemed to be making progress, this accident seemed to set her back to an even worse state than when she started with me. She blamed God and she blamed Sojah. If Sojah was supposed to be her Spiritual guide, why did he not give her any warning to prevent the accident from happening? When she needed him most, he was not there for her. Marjorie felt very sorry for herself. Sometimes she felt Sojah wanting to speak with her, but she blocked him off. She did not want to have anything to do with him.

However, through this crisis, Marjorie received a lot of support. Reg was by her side constantly. She also received support from me, other members of our Healing group and her Physiotherapist. Our Healing group continued to meet without her. Then, some weeks later, she finally agreed to listen to Sojah.

Sojah said to her that he wanted to help her. He was there for her. She had been blocking the channels. When the accident happened, he had not been able to reach her. While she was angry and frustrated like that, he could not get through. He could only communicate with her when she was open to receive. She could blame him if she wished, but really, she had free Will and she had brought the accident on herself. This was quite a hard thing to say to Marjorie, but it was the truth.

Perhaps for most of us, when we suffer misfortunes, it is easiest to blame others and to look for the fault outside ourselves. Sometimes, this may be justified. But we are also to a large extent the creators of our own lives.

Sebashan

LINDA POPE,

Gradually, Marjorie accepted this. She began to listen to Sojah again. He gave her much constructive advice which assisted her. Marjorie opened herself more to receive help. Mentally, she had become very depressed by this episode, and needed a lot of support to 'find her feet again'. However, eventually she did recover, and considering the complications of her condition, doctors were amazed at how well and quickly this happened. For Marjorie though, it was an experience which she hopes will not repeat itself.

The Work Goes On

The journey of discovery for Marjorie with Sojah continues. For me, my work with her has inspired me to help many other people to make contact with their Spiritual guides. It has also encouraged me to seek for more conscious connection with my own guides. Through this, my own faith has grown stronger as to the reality of the Spiritual realm and our ability to link with that.

Our Healing group has been another focus for these explorations to take place. With this group, through joining together and regularly asking for Spiritual support and contact, it has given the space for this to come more and more easily.

We have not been able to learn everything about the Spiritual realms and our Spiritual guides all at once. It has needed time for our minds to adjust, so we could assimilate our discoveries step by step. Too much too soon would probably have been very confusing for us.

This is how it has been with Marjorie - a gradual, unfolding process of learning and experiencing - going further and further into areas which previously had felt to be unknown.

Chapter 12

Sebastian

From the early days of exploring channelling with Marjorie, she was able to channel not only with Sojah, but also guides connected with me. One of these of course was Dagmar about whom I will write more later. However, soon she was introduced to another Spiritual being whose name was Peter. I was told that Peter was my personal Spiritual Guide.

In my sessions with Marjorie, I was used to having conversations with the various Spiritual beings that spoke through her. However, with Peter, I found this difficult. Marjorie described him as being a very big Spirit and several times he indicated that he was there to protect me and that he would be there for me all of my life.

Then in one session, Peter was gone. I could no longer speak to him through Marjorie. In his place was another Spiritual being called Sebastian. I was told that Sebastian was my new Spiritual Guide. Because I had now chosen in my life to focus on Spiritual matters, Sebastian was there to help me go further with this. If I had not decided to do this, Peter would have remained with me.

Immediately, I found that I could talk with Sebastian much more easily than Peter. Through Marjorie, I felt a heart connection with him. He seemed to understand me, and his counselling was helpful to me concerning my personal problems. I found this new relationship to be exciting and fulfilling.

However, I wanted more than just to hear Sebastian talk through Marjorie. I needed to have my own contact with him. First though, I needed to trust that what Marjorie was telling me through her channelling was accurate. This was a dilemma similar to that which had also occurred when I wanted to explore my own past lives.

I had become convinced though of the existence of Sojah. Marjorie had no reason to come up with imaginary information that was false just to please me. Also with the depth of trance that Marjorie entered, she really did travel astrally. Her consciousness left her body and travelled to inner states of reality where she would meet these Spiritual beings. They would appear to her and she would describe them to me. In her own training to be a channellist, Sojah would often tell her to keep her own mind and thoughts out of the way, so she could concentrate on the experiences being given to her and pass them on. As the weeks went by I became more convinced that not only was Sojah real, but also Dagmar and Sebastian.

The challenge then for me was to make my own contact with him. As I tried some experiments to do this, again I met with a familiar lack of confidence. Like the early stages of my exploration of past lives, it seemed easier for me to help others with this work than it did to help myself!

However, over time, I did start to make progress. On a few occasions when I was feeling upset and I asked for his help, I have felt his presence very strongly.

Most recently when this happened, I was experiencing inner turmoil about a number of crises I needed to resolve that were affecting me simultaneously. As I struggled with this emotionally, I went into a room on my own and asked for help so I could know what to do. I sat down in a chair. Then I waited. Next I began to feel a strong heat at the top of my head. Slowly this spread until it went right through my body. At first this heat felt a little bit uncomfortable, but then it brought with it a feeling of inner peace and well-being. As I listened, I heard Sebastian communicating to me through thought. He gave practical suggestions that I could do to help the various situations I was in. Afterwards I reflected that the ideas he had given me were not ideas that I had considered by myself. But then, by doing what he told me, some hours later, all the situations of turmoil had been resolved and my whole mood had turned around. I was grateful.

On another occasion, I was with a group of people at a house in the countryside. I felt that I wanted some time on my own, so I went for a walk and sat down on a hill side overlooking a river. It was a cloudy summer afternoon with a very light drizzle. Apart from the motion of the clouds in the sky, it was a peaceful scene. I was able to enjoy the beauty of it all. It felt like a wonderful opportunity to have some time with Sebastian.

For a while, I felt nothing. But then, it was as though my heart was melting. I felt this very warm feeling of love. It was almost overwhelming. Sebastian was talking with me and I was talking with him - nothing profound - just simple assurances of love and well-being. I valued these moments very much.

There have been other occasions too where I have felt that Sebastian is close by and my belief in his presence has grown. Often I have felt in my meditations that we could engage in an inner dialogue together. The thoughts coming from his side have been helpful to me. I feel though that we are still at the beginning stages of the potential of what our communication could be. I know that he wants me to open more psychically and I want this too. But one thing I have learnt in this work both for myself and for others is to be patient. Trust and belief needs time to build. We can only cope with so much new experience. Our ego needs to be nurtured so that it will accept these Spiritual experiences and allow them to unfold.

Recently I asked Sebastian some simple questions through my mind. Then I wrote down the responses that came as thoughts into my mind. I will share these with you now.

Conversation with Sebastian
Q: How do personal Spiritual guides function to help the one on Earth they are guiding?

A: *We try to keep aside from the ones we are helping so that they can make their own decisions. We are concerned and wanting them to make the right decisions for themselves and their future. But there is little we can do if they don't do this.*

We can easily feel quite protective towards the one on Earth we are helping, but our lesson is to let go. We know the Soul of our one on Earth and we know what he or she has chosen to do on a Soul level. So, when people on Earth turn to us for help, or even if they try to listen to their conscience so they are living according to their own inner truth, then we can come closer and try to light up those areas of their consciousness that will help them.

Our greatest joy though is when we can actually make contact directly and can be recognised by our one on Earth for who we are. This is not always easy to establish, as you know Paul. But it is happening more frequently and we are glad about this.

Some people prefer to ask for help and offer prayers to God rather than a Spiritual Guide or Guardian Angel. However, once people genuinely open their hearts seeking guidance we can be there to help.

We are also here to offer protection to your psychic body from danger. We do not want you to suffer any more than what you have chosen as a Soul. And even then we will lessen the impact of this suffering if we can.

Because we are attuned very closely to your energy frequencies, we also learn through your experiences. To some extent we go through those experiences too. We can feel your emotions and thoughts very strongly and clearly on our side. But then we are not allowed to interfere in your Will so we have to keep our own desires removed from you unless you need and are open for our assistance in that way.

If people make choices against their Soul's best interest, we have to withdraw. We can only come as close as our one on Earth wants to unite with his or her own Soul and is ready to do this. Then we can help this process take place. It is often quite complicated and there can be much going on with the inner realms of your consciousness.

However, it can be very frustrating when the one on Earth makes a mistake over and over again and keeps himself from living his life purpose by repeating this. We have to be patient then. This is another of our lessons. But then, if we are not wanted, we usually have other activities to do so we are not exclusively concerned with our one on Earth.

Q: How did you choose to be with me?

A: *The nature of the choice was made through love Paul. We are both Souls who have been through many lives. It was thought by the Masters that we could help each other.*

In my lives on Earth, I have not followed a path of Healing and Service such as you have done many times, Paul. But I am ready to advance on this level. And from the Spiritual side, I have access to many resources to help with this. However, on Earth, I have attained an emotional maturity and learnt how to be assertive about looking after my own needs as well as being respectful of others. I am quite well able to express masculine qualities of action and communication without being selfish about it. The Masters have felt that these qualities I have would serve you, Paul.

I have learnt through many mistakes on Earth. And so I understand when you too make mistakes. And I want you to know I am not going to leave you or give up on you. I do want to help you achieve what you set out to do. And I am committed to going through this life together with you.

Q: How is it that I have chosen to have two personal guides in this lifetime?

A: *Before you entered this lifetime, Paul, you elected to live a life where you would have to meet some early difficulties and overcome them. It was part of the life journey that you chose, that you would need to find your Spiritual path through your own efforts. It would not be handed to you. You had some Karma to overcome, and the fears and weaknesses you felt in your early life were indicative of this. But now that you have reached adulthood, you have discovered your nature as a seeker of Truth, and as one who wants to serve. Peter could help you survive and he also helped guide you towards opportunities that would bring you closer to your Spiritual path. With all this, he did his job well. But now that you have chosen this path, he could take you no further, and so I could come in to help you.*

You see Paul, for me to help you in the early part of your life would not have helped me in my development. Also, you needed someone with Peter's psychic strength to help you survive. It helped you and Peter for you to have him with you for this stage of your life. With the influences around you in your young life I don't think I could have helped you withstand pressures as well as Peter could.

I want you to understand Paul that you have needed to move out of the life circumstances of your early life and create a completely different life pattern for yourself on another part of the planet. Much of the change needed for you to adapt and move to these different phases of your life took place at a time before you had too much insight about what was happening. Peter's strength was very important to enable you to do this. He was there to support you as a backbone to your life, to help you keep faith that you could succeed. Without him, you could have suffered much more than you did.

But now, you are at a stage in your life where you can make further changes in your life more consciously. You are more aware psychically and this is a situation that is more suitable for me to be with you.

For Souls who go through important transformational changes in their life, it is not uncommon for them to have a change of guide. The qualities of one guide may be more useful for one stage of the person's life. The qualities of the second guide may then be more adapted to help at a time further on, depending whether the person actually decides to make the changes that have been suggested by the Soul.

169

Q: What is your place in the Spiritual world?

A: *Well, I am a Soul learning like yourself, Paul. There are many higher than me and also there are those who are more limited than me in their consciousness. At the moment my main task is to support you as your guide. This is work that I enjoy and that I have willingly chosen.*

I feel that we are close and becoming closer. I think you have chosen an interesting and potentially significant life. And I hope very much that I can help you so you will fulfil the main aspects of what your Soul wishes to do.

The work I do with you occupies quite a lot of my psychic space. However, there are also others that I help here on this side, especially those adjusting to living on this side after trials on Earth. My work at the moment is on a smaller scale, helping souls one at a time to adjust to conditions here. But I am also helping Souls learn how to guide humans on Earth. There are many Souls attracted by the work that you are doing. Some of them, I try to help so they can go further themselves.

I feel myself to be a small cog in a vast universe. I know there is a Plan and it gives me joy to be part of it working with you. However, I am a humble Spirit and I do not want to give you any false impressions of grandeur.

For all of us, if we are true to ourselves and we do what we can, then this is the path for us to find happiness and the rewards that would be due to us. That is what I want to do with you, and this is the main message that I want to convey to you.

However, Paul, I want to encourage you to persevere with the path you are on, even when it feels difficult. Every small action of yours can make a difference and the effects of your actions may extend far beyond what you realise. I know that my work as a Spirit is interlinked with the work of many other Spirits. And also in my relationship with you on Earth, we act together and our paths are interconnected. From this, there is hope that we can generate love, create beauty and share joy. This is what makes life worthwhile.

Q: How can I contact you if I need you?

A: *Just listen Paul. Ask for help and listen - listen with your heart. Sometimes I can communicate to you through your thoughts Paul, or if you feel a sense of peace coming to you when you are troubled, that may also be me, Paul.*

It is good for you to take time out of the daily demands of family and work so you can be alone and perhaps have some time with me. Meditation will help, if you could do that regularly. Also, you can ask questions, as you are doing now, and write down what thoughts come to you in response. Sometimes, what you receive may be a mixture of what I want to communicate and your own thoughts. Be aware that I can only communicate through your mind and so I have to use your mind to answer your questions. But by reading afterwards, you can determine more and more, which thoughts are from me.

Don't despair though, even if you doubt whether you are getting through. If you feel frustrated, then let go and try again later. Often, people may miss out on contacting their guide because they try too hard. So, when you can, just be still and listen.

For you, time in Nature can also help. The Spirit of Nature and the nourishing energies that are available for you when you are near trees, water or when you are in the open countryside can help quieten your mind. Then your heart may be more ready to open to me.

If in your meditations, you gently focus attention on your third eye, you may one day see me. When you see me, you will know I am there with you, communicating with you. You will have no doubts then. At the moment, you rely more on my thoughts to you.

Q: Are there any thoughts you would like to communicate to readers of this book?

A: *I only wish to say how privileged I feel to be able to speak of myself in these pages. As a guide I am learning all the time and I enjoy to be with Paul. We guides genuinely want to help you on*

Earth to live happy and fulfilled lives. We do exist and we are here for you.

The relationship I share with Paul is an intensely personal one and it is unique. However, there are many elements in the way guides are linked to their one on Earth that is common and shared by all. We feel that it is natural for us as guides to have contact with you on Earth whom we are guiding. We want this to be so. For such a chasm to exist between your Earthly world and our Spiritual world feels unnatural and we are trying to find ways to bridge this gap. In former times there were societies where the two worlds were much closer. So we hope that this can happen again.

Please do not feel that you are alone, or blame us for your woes. We are here to help you. We would like to bring some of the peace which we experience to your world, so that you can share this too.

For you to make contact with your guide, the first step is for you to want to do this. Once you have sent out this thought, then we can respond and start to find ways to help you do this. I wish you well. And thank you for listening to me, Paul.

Chapter 13

Contacting Our Spiritual Guides

Making the First Steps

According to the teachings we have received in our group, we all have a Spiritual Guide. Usually, this Spiritual being is with us throughout our lifetime to protect our psychic space, and to help us, as much as possible, to fulfil our life purpose. Our Spiritual guide knows us intimately, but will not interfere in our free will. Once we become aware that such a Spiritual being is there supporting us, it feels natural to me that we should want to make contact with our guide. And it seems that they too, want to make contact with us!

However, to make a decision that we want to make contact with our Spiritual guide is not necessarily an easy one. When I started considering whether I really wanted to make contact with Sebastian, I thought of all the parts of my life that I did not feel good about. I could recall actions of mine about which I felt ashamed and guilty plus thoughts which were not very noble. If Sebastian started speaking to me, he may say things that I did not want to hear. So, I realised that opening myself to Sebastian meant that I would need to face up to the truth of my life including the not very nice bits. I understood that this process would be similar for other people as well. And I know that for some people to confront the truth of their life can be very difficult.

Very often then, people can be a little afraid initially at the thought of contacting their Spiritual guide because it involves not only seeking the support and companionship which a guide could give, but also learning to live a life where we are being more true to ourselves.

Of course, it is common for people to experience doubt, wondering if they can really contact their guide, or if it will be just the imagination, or whether some trickster may come and pretend to be our Spiritual Guide so we get more confused. A lot of this is a question of building up confidence and trust. Usually, this needs time and for the person to engage in some practices regularly to encourage the contact to take place.

Generally the best practices to make contact with our spiritual Guide are to find a suitable form of meditation or inner reflection and to do that regularly. This will encourage our consciousness to go within our mind and open to inner dimensions of being. The more we can do this, the more our ego will feel safe to allow this and then Spiritual experiences can start to reveal themselves to us.

Some people, through reasons of inheritance or other factors, come into our world with their psyche already quite open to Spirit. These people then can communicate with Spiritual beings without any special preparations. However, most people can learn to do this safely under the right conditions.

For many people, when someone they love dies, this brings strongly an interest in Spirit. Sometimes it may even be that the inner reason a person dies is to help their loved one to gain an interest in Spirit. But then after their Death, people may sense the presence of their loved one with them even though they have passed over. This can be very real and convincing for the person concerned. That this contact is possible seems very understandable considering the intense longings that can be there, probably on both sides, after such a loss.

However, these loved ones are not our Spiritual guides. They will not be as familiar or connected to our life purpose as is our guide. They may want to console us, reassure us or even wait for us. But they have their own path to continue after they have died. Ultimately we need to let them go.

Meeting Our Guides

By using directed meditations I help people to make contact with their guides. People can develop their inner perception in different ways. Some people are quite strongly visual and will see images very vividly. Other people more sense what is around them with thought or feeling. By focusing on the third eye, in the middle of the forehead and just waiting for the darkness that is there when the eyes are closed, visual images may come and help to open this form of perception.

Many people are able to travel in their meditations and go on inner journeys. In these directed meditations I ask people's consciousness to take them to an inner place which feels safe and where there is love so that they can meet their guide there.

Doing this can be very effective. Often people find themselves going to a place in Nature, a place where they feel calm and peaceful. It may be a garden, the seaside, a clearing in the forest, by a lake or even some inviting building. the place will be individual for each person. Then as people are able to return to this place in further meditations, by asking gently, inwardly to be there, the place itself may become more and more like an inner sanctuary - bringing nourishment to the person's inner being. Once this is stabilised the conditions may be ripe for the person's Spiritual guide to appear.

In these meditations people need to learn to let go of control so the unexpected can take place and so they can open themselves to be surprised.

When leading these meditations I ask for protection and also that what the person experiences may be for the best and healing for them.

The first appearance of the guide may be marked in different ways. There may be the experience of intense light or colours. Other people may receive strong thoughts coming to them. Or there may be the powerful sense of a presence with a lot of love.

People may then see an image of their Spiritual guide as a person. At first, this may just be the side of a face or some portion of a body. Then in further sessions this image may expand and unfold, till the whole person is visible.

It seems that our Spiritual guides take on a specific human form mainly for our benefit. It would be an image that suits them and how they want to be represented to us so we can see them. Such an image is created through their thought. Then they also use a name for themselves. This name can be an easy form of identification and association to help our connection with them. The image of our Spiritual guide may be male or female but they can really express both qualities.

It may need several sessions to develop contact once it has been started. Communication may take place by telepathy, through thought transfer or else by your guide showing you things and giving you a strong sense of what it is about. Over time, communication will usually improve with practice and become meaningful.

The quality of being with your guide will be one of love. Usually, your guide will feel like your best friend, or someone with whom you feel very much at home. You may need time to adjust to each other and to get used to each other. It is quite possible that you may have known your guide in other lives, and there is a reason from this that has drawn you to be together again. Also your guide may be like an inner counsellor. But you are at liberty to let the contact with your guide unfold at a pace which suits you.

Usually once people make genuine contact with their guide, there will be a sense of certainty about this. Even if afterwards their rational critical mind wants to be sceptical, they will know the truth that they have met their guide.

Occasionally, especially with those who have been taught to be suspicious of the 'Occult', they may meet a Spiritual being who makes them afraid. This is not their Spiritual guide and can be told to go away, and the person can ask for protection. Otherwise, this appearance may in some way indicate some unintegrated part of the person that is needing help and psychotherapy could be recommended.

Sometimes a person will need psychotherapy to help remove inner blockages so that contact with the Spiritual guide can occur. Also once contact with people's Spiritual guide has been established this can help tremendously in Psychotherapy work. The guide can help people to find perspective and truth from inside about what they are experiencing. There can be many different pathways of self discovery possible when contact with our Spiritual guide has been made.

The Consequences of Meeting Our Guide

Once you have made contact with your Spiritual guide, there will be a challenge for you to decide how you are going to respond to this. There will be a question for you of deciding if your Spiritual guide is really an external being or whether it may be some deeper aspect of your Self. Also you will need to choose how much you can trust communication or information that is coming from your guide. I feel that it is important to ask these questions to yourself and to test your guide about this.

What we perceive as truth can be very coloured by our beliefs. If a person is not open to the idea of Spiritual guides then they will not exist for this person. Even if the Spiritual guide is around giving wonderful messages, then these experiences will probably be regarded as something else by the person concerned.

However, to make contact with our Spiritual guide and acknowledge that this is true, will entail a change in our belief system. This will open us to experiences that we could not have been open to receive before.

This change may need time and support for you to integrate. Once you have made contact with your Spiritual guide, there may be much that your guide wants to communicate with you. You need to feel sure that you are ready to receive this. It is possible for you to say 'no' to your guide. Even though your guide may find ways of making contact with you quite spontaneously, it is up to you to choose when you want contact and in what way. Usually your guide will be sensitive to this.

It is also quite important when communicating with your guide to learn to keep your own personal desires about what you want to be true out of the way. These personal desires will be like a block that interferes with your guide's capacity to come through to you. With these desires present, the experiences you receive may contain distorted information. Therefore, it is necessary practice when opening to contact your guide to learn to still your mind, and really open to the truth that is there.

Through listening to your guide and receiving love and inner support from this source, your life may begin to change. You may become aware of aspects of your Self and life path that you did not know consciously before. If there are areas of your life that have served their purpose, aspects of your life that are inhibiting your inner growth, you may be encouraged to let them go. If you have been living your life according to your life purpose, then the advent of your guide may result in feelings of peace and happiness about this. However, usually when people's guide appears then some adjustments are needed for the person to make. Sometimes there is the opportunity for a whole new phase of the person's life to unfold. From a situation of stable security, this may fall apart, and the future may seem very uncertain and unknown.

It is up to you how far you go along with these changes, and at what pace you say 'yes' to them. You need to feel what is 'right ' for you and with what you can cope. Ultimately though, if changes suggested bring you closer to connecting with your life purpose, then this will bring blessings as well as happiness and peace, even though there may be lessons to learn along the way. It is okay for you to live your own life in privacy without the intrusion of your guide for a time if you wish. Once the contact has been made, you only need to ask for help and your guide will be there, close by.

Channelling and Teaching Guides

Mostly people's Spiritual guides will be there to assist with their personal problems and their welfare and they will be important really to nobody else. This is because the guides will be tuned in specifically to the energy frequency of the one on Earth they are helping.

However, occasionally a person's Spiritual guide may want to teach and spread knowledge of a Spiritual nature to many people, as well as helping their one on Earth personally. It could be that these 'teaching' guides are more advanced Spiritual beings. Then, the person on Earth will need to decide if he or she wants to be a 'medium' for these teachings to be imparted. In these cases people who have Teaching guides have usually chosen as souls, before they were born, that they would offer themselves in service at a certain point in their lives so that these teachings can be given. But then the choice needs to be made again once the moment comes.

People who agree to this can learn to channel so that their Spiritual Guide can speak through them. To do this is also a process of learning on many levels and involves considerable trust.

When people first begin to channel, they may relate what their guide is telling them and say this aloud. Another less exposed way of doing this may be to engage in automatic writing, letting the thoughts of the guide come out quite quickly through writing them down.

But then, a more advanced stage of channelling involves letting the Guide speak directly through the person's mind. Then the consciousness of the person would move to one side so this can be accomplished. The person's guide would then take responsibility for the person involved from the Spiritual side. But then it can also be important for there to be someone who can help from the Earth side, particularly around the aspect of ensuring that the person comes fully into their body and back to normal consciousness when the experience is over.

This form of channelling can take a person into a very deep state. Often the Channellist will remember very little of what has happened afterwards. When I have been conducting channelling sessions of this nature, usually we have made some record of what has happened, especially for the benefit of the channellist.

It seems that much inner preparation is needed so this form of channelling can happen smoothly. However, people doing this as channellists are usually looked after very well in Spirit. They may be able to bask in some healing light or also join in the process while the teaching is taking place. Again I find it is important for me to ask for help and protection before I do this work with people.

A lot of this work is experimental until a familiar pattern of working is established. Therefore, sensitivity, caution and care is needed on all sides to ensure its success. There is learning for the guides about doing this, as well as for us on Earth.

It is also possible that other Spiritual beings besides people's Spiritual Guide may be able to channel through them. If there is a more advanced Spiritual being wanting to impart teachings, then again this process will involve preparation. People may have quite a number of Spiritual beings assisting at different stages of their life for different purposes. However, channelling Spiritual teachers is quite a different matter from someone who is a medium to channel messages from people's dead relatives for the purpose of proving there is life after Death. These Teaching guides come from much higher planes in the Spiritual worlds.

If you feel the urge that you would like to learn to be channel for your guide, I would recommend that you be careful and cautious about this. Find a group of people who are experienced in this work to help you. Be sure in your heart that you can trust the people with whom you are working. Also, you need patience. Often this process needs much time to unfold. However, if it is right for you to do this then you will be guided so that the people you need will come into your life to help you, at a time when you are ready to proceed.

Meditation to Contact Your Spiritual Guide

Find somewhere quiet where you will not be disturbed and the following meditation may help you to make contact with your Spiritual guide. This meditation is an outline and can be extended to last as long as you wish. By practising regularly, this will help the inner openings to occur.

Sit or lie comfortably. Close your eyes and take a few deep breaths. Breathe in peace, and as you breathe out, imagine that you are letting go of all the tensions in your body, your consciousness becoming lighter and lighter as your physical body becomes heavy and relaxed. Gently say a prayer asking for protection and that your Spiritual Guide may draw close to you. Find your consciousness lifting, being in a place where you feel safe, where there is love and you know that all is well. Slowly open your heart to breathe in this love and you may become aware of the presence of your Guide. Your Guide comes to you with love and only love. Let your inner eye now open to perceive your Guide. You may even see a vision of your Guide and talk together with your thoughts. Allow this interaction to unfold. Spend some personal, intimate time together. Your Guide is like a very dear inner friend. Ask any questions if you have them. If your guide wants to show you things, then let this just come to you. You are safe. Each time you do this, it gets easier and easier to find the way, to build the bridge, so you can be together, so you can gain the help and comfort that you need.

But now, just enjoy for a while, this space you share together. So that only when you are ready, in your own time, you can bring your consciousness into your physical body, returning to normal consciousness, closing your inner eye until next time. Then slowly, when you have adjusted, you can open your eyes, feeling refreshed and remembering everything you've experienced.

Chapter 14

Stories of People Meeting Their Guide

I would now like to share three stories of experiences from people with whom I have worked and how they were helped to make contact with their guide. Each of these stories brings out different aspects of the process involved in this work and exploration. Again, I would like to emphasise that the process how people can become conscious of their guide is unpredictable and is unique for each person concerned. However, the effect of doing this can be quite transforming as these stories will illustrate.

Dorothy

Dorothy came to me because she needed help. She carried a lot of pain and trauma inside of her. Her life had been in many respects, unhappy. However, she could laugh and her sense of humour helped her a great deal.

Born at the beginning of World War II, Dorothy never had any contact with her father. He died in the war. She was an illegitimate child and brought up with two other children from her mother's marriage. Here Dorothy felt neglected. Her mother was very busy.

Religion was very important in Dorothy's life. She was raised as a Roman Catholic but later became interested in Spiritualism through her mother who was a medium. Yet her dominating mother did not share much of this interest with Dorothy and Dorothy did not have the confidence to express her own wishes and needs aloud.

Soon after Dorothy got married in her early twenties, she was diagnosed as having Multiple Sclerosis. Although the illness impaired her mobility to some extent and gave her a lot of pain, it did not disable her completely. However, eventually she needed to retire from her teaching job. Then four years before meeting me, her husband died from Emphysema.

In my first work with Dorothy, we uncovered a horrifying Past life where, as a little girl, she had been physically and sexually abused until she gave up and died while aged about 7 or 8 years old. In this life her name was Cecile. Volumes of repressed thoughts, emotions and physical sensations had to be released through these sessions.

Then we searched for the Inner Child of Dorothy to try to help her. She could not imagine this child self to be happy. But we found a place within where indeed her inner child self could be happy and where Dorothy and her Inner Child could communicate. This was very healing.

Dorothy felt ready with a strong wish to contact her Spiritual Guide. She knew that she was quite psychic and she felt that she had latent ability to be a medium like her mother. However, she had always withheld this. She did not have the confidence to expose herself in public. It was easier to hide away.

As a child, Dorothy had often experienced visions of a priest who spoke to her. She felt this like her Guardian Angel. But she wondered if this might be some fantasy connected to the religious teachings she was receiving in childhood.

More recently, Dorothy had joined a Psychic circle and had been told by one of the mediums in the Circle that her guide was a nun called Sister Rose. Dorothy was given a description of the appearance of Sister Rose. Because she tended to adhere to what people in authority told her, she assumed that her Spiritual Guide must be Sister Rose. However, she had some doubts about this, because, try as she would, she could not sense any contact with Sister Rose. She could not understand this.

We began our session by asking her consciousness to help her to find her purpose Spiritually. Immediately she began to experience colours. Then when these cleared, she felt as though she was looking for some particular place. Then she sensed that she was in a church. She felt very comfortable. It was a Roman Catholic Church. She could see the cross and the Altar. As her vision became even clearer she saw that there standing in front of the altar was a Priest.

Dorothy felt very safe and very secure. Then she felt this Priest drawing her to him. Immediately, his hands went up in a blessing for her. It felt very good for Dorothy. She became very quiet. From deep inside, she could sense that he was the one for her. He was her Spiritual Guide. She realised that he had been with her all through her life. He gave his name as Canon O'Rourke.

When I asked him through Dorothy to tell why he chose the guise of a Priest, his thoughts transferred to Dorothy. He told her that the image of a priest was something she would recognise, respond to, and with which she would feel safe.

Later, Dorothy began to channel Canon O'Rourke more directly. When doing this, Dorothy's normal, nervous disposition changed. Instead, the atmosphere around her became calm and solemn. I felt really as if I was talking with a priest, and felt very humble in his presence.

Canon O'Rourke told that he and Dorothy had known each other in many lives. One life which was particularly important was in Tibet. In this life, he had learnt much and advanced to a degree that afterwards he no longer needed to return to Earth life. Meanwhile, Dorothy, in her incarnation at that time, had faltered. Now he was her Spiritual Guide because he wanted to help her.

With the past life where she had been abused as a young girl, the trauma of this had been so great as to affect her Soul. This damage combined with her unhappy childhood in her present life, had contributed to her contracting Multiple Sclerosis. Now, as a result of the releasing work we had done, she would not need to suffer more as a result of that life. She would still need to endure the physical discomfort of the MS but the mental/ emotional/ psychic debris left over from that life was gone.

This was all very reassuring for Dorothy. She now recognised that Sister Rose was not her Spiritual Guide. She realised she needed to learn to trust her own intuition rather than what other people told her to do. Canon O'Rourke told her that he was a Spiritual teacher, very interested in Philosophy. As well as helping her personally, he wanted to reach others through her as well.

In our next session, Canon O'Rourke led Dorothy to a place in Spirit where she could meet her father. This was a very joyful meeting. Her father had tried to have contact with her when she was a baby but her mother had chased him away. After he had died, he had watched over her and wanted to help her. He was very glad to tell his story. Actually, he was a very young Spirit and the life where he had fathered Dorothy was only his second life on Earth. He was still learning how to adjust to how to live on Earth. Dorothy realised that in nature she was much more like her mother. However, as a result of this meeting, Dorothy felt much more whole, as if a part of her was in place again.

Meeting Canon O'Rourke has given Dorothy much peace. Since meeting him she has been able to have contact with him whenever she wanted. He has been a continuing source of strength and support to her. This has helped her tremendously.

Mandy

Mandy was a young mother in a desperate situation. She had been receiving treatment for cancer on and off for a couple of years. Then she had become pregnant. While she was pregnant the tumour had re-emerged in her liver. The Doctors strongly advised her to have an abortion so she could receive maximum medical treatment. She refused. Mandy felt that she had to have this child. She was also committed and determined to get well if she could.

Instead of medical attention which her doctors could provide, Mandy sought for alternatives. She tried ayurvedic medicine, transcendental meditation and Spiritual Healing - anything which might help. Many friends gathered around her to try to support her. In the meantime, the doctors inserted a machine into her body to administer localised chemotherapy to the liver.

Mandy survived until her baby was born but the birth process almost killed her. Through loss of blood, she was in Intensive Care for about two weeks. Eventually she pulled through. After that, she had some weeks where she could be at home with her family and her baby, trying to pick up the pieces of her life. The doctors were waiting to perform a risky operation to try and remove the tumour from her liver. Mandy was not sure whether to go ahead.

When I came to visit the town where she lived I was asked if there was anything I could do to help her. She welcomed me coming to see her.

Initially I tried some Spiritual Healing with her, but I knew others were already doing this with her. So, in our second session I suggested to her for us to go into her inner consciousness and ask for Spiritual help. She was very open to this idea.

At first, this process with her did not go very easily. I asked for a door that might help her make the necessary inner transition. She became aware of a door, but it took her a great effort to open it. And then, as she went thorough, all she could experience was darkness. It was as though there was a lot for her to overcome to make contact with Spirit.

Mandy was used to doing things herself, with her own determination and courage. It was not easy for her to let go. But now she really wanted to contact Spirit if she could. We affirmed the presence of the light, and she pushed physically all the dark strands of substances to go away. The scene became more and more light for her.

Gradually she became aware that there was a Spiritual being in front of her. It was a male figure with a white robe, necklace, long white beard and strong. He gave his name as Paulo. He felt to Mandy that he was very loving, very supportive and wanting to help. We had some conversation with him and he said he was there to help her through her crisis.

In our third session, we attempted to contact Paulo again. This time he was quite agitated. He was distressed that Mandy was not getting enough space for herself. There were too many demands upon her.

By listening to this, the energy slowly became more peaceful. Mandy could feel enormous love coming from Paulo to her. This love felt stronger than love she had felt from anyone including her husband. There were tears coming down Mandy's cheeks. Paulo wanted Mandy to trust him and let him guide her on an inner journey that may seem dark and terrifying at first. Mandy hesitated but then consented.

Going on this journey, Mandy would need to leave behind her husband and children. This was very difficult for her to do. She sensed that the children were trying to cling to her. But she had to let them go. She cried but finally trusted to go on. As her vision continued she found herself going to a space away from them, plunging at first into darkness. This was terrifying for her and deeply distressing. But then as she more and more really let go, this experience became light and happy.

She felt her diseased liver taken out of her body, placed in light and returned to her body anew. Her children were then able to come to her in this place because they wanted to be with her.

This vision was extremely moving for Mandy. It taught her that she needed to surrender. She hoped that with this inner support, the vision showed that she would survive, but she needed to surrender first. I wondered if the vision was more a prelude to help her to die.

In any case, Mandy felt very grateful for this inner support. She knew that she wasn't alone from inside, and in Paulo there was someone with great love for her from within to help look after her, to guide her and protect her. She decided to go ahead with the operation.

Some months later, I heard the results of this operation. Surprisingly, the surgeons had found that the cancer was indeed confined to the liver. They were able to remove this. Perhaps all the healing Mandy had received from various sources helped! But then, in completing the operation, one of the surgeons accidentally severed an artery. This went undetected. Soon afterwards Mandy died from massive internal bleeding.

Chris

For some time, Chris had been having dreams and visions of an Old Viking King called Redveld. About twenty years earlier, Chris had lived in Suffolk, in the vicinity of the burial site where Redveld had died. In dreams about Redveld, he felt himself to be Redveld and the visions were very vivid. With an openness to belief in reincarnation Chris wondered if he may have been Redveld in a past life. When Chris shared about this with his wife, the dreams stopped. So that is when Chris came to see me.

It did not take long before Chris was taking on the persona of Redveld as a past life experience. We went through the story of his life, from his young life in Norway, his journey to Britain, right up to his death in a sea battle and beyond. For Chris, it was a very strong experience and he felt to be 'right there'. He very much became this Viking king. It was a life of power, but also bloodshed. Many people were killed through Redveld's direction. On the other side he was kind and loyal to his family and closest associates. But he remained suspicious of everybody else. He had some pride about the community life he started in Britain, and was a brave leader trying to defend and protect what he had gained. In the spiritual realm, after he died, he said that in this life he had wanted to show what he could do. However it seemed a life of material gain, but Spiritual loss. His world revolved entirely around himself. In Spirit, he felt that he would need to be there for a long time.

Chris was pleased with the session. For him it had answered a lot of questions. I did not expect to see him again. Therefore I was surprised when I had a phone call from him a few months later.

Some strange things had been happening to Chris. For a number of days after our previous session, he had felt very calm. But then he began to experience unusual things which he could not understand or control. His job was as a teacher for primary aged children. There was considerable stress from this job. It was worrying therefore for him to be suffering from short-term memory blackouts when he couldn't remember what lessons he had been teaching, where complete periods of time would seem blank. Also, he had noticed occasional personality changes where he would be much more short tempered than usual. It was as though he did not feel himself at these times. Then without warning he would sometimes also experience sharp pains in his side which would then go again without notice. In addition, Chris had been having some short bouts of depression. This had worried him because during these times he would tend to go out and spend more money than he could afford. All these phenomena, Chris traced back to our session with Redveld.

Chris told me that he had also suffered depression in the past. So this and the pattern of spending money then, was not entirely new. We wondered if this behaviour may be linked to Redveld as an expression of his excessive materialism and a part of Chris believing that he had a right to take things. Also the short temper could be linked to Redveld too. But with all the other phenomena, we considered if Chris may be suffering from some form of Spirit Interference, a form of Spiritual possession. His symptoms were consistent with this explanation. Chris speculated if he may have 'brought back' someone else when we did our past life work. I somehow doubted this because I was careful in my usual way how I closed that session. But I was surprised that Chris did not seem at all afraid.

We began our session to explore. Immediately, Chris was aware of colours - bright, bright colours - reds, yellows, greens, blues...colours everywhere. Then he was in the sky. He could see clouds. He was travelling fast across the sky. Next he realised that he was not alone. There was someone with him, a female Spirit being. She gave her name as Meanu. He was sure that she was separate from him. She was lovely. There was a feeling of love coming from her. Meanu was there as his Spiritual guide.

Chris rejoiced in this. She wanted to show him where they had known each other on Earth. Chris could see visions of beautiful designs and patterns. Then he could see buildings - huge, stone buildings. These were from the Mayan civilisation. In that lifetime they had been very close as brother and sister. But she had been tragically killed by a knife wound to her side. This was the pain he had been feeling - the pain of the wound of her past life death.

Meanu apologised that she had caused the pain and blackouts. For years she had been with him, trying to communicate. But Chris had not been listening. Because he refused to listen, she had resorted to drastic action to gain his attention. If he could accept her, he would not need to feel the pain anymore. She told him that she felt he had got lost. Redveld was not a nice person to be. Negative energies had become too important. Since then he had been trying to overcome these energies. But they were still there.

Meanu urged Chris to develop his Spiritual side. She wanted to help him but he needed to make more efforts himself in this direction. He had been dabbling in Buddhism, but she told him that this was not the way for him.

The energy of Meanu felt quite assertive but very loving and caring towards Chris. At the end of the session he again experienced vivid colours. He felt very happy and knew that she was the one for him. She had been quite forceful in creating symptoms that would prompt Chris to see me and thus, make contact with her. This was not typical for Spiritual guides to do this, in my experience. But for Chris, it was okay. Somewhere inside, Chris knew that he would meet her in our session. That is why he wasn't afraid. He was co-operating.

After our session, the pain in his side and memory blackouts completely disappeared and have not recurred. Chris has accepted Meanu as his personal Spiritual guide. This has been the beginning of a complete change of life for Chris. He has subsequently deepened his exploration of Spiritual matters and begun to follow a path of Shamanism. He has stopped his teaching job and is seeking work more attuned with the Spiritual side of his nature. He feels very good about this.

Chapter 15

Dagmar - and the Experience of Spiritual Healing

Opening To Be a Channel For Healing

From the time I helped Marjorie with healing so that the lump on her hand disappeared, I was eager to experiment with healing on other people. To my amazement I found that it was a very effective tool for bringing peace and relaxation and helping people. Some of my clients became more interested in receiving Healing with me than engaging in other forms of psychotherapy. It was a new world for me.

Central to the Spiritual Healing that I was doing was my relationship with Dagmar. Now again, I was introduced to Dagmar through the channelling I did with Marjorie. Dagmar said that she was with me helping whenever I did healing work. She could be there much stronger when I invited her to help. So it was up to me whether or not I believed in her.

When I did Spiritual healing with someone, I first asked for Dagmar's help and then took some moments to 'be with' the person I was wanting to heal and went from there. As I placed my hands on or around different parts of the person's body I often would feel heat, intense vibrations or other sensations. Sometimes I would know where to place my hands. On other occasions I would feel nothing very substantial but the person receiving the Healing may tell me afterwards of all the wonderful sensations he or she was experiencing. As I practised more, the results seemed to come more and more naturally.

What impressed me was that I was certain that the energy coming through my hands, helping people was not being produced by me. If it was my energy I felt I would feel tired afterwards. On the contrary, often I felt energised by doing healing and it brought a sense of peace to me too. I did need to concentrate and keep my attention with the person I was wanting to help. So there were limits to how long I could continue healing. Also, sometimes the healing energy channelled through me was so intense that I could only sustain this for a limited length of time. But I knew this energy was not coming from me.

The other factor which was important was that I could trust in this energy. It was not an energy that would hurt people in any way. Usually, unless a person was scared and unprepared for it, Spiritual Healing was an experience people could receive over and over again. People could feel the benefits of it. Invariably too, the Healing would go to the right place where help was most needed. Perhaps this would be evident through intense heat, cold or some other sign of energy being applied there. And of course, the effects of this would often take place with my patient without my conscious knowledge.

What I recognised then was there was an intelligence operating behind the application of Spiritual Healing. Because this energy was not coming from me, it was coming from beyond me. This phenomena helped greatly to build up my faith and confidence in the reality of Spirit.

I knew that some Spiritual healers tended to regard this energy as coming from a Universal source or God, and did not enter any more into the mystery of it than that.

For me though, it did make sense that there was a specific Spiritual being associated with me and helping the process of Spiritual Healing. I felt comfortable with this. Also, I felt no reason to doubt that this being was indeed Dagmar who had channelled through Marjorie - especially since the intervention of Dagmar in Marjorie's channelling had started me on to the path of healing in the first place.

As time has gone on, I have wanted to make contact more directly with Dagmar. At times I have sensed her thoughts coming to me making suggestions that were often very helpful, or giving me insights that were true. On other occasions I have sensed her busy impulsive presence in the background trying to help me. However, I know that there is still a lot of potential in my contact with Dagmar, waiting to be explored.

Recently, I had an inner dialogue with Dagmar during a quiet meditation while I was on my own for the purposes of this book. What follows are the questions I asked and the answers she gave to me as thoughts coming into my mind.

Q: Can you tell me about yourself and the work you do as a Healer?

A: *Thank you for asking me to communicate with you Paul. My name is Dagma. I am a Spiritual Being, a Soul who has lived many lives on Earth. At the moment I choose to be in the Spiritual realms helping people on Earth with healing. I work as part of a team of Spirits, and we help each other in the work that we do. Because of the experience I have gained, I am now in a leadership role of the team that is with me.*

Our work is essentially focusing and directing Spiritual energies to help those on Earth who need it. Also though, we work on this side helping Souls who may be distressed and needing the energies we can channel. I go where I am called to go. With my team, we act to support each other and our work is quite wide ranging. Therefore, we are kept rather busy.

I am linked to you, Paul, as your Healing guide. This means that whenever you ask for my help I come to you and I can then channel Spiritual energies through your heart centre and your hands and into the energy body of the person you want to help. Because you co-operate actively with me, this process now takes place very easily. Also in your prayers and Absent healing, I can listen to your thoughts and through your concern and asking for Spiritual help, this gives me permission to act on your thoughts and we can then attend to those people in need on your behalf.

Sometimes, other members of my team will assist and be the ones channelling Spiritual energies through you, Paul, especially in specific cases where energies of a particular kind are needed. Members of my team have different expertise. But I remain responsible for any Spiritual Healing which is done through you. It is a happy relationship and I am glad that you have accepted me to do this work with you.

Q: How do you operate Spiritual Healing to help people?

A: *In the Spiritual realms where I am working, Paul, there is much peace, love and inspiration. However, there are places within these realms where this energy is generated - places of great power from where love and the essence of all being seems to radiate. It is not possible to come too close to these wondrous energy sources without feeling very affected by it. It is like the power, love and creativity of God.*

Some of these energy outlets have tremendous healing potential. We can draw energy from these sources to be used to help you on Earth. They are a limitless supply of goodness and well-being. We can channel this energy through thought. By the concentration of our minds then, we can direct the energy and change the quality of it to suit the purpose of what is needed. It is an energy that responds mainly to love. So for you on Earth to care about the person you are wanting to help is very important.

People suffering from different illnesses or nervous problems will need a specific form of this energy to suit their particular condition. We have to be careful in the way that we adjust this. For instance, a person with low blood pressure may need a powerful burst of activating energy to get things moving inside them, whereas a person who has been over busy and stressed may need a very different form of energy to quieten the mind and slow down the person's nervous system.

Every person has an energy body consisting of different layers, and this is called the aura. The aura is continually changing according to the thoughts and the feelings of the person concerned.

Learning to channel and adjust these powerful energy sources is like a science to us. There are classes and gatherings of different Spiritual beings to teach us and where we can learn how to do this better. However, there are some illnesses on your side that only the most advanced healers on our side can help. Sometimes the Spiritual beings that teach us were Doctors or Alchemists in previous lives on Earth. The knowledge they have gained can be useful with the energies we are channelling here.

With so much illness and suffering on Earth, we are not short of work to do. It is good though whenever someone new from your side begins to ask us to help. This adds to the healing we are able to do, and creates more opportunities for workers on our side.

Q: What has made you decide to be a healer?

A: *In my most recent life on Earth, Paul, I suffered a lot from illness. Eventually, I died. But before then, I greatly valued the care of Doctors, nurses and loved ones who tended to me. There was little they could do to help me. But it warmed my heart that they cared. And it made me feel that I want to do something to help others who suffer as well.*

This was not the first life where I had suffered. But many times in lives I have wished that more could be done to help those I loved and myself at times when I really struggled to survive.

In this most recent life, towards the end, I found peace. I felt that God or Spirit was with me, and that it was okay for me to live and die in the way that I did. I felt a sense of being looked after even though I was very ill.

This inspired me, so that when I came over to the Spiritual side, I knew I wanted to help others who suffered in the way that I had suffered. This is something deep that my Soul wanted me to experience and the time was right. And so, from there I was given the opportunity to learn to do what I am doing now.

I love this work and it is very interesting and I am glad to be working with you, Paul.

Q: How did you come to be linked with me?

A: *We have met before, Paul. In the past there was a lifetime where I was your daughter. We lived in North America before the white settlers came. It was a troubled time though. You worked as a shaman for the tribe and you were devoted to your work. Some of your practices though were unconventional and you made enemies. Eventually you were killed and soon afterwards the rest of our family died too. You had a large family, Paul, and you cared for us all a lot. I very much admired the work you did and I wanted to help you with it. I was very sad when you died because my deep longing was to work closely with you.*

So then when we met in Spirit afterwards, it was arranged that we could have the opportunity to work together in the way that we are now doing. It has taken some centuries to pass before the conditions arrived where we would both be ready for this. But now the time is here.

I had begun my work as a Healer before you made conscious contact with me, Paul. I had to wait until you were ready to meet me. In some moments, I wondered if it would really come to pass. But then eventually it did.

Q: You have encouraged me to create a Healing Circle group. What is the importance of this from your side?

A: *When you are in a group and you ask together for Spiritual help, then we can be there with you in greater numbers and with more power than when you are on your own. We can also help generate love amongst you in your group so you feel companionship and the joy of acting together. For you on Earth to link together with love is very important for the healing of your planet. The key for such a group to be successful is for you to feel harmony amongst yourselves, for you to be clear about your intentions and for you to act together so that you can achieve this. It is usually better for there to be a leader, and we feel that you are suited for this role in your group. Paul.*

Once you are attuned together, you appear like a beacon of light on Earth for us. By inviting us to be with you, we can bring Spiritual energies down to your frequency on Earth and your collective presence is like a magnet that helps draw us near.

Of course there are those whose work with Spirit is more suited for them to approach us on their own. This is important for some and needs to be encouraged too.

You may notice at the end of your meetings though, how much peace there is in the room where you have been together. This is a sign of our presence and the energy we have been able to bring to be with you.

Through regular meetings and a simple ritual, it becomes possible for us to adjust to you and make an easier passage so we can come to you. Also, when you pray for Absent healing or channel Spiritual healing as a group, we can receive your wishes and focus Spiritual energies more strongly than when you act alone. When you are in harmony with each other, then your collective energies will strengthen and help uplift each one of you.

The object of such a group though is to learn to serve and to help others. By being able to be with you in your Circle, the conditions are created whereby your Spiritual awareness will be increased. So in time, as your group stays together, there can be much healing and personal development. Everyone can contribute to this. By becoming more Spiritually aware, your heart will open naturally to want to serve. And this is what we are aiming to achieve.

Q: How can I work more closely with you?

A: *Well, already we are working quite closely together Paul. But for you to improve this, you need to trust and open yourself more to my presence.*

Let me go through some of the basic elements of Spiritual healing that you and others like you need to learn.

As you know Paul, when I am working with you, you will often feel warmth, tingling, peace or other sensations indicative of the healing energies being channelled through you. This is Spiritual help being given to you. As you allow this to come through you without trying to influence it or to bring your own desires into the process, then I can work through you very easily.

You need to concentrate on your openness to let the healing take place, and your intention to help the person that is with you. But then you can listen. I try often to speak to you through your thoughts. There are places where your hands could go that would be most effective. Sometimes I also try to pass on information about the illness or weakness of the person you are helping.

As you become more conscious of the process of what is taking place, the healing we can do together may become more elaborate. Train yourself to be attuned to the energy system of the person you are helping and gradually you will become more sensitive to this.

The more of this work you do, the more you will unfold psychically, as long as you wish for this. And then, the more sensitive you become, the more closely we can work together.

Q: Why can't everyone be healed?

A: *It is interesting that people can block healing through their thoughts if they do not want help. This can happen on a conscious or subconscious level. It is like love. You can offer love to someone else. But they will not necessarily receive it unless they are open to it.*

A person needs to be ready inside themselves to receive Healing. Many illnesses are linked to the thoughts and beliefs a person has about themselves or circumstances which create negative conditions. Until a person wants to be well, genuinely, then we do not have much hope of being successful at providing a cure. Sometimes miracles do happen at a time when a person has become ready on many different levels for a change in their life. The help that we can provide may be just the final piece in a jigsaw puzzle to enable a cure to take place.

But people can suffer because on some levels they want to suffer or they feel they deserve to suffer. Then of course, they will most probably continue to be ill or suffer in the way they wish.

Some souls may plan an illness or death by illnesses as part of the learning they need to go through. We may not prevent such illnesses then from taking their course. But we can still help by bringing peace and psychological relief if the person is open to it.

There are illnesses, like some viral infections that are very difficult for us to help. The human organism is vulnerable to be attacked and disturbed by these agents.

Q: Do you have any advice for people who may wish to channel Spiritual healing?

A: *Let me say that if you wish to heal and help people, then do that. All you need is an open and caring heart. Ask for help and let us do the rest. If you want to help someone with healing, there will be a Spiritual being connected with you that will be able to help.*

If you can, join a group who are practising healing. If you feel comfortable in this group, then you can learn with them to attune your energy. Like any other skill, learning to heal needs practice. Try not to think that you are healing the person yourself. Otherwise the healing energy may drain your resources rather than coming from a Spiritual source. But Spiritual healing is very simple once you get used to it.

Not everyone in their plan as a Soul wishes to be a Healer. If it is so that in your plan, you do, then there may be a Spiritual being waiting to help you as I am here to help Paul. If this is the case, there may come an opportunity for you to make contact in some way. As your contact together can become stronger, your healing will improve.

Only do spiritual healing if you want to do it, if you really love doing it. Many people would benefit from this healing and it gives us joy to help through you.

Q: Is it important for people who want to be Spiritual Healers to belong to a reputable Spiritual Healing organisation?

A: *We urge you to respect the Law of your land and especially to work in co-operation with medical authorities. Basically, your work as Spiritual Healers is to try to help people and to co-operate with others who are wanting to do the same.*

To join a Spiritual Healing organisation may be helpful. Through this organisation you may meet people who can help you develop the Healing that you do. Also, many people in your society will be more open to receive your services if they know you belong to a reputable Spiritual Healing organisation.

However, being a member of such an organisation will not necessarily make you a better Healer. The gift of being a Spiritual Healer comes from Spirit. Trust your own intuition about what you need to do.

If a person is meant to come to you and receive Healing with your help, then usually circumstances will coincide to find the way how this can happen. Life can be very mysterious, but is not without its purpose.

It is mainly through us in Spirit that you will learn what you need to learn to be a Spiritual healer.

Chapter 16

Creating a Healing Circle Group

'Love is the most important thing and the strongest energy and it overcomes evil and hatred. The best advice I can give you is to spread love where you can and where you will and care about other people. It is not always easy if you, yourself, are in pain or if you've got your own problems to have to start worrying about other people. But the happiest of people, if you notice, are the ones who are trying to help others. And you find happiness that way, and you also spread it - being helpful to other people. If you care at all, and if you love at all then you can do nothing better than that'. - Sojah

The Main Elements of Our Healing Circle Group

A Healing Circle group is a group of people who meet regularly to channel the energies of Spirit, with the purpose of generating love and healing, and learning through Spiritual development. To belong to such a group can be very rewarding and bring much joy and fulfilment. But it also needs a strong dedication from its members and a willingness to serve. It is important that attunement to Spirit be at the heart of such a group, that ego and personality concerns be secondary to that. Within group meetings there needs to be some elements of Spiritual Practice which can help members of the group learn to be more fully attuned to Spirit. It may be helpful for one person to be in the position of leadership or facilitation of the group to give a clear focus for its activities.

In this chapter, I would like to outline some important aspects about the Healing Circle group in which I have been associated and how this group has functioned. This group has been maintained for a number of years. Although there have been many changes, the essence of what we do has remained simple and has continued to unfold.

My own belief is that Healing Circle groups tend to come into being not so much because a group of people decide to create one, but more that there is a Spiritual plan with different Souls involved, for such a group to exist. If people decide to form a Healing Circle group from their own desires, but without having the necessary inner Spiritual support, then I do not feel it will succeed for very long.

So when people feel the yearning in their heart to join a Healing Circle group or to help form one, it is often quite mysterious circumstances how people meet to come together for that. Because Healing Circle groups are Spiritually inspired, it may be that a person is guided in a surprising way to meet somebody else with whom there may be a compatibility to join together in such a group. These meetings do not happen by accident. Certainly, in our Healing circle, many of our members have experienced this in the way they joined the group.

We have been told that when we meet together as a group, not only do we sit together in a Circle, but there is a larger Circle of Spiritual Beings also gathered to be with us.

With our group, we try to meet on a weekly basis, on a Friday evening. Our meetings have maintained a similar structure from one week to the next, so our members could become familiar with that and know what to expect. However, we have also tried not to be too fixed in what we do to allow space for innovation and evolution and also to keep our meetings interesting.

Many of our members live busy lives outside our group and so not everyone can attend each meeting. We have tried to be flexible with this. By having a regular format it has meant that our members could easily slot into 'the flow of things' after an absence. We have kept our group open so that new members could join and people could visit our group meetings when they had an interest and it felt appropriate to invite them. This has helped to keep our group alive and provided fresh input at times.

By having a regular rhythm, this has added a ritual element to our proceedings. With this, we could go deeper into our attunement with Spirit over time. We have found this helpful.

The main components of our meetings have been as follows. First we discuss any practical matters which need our attention and we share together how our week has been. Once this is over, we begin with a meditation and invocation to link us together, and to call upon the presence of Spirit. Then we have a round of Absent Healing to send out Healing to those we know who need it outside our Circle. Next, we share an Earth Healing Meditation together. I will write more about this in the next chapter. Then we engage in channelling Spiritual healing to each other in pairs - either giving or receiving. We share with each other about this afterwards. Following this, if we have time, we have a silent meditation for each of us to connect with our Spiritual guides or to open to some inner healing experience. Then we conclude with a session of Channelling from one of the members of the group. This may include questions and answers. We finish the formal part of the evening by giving thanks for the Spiritual help we have received and asking the Healing energies to go where they are needed. Afterwards we have some social time to chat and share a cup of tea together.

Altogether, our evenings are usually very enjoyable and there is a very happy atmosphere amongst us when we close.

Now I would like to explain in more detail about the Absent Healing and the Spiritual Healing which we do.

Absent Healing
Absent Healing is sometimes also called Distant Healing. Basically, with this, we are asking the Spiritual beings working

within our Circle to channel Healing energies to people (and perhaps animals) who are not with us physically, to help them. From within our Circle, we open our hearts, our imagination and our intention that the people on our Absent Healing lists may receive Healing that they need and that they can accept.

The way we do this is for us to go around our Circle. Then each person in turn can say the names (often just the Christian name) of the person to whom healing is being sent, and maybe a few words about that person's need. When we have all had our turn, then we have a silent space in which members of our group can focus on sending help to people whom they do not want to mention aloud, or give more specific time and attention to sending healing to someone on their list. We have found this silent space at the end very valuable.

We have been told that the Spiritual beings wanting to help us with healing pick up our thoughts, and can then channel healing energies in the direction of our thoughts to the people concerned. So, if we can really open our hearts and imagine healing rays reaching the people on our list, then this will help.

Sometimes in an emergency where someone needs help desperately, we will hold hands together and concentrate as much as we can upon healing help for that person.

People in our group have developed different rituals for doing their own Absent Healing. One imagines the people on her list in a Crystal cave receiving Healing. Others imagine the people one by one in the centre of our Circle, filled with Healing Light. Different approaches can be adapted to suit the person who is doing the Absent Healing.

I imagine that Absent Healing is very much akin to Prayer. Once we have spent some moments to attune to each person on our list, we release the Healing to the loving powers of Spirit, working with us. It is not us who do the Healing, but we are instruments through which the Healing can take place. By invoking the presence of Spirit or our guides and through our Healing wish and intention, this helps to create a link with the Spiritual beings working with us and gives them permission and the ability to go to the person in need and help. We have been told that this usually takes place at night while the person is asleep. Spiritual beings are not limited by time, space and distance in the same way as us and therefore they can provide help at the moment and the place where it would be most appropriate.

We have been encouraged to practice Absent Healing on our own outside our meetings as well. For this, we need a quiet space once a day where we can have some moments asking for Spiritual help and inwardly be with the people needing our healing help. Our members have willingly done this. I have found that it suits me to do this practice at the end of my day's activities. Then, this meditation gives me feelings of peace to open my heart to care for people in need. I often also feel close to Spirit when I do this.

One question we have faced is about whether it is necessary for people to request Absent Healing from us before we send it to them. Certainly if people request healing I feel they are more likely to co-operate with the process and open themselves to receive. But we have decided that it is fine for us to ask for healing really for anyone whom we choose. We feel that Absent Healing is like other forms of caring. We do not need people's permission in order to care about them.

When Absent Healing is directed to people, they still have the free Will on many different levels to decide whether to accept this healing or not. However, it could be that some people will very gratefully accept this healing even though they have not asked for it. Also, sick or injured children, animals, or people who are suffering severely may not be in a position to ask for help. Yet in our hearts we would not hesitate to help them if we could.

The Absent Healing is a very important component of our work as a Healing Circle group. It helps to give a meaning and purpose to our activities beyond just the circle of our group itself. Our members have been quite enthusiastic to include Absent Healing as part of their daily rhythm of activities. One of the main reasons for this is that it does achieve meaningful and successful results. We have had some quite spectacular instances of this.

Examples of Absent Healing

One woman phoned me once from Scotland requesting help through Absent Healing as she had been suffering from chronic sciatica and severe discomfort in her lower back. I included her in my list. Then a letter from her three months later confirmed that she had been pain free and experiencing excellent health from the time we started sending the healing.

My mother in Australia has suffered from chronic neck pain for much of her life. Doctors diagnosed Arthritis, but nothing over the years has really helped. Sometimes the pain has been worse and sometimes better but it has never really gone away. This continuing discomfort has bothered my mother and caused her much depression.

I offered to send her Absent Healing regularly. She accepted this. Since that time she has been pain free in her neck. She has become convinced of the power of Spiritual Healing and she has asked me a number of times to continue.

One of our group members had an elderly male friend dying of cancer. As a group we sent Absent Healing to this man. Our group member did this on her own as well. This man did eventually die, but the doctors were amazed that over the last weeks when the cancer had reached a very advanced stage and they would have expected him to be suffering extreme pain, he remained relatively pain free. His death was remarkably peaceful.

A woman whom I will call Marilyn asked one of our group for us to send her Absent Healing, as she had been suffering severe psoriasis since she was a young girl. From the time we began sending her healing as a group, Marilyn noticed an improvement in her condition. She wrote to tell us of this. But then, for some weeks, our group member with whom Marilyn was in contact, was ill and taken up with other responsibilities. In this time, she could not attend our group meetings. Unbeknown to Marilyn, during this period we did not send Absent Healing to her. A few weeks later, Marilyn was in contact again. The psoriasis had flared up again during the time exactly corresponding to that when we had stopped sending her healing. Once we started with the Absent Healing again, her psoriasis settled.

Marilyn had a cat who was dying. She requested Absent Healing for her cat and the animal survived. Some months later her cat was still alive and well.

Absent Healing is able to help people in many ways. Many people to whom we have sent Absent Healing have recovered from injuries or illness quicker than expected as a result of the healing. Absent Healing can also help to bring peace of mind to those who are troubled.

Our Absent Healing Cards

Some time ago, in our group, we were guided through the Channelling to create absent Healing cards. These cards could act as symbols to enable people more easily to connect with receiving Spiritual help. They could be given to people who believed in Spirit and who wanted our support.

It was suggested to us that we design the cards using some simple symbols that could act upon the consciousness of the person looking at the card and help bring peace. Therefore, on one side of the card we had printed a rainbow with a white dove and a pair of hands holding the globe of our world. On the other side some green leaves, growing and reaching outwards were illustrated with a text that said 'May spiritual love enfold you giving you Strength and Healing. May light shine upon you bringing Comfort and Peace.'

These cards have proved very popular and have become very precious to many who have asked for our help.

It was quite a magical process for us how these cards were created with the help of inspiration from our channelling sources and different people, who contributed along the way. When we finally got the cards printed, we thought they may be too expensive for us, due to the complicated layout and the different colouring used. However, we asked if we could have a discount on the price of them. Then when we received the bill, the amount on the invoice we received, corresponded exactly with the amount of money we had accumulated from donations in our bank account to pay for this.

Spiritual Healing

Many of our group have been surprised and delighted to develop the capacity to channel healing to help other people. As well as doing this 'absently' through meditation, we have also practised this directly using the hands and heart primarily as instruments for passing on Healing energy.

Much of our learning about the Healing has come through Channelling with Dagmar and the prompting of other Spiritual guides working with us.

The mechanics for doing Spiritual Healing are quite simple. Except in emergencies or perhaps with animals or children, it is important that the patient has requested the Healing and therefore is open to receive. Then, with the patient either sitting or lying, the first step is for the Healer to take some moments to attune to Spirit and to the patient, asking to be an instrument for the healing to take place. Then, either by making physical contact by touching different part's of the person's body, or by working more with the energy field or the 'aura' of the person with hands not touching the physical body, the hands of the Healer can stay or move to different places around the patient's body where healing may be needed. Some Spiritual Healers follow set procedures of where to place their hands to offer Healing in a more systematic way. However, I believe that a more intuitive approach is often most beneficial. The Healer can then be more open to Spiritual influences and guided to where the healing really needs to be focused. When the Healing is completed, a few moments of giving thanks to Spirit and asking for continued help for the patient can end the session. This can be done aloud or silently.

To be a Channel for Healing is a humbling experience. To call upon the power of Spirit to help with Healing brings peace, love and energies far more than what we can usually express through our personal selves. It works only as we offer ourselves in service and we care about the person we are trying to help. As this attunement and surrender to Spirit becomes greater, then the capacity to heal increases too.

I have noticed with my own healing that as I have gradually developed as a Channel for Healing, my own inner perception and intuition has also grown stronger and I have become less self-centred in my thoughts and more able to tune into the needs of my patient.

It has been important for us to practise Spiritual Healing in our group with each other and also when the opportunity has been there, with people outside our group. With many of our group living quite stressful lives there has rarely been a shortage of volunteers to receive healing! Through feedback, we have been able to gain confidence that it really works. Our group has felt to be a safe space for us to experiment doing this with each other. Then as members of our group have gained confidence that they can do it, this has fed their belief in the process and this in turn has helped to open the channels for the healing energies to come through more strongly. We have found it to be essential for us to be as positive as we could be. This helps the healing channels to be open. Also, it helps our patients have confidence in us so they will believe they can receive help.

Naturally, there have been times within our group when some of our members have found their self-confidence lapsing. Often though, the feedback we get from those receiving healing can be very affirming that we are achieving far more than we thought possible.

We have been told that there are surrounding and permeating our physical body, different layers of more subtle energy fields called the 'aura'. This aura also has associated with it, a number of nodal energy centres connected to our body called energy 'chakras'. Much has been written about this. Some people with

210

psychic sight can see the aura or aspects of it as colours and energy fields around us. The aura is changeable and varies according to our moods, health, the thoughts we have and our general vitality. When we are sick, our aura tends to become much duller and less vital in different ways. Physical illness is usually preceded by disturbances that occur on a subtle level with the aura first. It is also on this subtle energy level where disturbances from the past may be stored, affecting us negatively until they are somehow liberated.

Spiritual Healing then, tends to act directly upon our subtle energy system, providing it with energy inputs and helping to draw away negative energy residues. After a healing session, a person's aura will be generally brighter and the person will feel better.

If a person has been injured, then there will be corresponding disturbances in some layers of the aura. So manipulations of the aura can help physically to restore harmony and heal something that has been damaged.

Several times I have found this to work on Marjorie, when I have been doing healing with her. Because of her fragile arthritic condition Marjorie sometimes suffers from dislocation of her joints, particularly the shoulder and elbow. When this happens she can be in extreme pain. With Spiritual help then and by manipulating her aura, without touching her physically, it has been possible to ease the joint back into place so that she felt an immediate easing of her condition and within a few days the pain from this area has gone. I have been able to help Marjorie a number of times with this so she did not need further medical treatment.

I feel that there are many situations with healing, when having the hands in direct physical contact with the patient can also be very helpful. This way, the energy can be applied directly to the nervous system, to the blood stream and to other physical organs. Sometimes, people need and really appreciate too, the comfort of human touch. As humans, we all have a need to feel that we are loved and cared about. We need this physically as well.

Spiritual healing does not help everyone. Nor do its effects always endure. People may not be open to receive healing on an inner level. A person may feel undeserving to be happy and well or even not believe that this is possible. Often the conditions of illness, depression and anxiety may be sustained by negative thoughts and belief patterns generated by the patient. Environmental factors may also have a negative impact. Someone whose life is governed by habits and ways of being that are unsupportive may easily slip back into these patterns again shortly after a session of Spiritual Healing is completed. In these cases the effect of the Spiritual healing will be quite short term.

For such people to find enduring benefit, they must also be prepared to change the circumstances of their lives as well. Doing this, Spiritual Healing on a regular basis may provide a space in someone's life to encourage changes to be conceived. For people needing to make fundamental changes in their lives, Spiritual healing may be very helpful in conjunction with other Psychotherapy to enable them to become aware of negative patterns in their lives and through unblocking stuck energies, start to create something new.

Public Healing

With our Healing group, we reached the stage where practising Spiritual Healing upon each other was no longer enough. There was the desire to extend this Healing as an activity beyond our group. However, others in the group were not in the position like me where they wanted or could take patients privately. So, after much discussion, we hired a Public Hall one evening a week and started to offer healing to members of the general public.

Although some members of our group were rather nervous about doing this in the beginning, it soon proved to be a great success. Doing this spurred on several of our members to seek professional qualifications to practice Spiritual Healing. But people came to receive healing and they seemed to really enjoy it.

From the meditations we have had at the beginnings of these evenings it has felt as if a tremendous feeling of love and peace has descended into the room. This has been a strong indication of the presence of Spirit working with us.

Over time we have acquired 'regulars', people coming to receive healing almost every week and others coming and going, plus many people who we may treat only once. To me the space we have created to provide this healing has felt like a Sanctuary, and we have joined together as a community of people to welcome Spiritual energies. I am not sure how people have been drawn to come to us. Many have come through word of mouth.

The Challenges of Maintaining Our Healing Circle Group

As a group, we have been through personal crises, power struggles, emotional upsets and illnesses. At times we have wondered how we could possibly go on. However, as crises have come and we have reminded ourselves that at the heart of our activities was Spirit, then this has steadied us and we have been given the strength to continue.

As leader of the group, I have tried to be sensitive to other members' needs and wishes. My actions have not always been perfect but I have done my best. I have also felt it to be important to maintain a vision of continuing unfoldment for our work together.

Some of our long standing members have left the group at different times. The rest of us have sometimes felt guilt, wondering what we did wrong to make the person leave, or blaming the person for their actions. But usually people left the group because they had gained from it what they needed for their own personal development and they were now ready to move on to other spheres. In many ways this is a natural outcome for our group, and important for us to accept this as a means to spread what we do further.

As one person has left the group, it has left space for another one to join us. This has not always been easy at first and we have needed to adjust to accommodate new people. Many of the needs and questions new members have brought into the group have been similar from one person to the next and so we have needed to be patient with this. But new members have also brought new enthusiasm and specific gifts for which we could be grateful.

I do not know how long our group will continue or even how it will eventually unfold, but it has touched the lives of many people and been an important place for learning and service for Spirit. I trust that this will continue to be so.

Joining a Healing Circle Group

What I have written concerning our Healing Circle group could serve as a model for the formation of new Healing Circle groups, but other models may serve too. For much of what we have done in our group, we have not tried to copy what anyone else has done, but abided by guidance we have received, listened to our own intuitions and instincts and acted upon this.

I feel that there is much need for Healing Circle groups in our world today. As part of my work I would love to help in the formation of these.

So, if you feel inspired that you would like to join or lead a Healing Circle group, then I suggest for you to seek to do this. If this is part of your life plan, then deep inside you will know how you need to do this and who you need to meet along the way to accomplish this. Ask for help inwardly and find the help you need from people so you can discover this path. If it is right, then I know from my own experience that it may bring you much joy to succeed.

Chapter 17

Earth Healing

Our Earth Today

Our Earth is a fantastic organism. It is teeming with life of myriad form and description. Really, it is a miracle to be alive and to be conscious and able to appreciate the wonders of our life. When we are aware of the links we share with other creatures and life forms on our planet - when we truly open our hearts with love to this, then we can feel joy at our togetherness.

However, as human beings we can also experience much sadness and suffering at what we are doing about this. With our fellow creatures, our precious plant life and trees, the life sustaining elements of air, water and earth, these are all sacred. They are worthy of their rights to exist in connection with us and their need for us to nurture them. But we as humans tend to use our free Will to exploit the Earth's resources, to manipulate life around us to fit our own purposes, individually and collectively - often with little regard of how our actions may affect the balance of Nature and the ecological needs of the different life forms cohabiting with us.

Physically, our bodies are created from substances of the Earth. We cannot escape from the intimacy of the relationship we share with our Earth - except through denial and ignorance. To live, we breathe the air, eat food, drink water and warm ourselves through the materials of the Earth. Without this, we could not survive as human beings. The Earth is our physical home.

Our consciousness and Soul do not originate from the physical Earth. Our Souls come down to the earth from Spiritual realms to inhabit a physical body. So in some ways, we are guests on our planet Earth. We are given the Spiritual gifts of consciousness and free Will. Our free Will gives us both a challenge and an opportunity. The opportunity is one where we can learn skills and gain awareness, and through the opening of our hearts, we can become ever more conscious with love to fully participate in the process of creation and evolving life on our planet. The challenge is one where we can misuse our powers, making mistakes, causing suffering and pain to others and ultimately ourselves.

So, what are we doing to our precious Earth, that force and organism which pervades us and sustains us in so many fundamental ways? It would be desirable if we could honour and cherish our Earth and all that comprises, treating our physical home with care and respect. Is that what we are doing though? The evidence would suggest the contrary. We are destroying the Earth. As our capacity to manipulate the Earth increases further, we destroy more and more of our physical world.

The soils of our Earth are being covered in concrete or despoiled by pesticides, radioactivity and other poisons of our own making. Our seas are becoming rubbish dumps for the many chemical waste products we don't want. Our animal life is being exterminated and many species are becoming extinct. Great areas of native forest and jungle are being cut down, leaving huge expanses of waste land. Our air is being polluted and the upper reaches of our atmosphere damaged. Global warming is a phenomenon happening because of the blanket of carbon products we are spewing into the air. With bio-technology, genes are being manipulated to alter the very fabric of life on our planet. Yet many people congratulate the 'advances' we are making in our world as 'progress' and 'growth'. Even in outer space we are filling the area around our Earth with junk we no longer need.

We are largely responsible for what is happening on our planet at this time. We are the ones damaging and destroying the Earth. And many people don't seem to care.

The forces of greed and selfishness within people and organisations seem to be creating the most damage and destruction. Greed makes people obsessed with making money at all costs, driving for extra profits, exploiting and abusing others in order to gain some advantage in our competitive society.

People who do care try to struggle against this. But it is not easy. Governments also wheel and deal against each other. For every action though, there is a reaction. Our Earth cannot endure endless battering and destruction. It contains finite resources.

As a collective race, we humans have the capacity to care for our Earth if we wish. But greed and selfishness closes people off from the perception of caring. With greed and selfishness, people cannot see further than what they want. This is very sad because if the Earth is destroyed, then we will all suffer tremendously. No one can escape from that. But our collective orientation as a humanity towards money, 'progress', war, competitiveness, profit and exploitation has had its effect too. We have tended to lose sight of the beauty and fundamental Spiritual qualities of our Earth.

So, if we do care, what can we do to help? With a huge human population on our planet, and with large organisations seeming to rule over our lives in so many ways, it is easy to feel powerless, as if we can act only to make the tiniest of differences in outcomes. By ourselves, if we feel isolated, there is not much we can do. But if we link with others, perhaps we can achieve more.

To help our world, it would seem that the values of our cultures and our societies need to transform themselves. Our attitudes need to change collectively if we are going to be able to help. Also if the motives are coming from a loving caring source, science and technology could bring much good. For me, the key issue concerns motivation. We cannot force people to be less greedy and selfish. We each have our choices about that.

There are organisations like Greenpeace and Friends of the Earth who have tried to influence people and governments to become more environmentally aware. The aims and intentions of organisations such as these are becoming much more socially acceptable than they were, say ten or twenty years ago.

In my own life, I have tried to make some token efforts towards environmental action. Our family have eaten organic vegetables when we could. We have participated in recycling schemes. As a hobby, I have grown some trees from seed and found homes for them. When I've felt strongly about some environmental issue, I have written to my member of parliament.

But then I know that many of my actions have not supported the environment. I have tended to feel inadequate in my own small efforts.

As I have shared, my own life path has been towards helping people and healing, so I have not chosen to be an environmental activist even though I appreciate the work of these people very much. I have often wondered what more I could do?

From my work with Spiritual Healing, I have been amazed at how much peace and well-being this can bring to people. Sometimes I have wondered if such Spiritual energies could be directed to help the living being of our planet Earth? I have known that with Spiritual Healing, this required someone on Earth to channel the healing so that it could be focused on the person who needed it. Perhaps our Earth also needs people to channel Spiritual energies so that peace and well-being could be restored to it? This could help our collective 'karma' if we are able to do this. But how can Spiritual energies be channelled effectively to help the Earth?

My longings in this respect have been answered through a member of our Healing group whom I will call Naomi, as she wishes to retain her anonymity and I respect that wish.

Naomi has made contact with two Spiritual guides wanting to work through her. These guides have wanted to use Naomi as an instrument to teach about the Earth Healing and ways in which this could be done Spiritually. As a result of this, we have learnt an Earth Healing meditation and adopted regular practices within our Healing group so we could make efforts to channel Spiritual Healing to our Earth.

Because Naomi's guides have wanted their teachings to be spread, and with Naomi's kind permission, I would like to include some of their teachings in this chapter plus the Earth Healing meditation we use. First though I will share some details relating to the process of how these teachings were given to Naomi and our group.

Meeting Thundercloud and Cariadd

Thundercloud and Cariadd are the names of Naomi's two Spiritual guides. She initially made contact with them through individual work she was doing with me, as well as her activities in relationship with our Healing group.

Naomi came to me because she wanted to learn about past lives that she had lived. As we went on with this work she became very interested in the knowledge of herself she was gaining through this. Because of the nature of the experiences emerging for her, I felt that it was appropriate to ask her if she would like to join our Healing group.

Naomi agreed to this and when she came at first, she was a little unsure about what to expect. This was all new to her - at least in her present life! However, Naomi was then surprised to find how interested and involved she became in all that we did together. Naomi became one of our most dedicated members.

After a while Naomi was able to learn to 'travel' in some of her meditations. With her inner visions she went quite a number of times to the side of a lake with a large tree beside it. Here she became aware of the presence of a majestic male Native American. Gradually this Indian was able to communicate to Naomi and teach her by showing her things. Usually he remained at a distance whilst panoramic scenes slowly revolved before her. This is how Naomi met Thundercloud. He was her personal Spiritual guide.

Nearly always, Naomi became aware of a bird: large, brown, powerful and eagle like. Naomi found that she could move her consciousness into the bird and then fly. This was her first experience in Astral travel.

Initially, she was rather clumsy at this and could not control it very well, often entering rapid, terrifying spins. But the consciousness with the bird tried to help her.

On one occasion she was able to visit a Spiritual temple of learning with a vast landscape around it. On another journey, she went to a place resembling the meadow where Marjorie would meet Sojah for our channelling sessions. The thought came to her through the bird urging her to learn to 'fly free' in her life. This was repeated like a mantra. Later Naomi became aware that this bird was another representation of Thundercloud.

In one session with me Naomi saw that there was a door in the sky. As I coaxed Naomi to open this door, the most brilliant golden white light streamed through. As I gently supported Naomi to go through this doorway she was able to adjust to the love, peace and brightness of the atmosphere that she entered. Naomi was then able to meet Cariadd, her Healing guide.

To Naomi, Cariadd had a very beautiful appearance and was able to talk with Naomi more easily than Thundercloud. Cariadd shared with Naomi that in her last life on Earth she had been a Celtic High Priestess and she had worked with Naomi then. Their association could be developed further now.

Cariadd was able to teach Naomi to channel. Naomi's consciousness could move aside and Cariadd could then speak directly through her. Naomi was a gifted channellist and much of what Cariadd said through her was inspiring. However, Cariadd spoke somewhat in the manner of the High Priestess. Her personality was very directive, authoritative and obviously used to having her words and edicts obeyed without question. Naomi did not feel comfortable for Cariadd to speak to people like this. It was not a way how Naomi wanted to relate to people. Also, while she was channelling, Naomi felt she could do nothing about what was being said through her body.

Later on Cariadd mellowed and became more humble and receptive. She developed ways of working with Naomi so Naomi could feel more included. Naomi, though, also had to learn to express what she wanted. This is one example of how a person and their guide needed to learn to adjust to each other so that communication could flow more easily.

Both Cariadd and Thundercloud were strong personalities. It became clear that their intentions with Naomi were more than just to guide her personally. More and more in Cariadd's channelling the orientation of her words moved towards the need of healing for our Earth. In the meantime Naomi struggled with her own doubts and fears about the reality of the channelling she was doing and what her guides wanted from her. She had to make her own choices too.

During one session Cariadd spoke about the damage that had been done to the Earth through the abuse of human beings. She suggested the need to establish a Spiritual network all round the world, of people channelling Spiritual healing to our Earth. This was surely needed. There were other Spiritual beings also trying to help people to make this network stronger, so that if enough people could be engaged in doing this work, linking Spiritually together, then it could reach a critical point where this healing could really penetrate into the Earth and release blockages that have been there. Then healing energy would bubble up from within the Earth itself bringing with it peace and well-being for all on our planet. This was the goal for which Cariadd and Thundercloud were working.

Hearing these thoughts I felt profoundly moved. I wanted to support these efforts all I could.

Thundercloud's Vision

In my channelling sessions with Naomi, it became a pattern for me to relate with Cariadd rather than Thundercloud. Thundercloud had the stronger presence but Naomi could not yet cope with his vibrations if he came too close to her. What he could do though was to take her on inner journeys, teaching her this way.

During one session, while Cariadd was speaking through Naomi answering questions to the small group that were present, Naomi's consciousness was taken by Thundercloud on a journey. As usual, they travelled in the bird and Thundercloud communicated to her that he wanted her to go with him into the past.

Together they flew to the forests of North America. However, these were the forests as they were before the European settlers came. As she was taken down to ground level, the wonder and beauty of the landscape filled all her senses. She could smell the trees and there were so many. The water was clear and fish formed streaks of silver in the spray. It was untouched and unspoilt - pure and known only to those who lived there.

Thundercloud communicated to Naomi that he wanted her to see and smell and hear and understand the beauty as it was - so that when she returned to our time to learn about the Earth Healing, she would understand the urgency and why she had chosen to do this. He was wanting to show Naomi again the Truth of what her Soul knew when she asked for this Incarnation. Thundercloud emphasised to Naomi that she needed to be reminded of this so she would not reject Cariadd as being false.

To end this vision, Thundercloud flew Naomi back to the present time by going over the forests of Sweden and Finland. He communicated to her that these were places where the forests in present time do not look like they should anymore, because of the greed and the toxins that have come through our human interference.

So Naomi experienced the Scandinavian forest devastated by acid rain, immediately after the wondrous experience of the pristine forests of the former North America. The result of this left Naomi shaken and disturbed. When her consciousness returned into her body, Naomi did not look happy and refreshed. She was more quiet and deeply thoughtful.

222

Much later Naomi shared with me that his vision gave her a burden of sorrow and loss. She felt it was too much to bear. Once she was away from the group, her tears flowed often.

Some days after this, Naomi had another opportunity to do some channelling. This time she was hesitant, not sure if she was ready to do any more just yet, afraid of what may be revealed, fearful of being unable to cope with the responsibility of knowing. But then she agreed to go ahead.

Thundercloud was not finished with the vision he wanted to show Naomi. There was a second part to it.

Again Naomi went with Thundercloud in the bird. They travelled once more to the beautiful North American forests from the past. However, just as she was soaking up the joy, marvels and vitality of this landscape, she was switched in her consciousness to the future. This was an abrupt and violent alteration for her. It was shocking!

At first, she noticed the poisoned water, stretching far into the distance, the dead fish, a vast cracked dry lake and the defoliated trees. The panorama was infinite for Naomi - slow, painful visions of devastated Earth scenes - endless for her. It went on and on, much, much longer for Naomi than for us who watched her crying.

The message was clear. This was a symbolic and 'real' vision of how the future of the earth could be - all life and beauty ruined, unless there was action now to help the Earth. In a most poignant and dramatic personal way, Naomi was being shown the consequences of what may happen if she and many others together do not fulfil their purpose and make efforts to help the Earth now. People's greed could destroy the Earth unless we can all help and find help.

At the end of this session, the mood in the group was sombre, sad and almost despairing. We were all concerned for Naomi. I did not know what would happen with her as a result of this. I was used to Spiritual guides bringing joy and happiness to people's lives - not this. Inside myself, I felt guilt that I could not have protected Naomi from these visions. I was not certain anymore if Thundercloud and Cariadd were in fact suitable guides for Naomi, or whether they were too strong for her and overruling her needs.

It came as a shock but no surprise when a few days later, Naomi informed me that she wanted a break from the group and from channelling. She needed 'time out' for reflection. I wondered if that would be the end of the Earth Healing for our group.

However, it was not all over. Naomi needed time to digest and assimilate her experiences, time to form a new relationship with her guides where she could be more in control, and time for her to discern from within herself what she really wanted.

After some months, Naomi returned to our group. She was ready to continue her participation and work with us. It was soon after this that Naomi was given the first information which has become the basis for the Earth Healing meditation which we now use.

Cariadd's teaching

One evening while Naomi was doing some paper work at home, she felt the presence of Cariadd wanting to communicate with her. Naomi felt that she could shut Cariadd out if she wished, but she wanted to know what Cariadd had to say. So Naomi allowed herself to write automatically, making notes on the paper of the thoughts coming into her mind. Reading this afterwards, this communication was a meditation and a visualisation, the beginning of rituals and practices our group could use to help heal the Earth Spiritually. Naomi sensed that this information was important and she wished to pass it on.

Soon, Naomi agreed again to allow herself to be a channel for Cariadd to speak through her. We listened with interest to the teachings Cariadd wanted to impart about Earth Healing.

Cariadd conveyed that just as human beings have a Spiritual aspect to their nature, with Chakras - energy centres, and with many different aspects of us needing to be operating in harmony for us to feel happy and for us to be 'whole' and at peace, the same was also true for our Earth.

The Earth could be experienced as a living being with different Chakras, energy centres and with many different multi-dimensional interrelated facets which needed to be operating in harmony for the Earth to be in good health and functioning well. Unfortunately, this was not the case. There were many dangerous imbalances occurring in the energy system of the Earth, imbalances precipitated by the activities of human beings.

Cariadd blamed the imbalances now existing within the Earth as primarily coming from the greed of people. She spoke how in evolution from earlier times there had been a taking from the Earth first for need, so people could survive. This had become a taking from the Earth for profits, and then a greed for more profits, which has turned into being from some quarters, a massive exploitation of every aspect of our planet and its life. She told how if action were not taken to stop it and turn in another direction, the future of our planet and our environment would turn out as ruined and destroyed as in the vision which Naomi had been given of the future, with Thundercloud.

Practical action was needed to influence governments, multi-national companies and all those in power, urging them to adopt more sustainable practices and policies. She said that many young people were being inspired by those in Spirit caring about the Earth to engage in protest and join groups that could make a difference.

Cariadd explained that she felt that the Earth was sick. It was actually ill, physically ill. She said that in the natural state of health, the colours of the aura of the Earth were beautiful, vibrant and even. But now, the Earth colours were clouded. She suggested that if we could stand on the moon and look back at the Earth, seeing the globe of the Earth, as we would in a picture, and Spiritually see the colours that emanated from this, they were not there. The colours would not be there. At the moment the planet was surrounded by a murky mixed up confusion of clouds. We would not see this physically, but psychically or Spiritually. We could look at the Earth and we would see this dreadful shadow and cloud around it. Now this should be pure. The colours should be there. If the Earth were not sick, they would be.

So, was there anything besides practical action that we could do to help? Cariadd replied that by using simple symbols, visualisations, mantras, prayers and focused positive thoughts, we could help channel healing Spiritually to the Earth. Doing this in groups, as individuals and in ever greater numbers could really make a difference.

Cariadd suggested that as more people began to be aware Spiritually, and as they linked together Spiritually, the power of positive thought was very strong, really strong. If we added to this what people were doing on a practical level, then areas really could begin to improve.

With a common intention, this could form a network and web of healing around the Earth, channelling healing Light to our planet. Prayers were also needed for the greed of the people, that this could be assuaged. Without this aspect of our human nature being placed in much greater check, little progress could be made to help.

Cariadd had referred in earlier channelling sessions to a New Age of consciousness that was coming to humanity. When I asked her to say more about this, she told that this was the age where the Spirit - the Spirit of goodness, Spirituality - where we had the chance for that to become all powerful. This was the Age where the natural world should be valued, protected and nurtured - the Age where people should move from the levels of materialism and greed, into the levels of sensitivity and understanding - the Age where we should achieve telepathic powers and high levels of development in our minds. This was the time when all of this should happen. This should be the beginnings of the salvation of our world. However, then she warned that what was significant was that this was no longer a guaranteed process.

Cariadd spoke of a time in the past when people were able to develop and where they still maintained a link with the natural world. They respected the world in which they lived. They took from the Earth, but also gave back. Now in the Age of consciousness that we are entering we should return to that balance where we respect and give back. We have the chance to do this if the awareness of all is raised. However, it will take much work, dedication and co-operation with Spirit to enable this to happen.

Preparations For Earth Healing

To prepare us for the Earth Healing meditation, Cariadd taught us about the seven energy Chakra aspects of our Earth and gave a colour and a symbol to associate with each one.

For the upper atmosphere and outer space surrounding the Earth, she gave the colour violet and the symbol of a slowly revolving crystal. Next, for the sky, the main atmosphere around our planet, bird and insect life, she suggested the colour indigo with symbols, a snowflake for the polar regions, a feather for the temperate regions and a butterfly for the tropical regions. Then, for the oceans, rivers and aquatic life she gave the colour blue, with a smooth pebble or shell. Next, for the trees, plants and land life was the colour green with the symbol of a leaf or flower. The following Chakra was represented by the deserts with the colour yellow and the symbol of a candle flame. Next were the soil and the upper soil stratas of the Earth, associated with the colour orange and with a rough stone. Finally, the inmost Chakra was the inner Earth and given the colour red and the symbol of the crystal.

Thus the seven Chakras of the Earth formed a clear analogy with the seven major Chakras of human beings and colours normally associated with them. The crystals, as symbols, would mark the 'poles' of our Earth's equilibrium and balance, from the outer to the inner and vice versa.

Together the different colours made up the colours of the rainbow. The rainbow was another important symbol within the meditation representing like a bridge or arch that could connect different people and groups from various parts of the world together, and could also unite the different facets and Chakras of our world together into wholeness. Therefore, when working with other Healing groups with the Earth Healing meditation, we could imagine our group being at one end of the rainbow and the arch reaching down to other groups and so link together.

The intention of the Earth Healing meditation would be to balance and purify and bring healing to the seven Chakras of the Earth and its wholeness.

Cariadd suggested that as a prelude and opening to the meditation, prayers could be offered to our humanity asking that we may learn once more to respect the Earth, to be less greedy and selfish in our actions and more in harmony with the needs of the whole. She told us that if a man was to offer these prayers and then a woman speak the visualisation of the meditation that followed then this would help balance the male and female energies which would be another aspect of healing in the process.

Different versions of the Earth Healing meditation have been channelled by Cariadd. What follows is one version with all the basic elements that could be used.

I include the text of this Earth Healing Meditation with the kind permission of Naomi, who channelled this directly from her Spiritual guide, Cariadd.

The Earth Healing meditation

Quietly close your eyes and ask for spiritual help, that the greed of the people in our world may be lessened and that Man may become much more in tune with and less destructive of, our environment. In the ensuing peace, allow this visualisation to build.

Imagine a rainbow steadily building a graceful arc across the sky. Its colours are vibrant and clear. As it builds, imagine floating gently with it, rising upwards until you reach the top. You surround yourself with the colour violet. Violet is everywhere around you and it is beautiful and rich. In the violet float a clear crystal. See it turn, catching rays of light in the process. Imagine the rays, travelling outwards through the darkness of space where all life begins and ends, purifying everything.

Gradually allow your violet to change to indigo. Make it a velvety colour that you can almost feel the texture of. Allow your thoughts to come nearer to our planet and think about the higher atmospheres and then the skies and everything that flies within them. You may choose to channel your healing to the polar region. If so, in your indigo float a snowflake, rotate it slowly and see the perfect filigree pattern and purity. Imagine the damaged ozone layer healing and closing and clear the pollution higher above. Imagine Antarctica free of human interference and the ore deposits being left untapped, the natural world being left undisturbed. You may choose instead to channel healing to the tropical skies. If so imagine a butterfly fluttering through your indigo. See its brilliant colours and its symmetry, its perfection. As you are aware of it flying, imagine the tropical skies being purified. The air is wonderful to float in. For those skies in between the two regions, imagine a feather floating down through your indigo, turning as it floats. Imagine healing spreading outwards, linking up with the other two regions.

Let the colour indigo slowly change to blue. As the blue becomes a strong vibrant colour allow your mind to travel to the oceans, rivers, lakes and everything that lives in our waters. Sense the colour all around you. To channel healing to the oceans and seas float a shell in our blue. See it turn. Look in to the mother of pearl interior and see the smoothness and reflected light. Hear the sound of the sea inside it. Imagine the waters being cleared of toxins and pollutants. Imagine krill multiplying and the sea's ecology being balanced. See fish swim in increasing numbers and all life thriving. To channel healing to the rivers, lakes and streams, imagine a smooth water pebble in your blue. It is pleasing to hold and its colour is gentle. Imagine pure, clean water above your pebble. You can see it clearly because all the pollutants have disappeared. Imagine farm lands being cleansed of pesticide and herbicide residue so the irrigation routes are clean. See rays of light shine from the oceans, seas, rivers and lakes everywhere.

Let your blue slowly transform to green. Direct your thoughts to the ground and everything that grows and lives upon it. In your green float the image of a perfect flower head or a leaf. Sense the life emanating from it, healthy and strong. Imagine all life sharing that health and strength. Imagine lifting suffocating toxins so that all the leaves and flowers of the Earth flourish like yours does.

As the image of bountiful health fills your mind, slowly allow the green to change to yellow. Let your thoughts travel to the arid lands. Surround yourself with the colour yellow, and in it see a candle flame burning. Watch it flicker and dip. Send healing thoughts to life that struggles in precarious survival. Imagine the fires of the oil wells dying and pure clean air replacing smoke. Imagine land mines being cleared without harm. Feel the rare torrential rain on your skin as you imagine it falling where it needs to. Let the yellow become bright and beautiful. See the light shine from the candle.

As the flame flickers let your colour change to orange, warm and vibrant. In the orange float a rough stone. Revolve it slowly. Channel healing to the soils and all things living in them. Imagine waste dumps and chemical spillages being cleansed. Work hard on clearing thoughts for radioactive waste. Imagine primitive and unspoilt health returning. Allow the orange to spread around the earth shape.

Finally let the orange become a deep rich red and in the red rotate a crystal. As it turns imagine red rays of healing travelling directly to the inner Earth where molten life circulates. Powerful healing thoughts will help.

As we finish our journey through the colours from the clear crystal of the violet to the red crystal of the inner Earth, imagine all the colours and symbols aligned, so that all the Chakras of the Earth are balanced. Harmony can be achieved between Man and all life. There is time.

Allow yourself to see the rainbow as a whole again. Gently float down the other side. As you softly land, look where the rainbow reaches. Imagine it spanning large areas of the Earth linking other groups like this one, where healing will gain strength because it is amplified. Now you are grounded and united in a common thought, open your eyes in your own time to continue with the healing work.

FuRtheR Thoughts

Cariadd taught us that as well as being shared in a group, the Earth Healing Meditation could also be done alone and in abbreviated form. If you have a stone, crystal, feather or shell or another symbol representing one of the Earth Chakras, you can hold this to help focus your energies on a particular area of need.

Perhaps if there is a news item one day relating to an environmental disaster in a rainforest, for example, then by imagining the leaf or flower and sending green energy in the direction of the area concerned, then if many people do this with a common symbol and intent, an energy field will be generated that may really help. This could be an immediate type of inner action we could do to help with any disaster or disturbance of which we become aware.

Generally, our actions on Earth begin with thought. Individually and collectively, we can be greatly influenced by the thoughts that have been generated around us. Therefore, if we can help so that the thought field of our humanity moves more towards having respect and wanting to care for the Earth, then the physical actions of our collective society can follow suit.

Chapter 18

The Wisdom of Sojah

Sojah, Marjorie's Spiritual guide, has spoken many times about his wish to impart his teachings about Spiritual life to people 'on our side'. To some extent he has done this. Members of our Healing group and people who have attended our 'Healing with a Spiritual Guide' workshops have been enthusiastic and grateful for what Sojah has told them. Sojah seems to have a way of expressing quite complex concepts, like basic issues concerning Life and Death, in a kind and simple way which can be easily understood by his listeners.

For my own inner journey I feel I have gained much knowledge and guidance from Sojah that I feel has been very beneficial and helpful to me.

In what follows, I would like to include the answers which Sojah gave to questions I posed to him during a special session with Marjorie. I tried to select questions that would be of some interest to people in general - questions also which I knew that Sojah could answer well..

During the session, it was as though Marjorie experienced what Sojah described as a sweet sleep. She awoke feeling refreshed but remembered nothing of what had been spoken. Usually, Marjorie's consciousness would be somewhat present in the inter-actions between Sojah and me. However, with Marjorie 'sleeping', it gave Sojah the opportunity to share all that he wanted, without Marjorie's influence.

Session With Sojah

I began this session in my usual way by guiding Marjorie through hypnosis so she could go into a restful state of trance. Next, I asked Marjorie's consciousness to be somewhere that would be nourishing for her and I invited Sojah, with Marjorie's co-operation to 'overshadow' her. Then, after some pause, Sojah began speaking using Marjorie's voice with low, slow tones. It seemed to generally take a minute or two for Sojah to adjust the 'channels' to be able to speak through Marjorie normally. Soon though, Sojah was speaking through Marjorie in a bright and animated way, ready for the questions to begin. At the outset, Sojah wanted to explain to me that he would do his best to answer the questions posed to him. However, he said that he did not know all the answers and that if he did not know the answer to some question he would tell me. So we started.

Paul: What is it that happens to us, Sojah, when we die?

Sojah: *Well, of course, two things are in progress - the breaking down of the physical body and the uplifting of the Spiritual body. As you know by now and have learnt, the Spiritual body is enclosed in the physical body, waiting to be released. It can leave the body before Death and travel, or come out in any state of shock. And then if it is not time for Death, the Spiritual body will enter back again into the physical one.*

But when it is time for Death, one cannot say that one Death is the same as any other. As there may be differences in Birth, so there are in Death. But I will try to explain just how the Spirit leaves.

You see, if it was an accident, then the Spiritual body would immediately leave the physical one and if Death occurs, will not return. If you have someone old and dying over a period of weeks, then the Spiritual body will slip in and out of the physical body from time to time, but will not leave completely until the Silver Cord is broken.

Each and everyone is attached to a Silver Cord - just as a baby is attached to its mother in the same way, and this has to be cut

233

away at Birth. So it is a similar process at Death. Usually, when it is time for Death, the Spiritual body leaves and one can see the Silver Cord becoming like elastic and gradually beginning to part.

There are occasions when it is difficult and the Silver Cord will not come apart easily. Then as I think I have mentioned before, we have Deliverers who help them on their way. But it all depends on the circumstances of Death, you see.

A young person usually dies in an accident and will be far more confused when they find themselves out of their body, than someone who has been old and ill, and for some time being aware that they are going to die. However, what happens basically is that the Spiritual body leaves the Physical body. If it is time for Death, then the Silver Cord will snap and the Spirit is free.

Now what that person perceives all depends on what that person has been and what they believe in, and how much Spiritual goodness and Light they have put into their lifetime. Anyone who does not believe in an afterlife, has learnt nothing, will be more confused, wander around hopelessly, not understanding that they are even dead. There will be people there to help them, but they cannot help them if they do not ask.

That is why it is so important - we must get across to people while they are alive just what is happening, so that they understand in Death as to where to go and who to look for.

There are many who do believe. And if they know that they may be about to die, they may ask for a loved one to be there. And believe me, if it is possible at all, then they will be. Whoever is there, eventually, if they follow the right path, they will reach the Spiritual plane nearest to the Earth, which we refer to as the 'Summerland'. And there they will remain until they have become adjusted, learnt that they have died, if they do not know, and discover just where they need to go next.

Paul: Could you tell about the Hall of Memories and what happens there for people after they have died?

Sojah: *Well, the Hall of Memories is almost like what you have today of a video re-run. You place a video into your video set, press buttons and immediately comes before you the programme you have recorded previously. This is a similar process, but much quicker.*

You go to the Hall of Memories and you see the whole of your life from Birth to Death. You see everything you have done and not only see this, but feel it. You feel all the sadness and misery you may have caused. But also all the kindness and goodness and joy you've brought to people, you will feel too.

It is a very worrying time for many Spirits because they are a little afraid. There are many who have not realised how bad and selfish they have been. It is a rather rude awakening when they see this. But then there are Spirits to help sort themselves out.

Of course, the very wicked ones don't even get as far as the Hall of Memories, because they haven't even cared about what kind of lifetime they have had. And therefore they just go down into the lower regions and live in their misery there. They will of course know and feel what they have done. But this is slightly different. They will not go to the Hall of Memories or the Higher planes.

I will try to describe it to you. It is a large building with many steps leading up into doors. Although many Spirits go in together, once you are in there, it is as if you are alone. You sit in your own space - with your guide, I may add, and the re-run of your life. Some are unhappy; some feel better; some even feel pleased that they managed to achieve what they did in a lifetime. It is an experience. But of course, if you have lived many lives, then you will know what it is all about and not be as nervous as someone who is doing it for the first time.

Paul: And what is the result of having been in this Hall of Memories?

Sojah: *Well, of course, you see how many mistakes you have made, and how much goodness you have done. You see, before you were born, you could have taken on the task of doing so many things in this lifetime. Now, you could have opted out. You could have avoided the things that are important. You could have changed the path that you were supposed to take. Well then, of course, you see this. For what reason you chose it in the first place, that life was possibly for you to move on. If you made a blunder of it then you cannot move on. So therefore, you must come back and live those lessons again.*

But I do stress here, no-one is forced to be reborn. It is entirely up to the Spirit. If they wish to stay forever on a lower plane, or wallow in self-pity, even in the lower regions, then they can do this. It is entirely up to the Spirit themselves if they wish to progress and try again.

It is almost like taking a degree in a course. You take this, and if you fail this, you say to yourself, I must sit for this exam again. Or you decide not to do this. For, where you were wishing to become a Scientist or Doctor or whatever, if you fail the first time, if you do not take the exam again then obviously you will not become one of these things. You will have to look around and choose something else to do with your life. This is similar. If you have failed in a lifetime, if you want to progress, then you must come back and learn the lessons again. Otherwise, you cannot go further.

Paul: How can we live our lives on Earth in the best way to progress Spiritually?

Sojah: *Well, of course, you need help. You cannot do it alone. That is why we are here to try and help you. There are certain people such as yourself, who devote their time to this. There are Masters who choose to come back and appear into people's lives and try to instil into them what Spiritual life is all about. It all depends also on the type of life you have chosen and why you have chosen this.*

Some choose very hard lives for obvious reasons. And life is very hard and a struggle. But if they can overcome everything they set out to do then at the end of their life span they will be able to rise to many higher planes or it may not be necessary for them to be reborn again.

It is all a question of learning and also helping others, because when you choose to be born you choose to help others as well. People do not always do this. If you take a wrong path, you do not do what you say you will. But originally, it is a case of how much love you can give and how much help you can be to human kind in this lifetime.

Someone will say, if I choose to be born to a poor family and have to struggle, but by struggling I win through, become important, pass all my exams - then it is my job to help others who are struggling, having known what it is like to struggle, if you understand me. It is all a question of sharing and caring about human kind, far, far more than it is on this side. On this side, it is so easy and when you plan your life it looks so easy. But believe me, it is not so. It is difficult and hard.

Paul: How does suicide fit into the scheme of things?

Sojah: *This is a very interesting subject because it varies. There are really three types of suicide. The first is where one is completely out of their mind and utterly not responsible for their actions. The second is one who is filled with depression and remorse and sees no other way out or wishes not to carry on living. Actually they do know what they are doing. The third is rather childish, where one is immature and wanting to be taken notice of. Things have not gone their way and they want to show people. It shows nobody but themselves and this is very selfish and is a very selfish act in this case.*

But all suicides are received on this side with love and there they see their lives before them and know what pain they have caused to those left behind. They are not condemned. They are not punished. Only they punish themselves. But they will have to come back and finish the lifetime they started. This in itself they are not always happy about. But if they do not, they will stay in a rather grey place. And they will not be able to progress.

Paul: Can you say about how the cycle of reincarnation operates?

Sojah: *Well again, as I have said, the Spirit leaves the physical body and goes home. You could almost liken it to an artist, an actor or actress who finishes the play, the curtain comes down, the make up, the costumes come off and home they go. And this is very similar too.*

You have chosen a role in life; you have played that role well, or not well; given, if you like, a good performance or a bad performance. And at the end of it, the curtain has come down and there it is. You cannot do that particular performance again. If it is a bad one, then it is just too bad. If it is a good one then you will feel satisfied.

It is very similar - much, of course, more involved, but once you are in Spirit you are not the person you portrayed. Your Spirit is the same. You have built it up. And you still feel the same. If you've been a happy person, then you will continue to be a happy person. If you have been a sad, depressed person, you may find in the beginning that you will continue to be so. You do not change your personality. But living the life that you have lived is over. You have to then learn how to cope in Spiritual life. And as I have said, you decide with yourself and your guide and many others whether it is necessary to be reincarnated.

If this is so, then it does not happen always just at once. You may have a long time on this side and decide to be born into another century. And all the time you are learning on this side and gaining knowledge to help you.

Then, when the time is right, you will get together with your Spiritual guides. One will be chosen specially to spend a lifetime with you. You will plan out your life. You will decide which the best parents will be.

A lot say when they are not happy with their parents - 'Surely I did not choose this father' or 'Surely I did not choose this mother'. But you did. And you did this for a purpose. It is all planned. It is not just chance.

So when the time comes and you need to be reincarnated, it is all put into motion.

The Spiritual body usually enters the mother when the mother has become three months with the child. It is then that the foetus has become whole and settled into the womb. And that is when the Spirit usually enters the body. But believe me, it has been hovering around before that. It has known all about the mother and all about the parents. And it is just waiting for the time to enter.

Then you will experience, although you don't remember, the growing and developing in the womb. You will forget all about the Spiritual life. And when you are born, a good birth or a bad birth, you will know this. And everything on the Spiritual side, you will have forgotten.

Vaguely, you may as you grow up in childhood, feel you remembered things - depending on how Spiritually minded you are, and how many lifetimes you have lived. You do sometimes feel still in contact with Spirit.

But normally it is not good to know about the other life, because if it was so, you would wish to come home straight away. You would not do the work you have chosen to do. You would only wish to come back to Spirit. And that would be no good at all.

So it is better really to blot out Spiritual life in the beginning and just live in your physical body and learn about life on Earth.

Paul: How is Birth related to Death?

Sojah: *Very similar really. The baby comes down the channel the same way, the cord is cut. And then the baby is laid into the mother's arms.*

In Death, the Spiritual body rises out of the physical body, still attached by the Silver Cord and will be so until, as I have explained, it snaps. If there is any difficulty in this, there will be help there to guide you.

239

There is some saying that sometimes the Spiritual body remains with the physical body two or three days after Death. But this only happens if no one calls for help or does not quite understand. This is why they always say that cremation should not be too early, because the Silver Cord has not been snapped. And sometimes the Spiritual body can suffer under these circumstances.

Paul: How are human souls formed in the first place?

Sojah: *Well, this is made up of energy, Paul. God is the greatest energy of all. In our Universe, it is all energy and matter that creates Spirit. I myself, cannot answer that question fully, because I do not know. And I have not met anyone on my planes who does know.*

What I can tell you is that one becomes perfect on this side through work and trying. Spiritual beings rise higher and higher until they become pure Light and energy. And it is these Spiritual beings who can create life.

That is all I can explain to you, because it is very difficult. But the Spiritual body is first created by matter and energy. And then the physical body is created also.

Paul: Are human Souls still being created at this moment?

Sojah: *Well, of course, and will continue to be so forever. There will be no standstill on this side. Your Earth will one day burn itself out and be no more. But there are other worlds. For ever more God created, and life will always exist. You cannot stamp it out. Many times in the Centuries of long ago it has been tried. But always it will survive exactly as Spring comes back after every Winter.*

Paul: What does a Soul need to attain so it will not need to return to Earth anymore?

Sojah: *Well knowledge, Paul - knowledge and a lot of life and people and caring. But you see, no one is born a Saint. No one can possibly learn this in one lifetime. It takes many, many lifetimes and much time on this side to learn. You cannot create a perfect being - not without a lot of hard work, understanding and I am afraid, suffering also.*

I think I have said before, many retarded people who appear to do nothing all day except sit and stare into space - they have to be looked after - but inside the physical body of this person could be a very old Soul who is learning a lesson or maybe for the last time round suffering and learning so they may rise higher when they come back home.

It is as I say, all planned. And it takes many lifetimes. However, you do get in the lower regions, and not always the dark ones, situations where someone is quite happy to be ignorant and lie around forever - not wishing to develop any further or to be reborn. These Souls would in time, as a child would, become bored of their surroundings and finally realise they need to learn something. Well then, of course, we are there to take them and teach them. And they may later once again decide to be reborn and learn some more.

Paul: Are there people on Earth at the moment, perhaps incarnating for the first time?

Sojah: *Well, yes of course, Paul. There is a first time for everyone. They are usually more of a simple Soul, but not always if they have chosen to be brainy. However, as it is their first time, they tread carefully. They are not given hard tasks as much as those who have been born several times.*

It is, I say, like sending a child to pre-school, then to Junior school, Senior school and then on to university. Gradually, you learn bit by bit. So you usually find someone who is around and is not terribly intelligent. By that, I do not mean wicked or unkind. But they may not quite be able to grasp things as some can. It could be that they are just beginning to find their way.

Often there are others who are born to be with them to help them. They may not know this, They have chosen to be born at the same time as a very young Soul to help them along if they can. You,

241

yourself, have done this, Paul, although you may not be aware of it. This is part of the work that you have chosen, to help young Souls.

Paul: What practises should people do to develop themselves Spiritually?

Sojah: *Meditation is the best answer, and also prayers and thoughts. Sometimes people find it easier to say some Spiritual words to bring comfort, and this helps.*

It is a case of reaching your Higher Self. This can only be done through meditation and thinking deeply. Also, caring about other people brings you closer. It is amazing that while you are caring for someone or looking after them, or concerned about them, you find yourself becoming more Spiritually minded, because you are caring for them and you are bringing down the right energies. But all you need to do is just believe. You have come from Spirit and you will go back to Spirit in the end. In the meantime you have to learn to live in your physical body and face quite a lot of difficulties. Life is not easy.

You are Spirit and you can be Spiritually minded. It is just a case of believing, sitting quietly and thinking. You can reach your Higher Self in this way. And believe me, once you have done that, you have all the answers you need, because your Higher Ego - Spiritual Self is in the Spiritual realm anyway and therefore knows all your past lives and even your future. And once you can tap into that, you are on your way.

Paul: If we say, form a love relationship with someone on Earth, will we stay in contact with that Soul whatever happens afterwards?

Sojah: *If you wish this. Many questions have been asked around this theme. One of the most popular ones concerns someone who has had two husbands or two wives. What happens on this side?*

You see, it is very different on this side. It is love. What causes jealousy is sexual matters more than love. And this does not exist in the same way here as in the physical body. It cuts out envy, jealousy and a lot of dispute.

So, if you have loved five people very dearly and they have loved you, then yes, you would all be able to live in harmony and share your inner life in Spirit. You may have to be separated from time to time if one of you wishes to be reincarnated. Otherwise, if you wish to go as a group so that you will all be born together around at the same time and once more develop, this too can happen.

You see, love is the strongest bond of all. The more you love, the closer you become to that person or those people. And nothing can break that love. It will always be there. So, yes, you will be able to share both worlds together. And at the end of time when you no longer need to be reborn, if each and everyone wishes this, then you can all live your lives in harmony together still loving one another. It is the love that keeps you together. And that is the strongest bond that can possibly be.

Paul: Can you say a little more about how Souls sometimes incarnate together in groups?

Sojah: *Well, they wish to work together. This is the main thing. They have been working together in Spirit.*

Say, for instance, they have been Healers on this side. They wish to be born and they wish to do similar work on Earth, whether to become Doctors or nurses or to channel Spiritual Healing as many are doing now.

They have worked in a group on this side and they feel they would like to work in a group on Earth. So then, they will all choose to be reborn about the same time. And of course, growing up, they will not be together. But gradually, if they follow the correct path and they will if it is planned, they will eventually come together when the time is right in life and then they will work together as they planned to do.

Quite often, there is a lot of love and caring again in this group. Therefore, if one or two of the group die, either from old age or accidentally, or that they have chosen to live only so long in this life, they will wait until the rest of the Souls they have been united with join them before they move on - so that they can remain together.

Some Souls prefer community rather than being alone. And of course, this can be so because on this side, you do have choice.

There are a lot of loners who are happy to be by themselves or just share occasionally. But there are many more Spirits who are happy surrounded by other Spirits and work and feel better in this environment. So that too can be arranged. It all depends on yourself really.

Paul: Can you explain about twin-Souls?

Sojah: *Twin Souls is a word that perhaps I would not use too much. If you are referring to someone who meets their twin Soul, well this again is two Spirits where love binds them together so much that they cannot bear to be parted. And therefore their choice is to keep on being reborn so that they can be together.*

Sometimes this cannot happen because one of the Souls has not quite fulfilled the lifetimes that the other twin-soul has. So they do become separated. And all their life seem to be searching for someone or something that they just don't find. They make the best of life and are probably very good. But somewhere there is an emptiness within them and they do not understand what this emptiness is. They say to themselves 'I am being as good as I can; I have a good wife or husband; I love my children. What is this emptiness?' When they come back to Spirit and there is their twin Soul waiting for them, then they know.

I can only explain it like that. It doesn't always happen. Not everyone has a twin Soul. It all depends on how much love and how much caring you have.

Paul: Can you tell me a little, what it is like to live in Spirit?

Sojah: *Well, of course. Again it depends on which planes you are on. I can only tell you perhaps about the lower planes - I don't mean the bad regions. I mean starting with the Summerland.*

You'll come over to this side and it will depend on how much you've learnt in your lifetime about Spirit as to how confused you will be.

And let's take someone who is confused. They find themselves on this side in what looks like a more glorified place than what they have left behind. There is, as I have explained, the beautiful trees, the rivers, the meadows, the mountains - all bursting with energy and joy. And this is the first thing they will experience. And how marvellous it will be.

But, as I say, after a time, they will wish to know where they are going and what they are doing. And it is only when they are ready, that Spirits will come forward and ask them just what they would like to do. And then, bit by bit, they travel around the plane. If they are not entitled to go up to a Higher plane, they can visit with someone but they must come down again. This doesn't happen often unless it is to do with some work. If someone they love is on a Higher plane, that Spirit can come down to them but they cannot go up, unless as I say, it is a planned thing to do with work and maybe reincarnation - and they have to visit this particular plane for a reason.

But everything is mental. There is nothing physical. When you first come over, habits die hard. They possibly think they need to eat. If they think they need to eat, food will be there. It will appear before them, and certainly they can go through the motions of eating.

But as they become more accustomed to Spirit Life, it will suddenly dawn on them that they do not need to eat to survive. The energy in this world is so different. That is what gives you life and you do not need food because obviously you are no longer a physical body. But that takes time.

The other thing is that you work and speak with your mind. And sometimes this is difficult, because your mind can jump about as it does on Earth. You can see a tree in the distance and think 'Oh I'd like to be under that tree' and there you will be before you have had time to realise. You think 'that mountain' and there you will be again. And you have to learn how to adjust your mind and go slowly. Otherwise, you will be buffeted around, learn nothing and not enjoy your new life.

Sometimes you need rest - and we have, as I have explained, hospitals, Spiritual Healing Sanctuaries, where you can come and rest and learn and receive Healing. It will be all Healing of the mind, because as I have said, you left your physical body behind.

But the mind can be in turmoil. There is also the question of having left someone behind whom they love very much. And they cannot settle in Spirit, because they are concerned about the person they have left behind - a child, or a husband, a wife, a lover or a brother or sister that they were very fond of. They know this person is grieving and therefore they grieve themselves. And they need a lot of help from Spirit to adjust and realise that this person one day will join them. All they can do is to send out love and care, go to that person. If the person is in any way psychic, then they may be able to pick up what they've been trying to say and feel better for it.

But many are not. Many Spirits have gone back and tried every way in which to meet the one they love. But they are talking to deaf ears because they do not hear them. Then they are very sad. But there is always someone on this side to help them. They also know on this side how long that person has to live. So although they know the person is suffering, they can be content knowing that the person has not long to suffer, although, unfortunately, the one left behind does no know this.

The thing that they worry about most is that the people left behind may wish to take their lives because they cannot live without the one who has left them. This causes great concern and Spiritual beings try very hard to help the person on Earth not to do this because it would not solve any problems, and they would not be

*able to be together for very long before they would have to part
again, if you understand what I mean.*

Paul: Could you tell about some of the work and activities in
which Spiritual beings engage?

Sojah: *Well, they are endless. I could go on forever. But you don't
want me to do this, so I will try to give you a few examples that
perhaps you could understand.*

*Of course, you know there are many groups of Spirits who wish to
help with Healing on this side and on your side. There are many
groups. They come together. They work together. They choose the
people they can work through, and they wish to do this, because
possibly in their lifetimes, they have seen much suffering, have
suffered themselves and want to make it easier.*

*There are as I have said, Deliverers. These are on the similar lines
to Healers, but their work is mainly receiving the Soul after it has
left the body and encouraging and helping it over to the other side.
Not everyone needs their help because they have someone there they
love waiting for them. But there are also a lot of lonely and
confused people and their Death may not be quite as easy and this
is what the Deliverers are there for.*

*My work, as I have said, has dealt with the Souls of the lower
regions and the Earth bound Spirits. This is worthwhile work,
but very hard. It is very hard to reach these Souls and get them
into the Light. But it is good work and it is something I have done
for many, many, many lifetimes and also in Spirit, because I care
you see, very much about Souls and raising them out of the
darkness, and I chose to do this work.*

*I also chose to be Marjorie's guide, because I knew in later life we
would be able to work together in this way. This is something I
also care about because I do care about Souls, you see.*

*Other work - there are young babies who come over to this side,
and tiny children. They need help and there are many Spirits who
call themselves Mother Spirits who help to rear these children.*

There are also Spiritual beings being created and learning on this side before they are born. These have special teachers to help them, because they will be learning for the first time - first how to live in Spirit and then how to live in the material Earthly life.

The babies who die and the children who die, possibly remember another lifetime. But they still have to grow. They do not come over and immediately rise to be young men and women. They have to live a life-span on this side also. Children here are very, very happy because you see, imagination creates, so therefore if they wish to imagine themselves in a ship, then they will be so immediately or wherever they wish to be. It is good to see such happiness in children.

There are problems with children who have come home before their time, when they had to leave their parents - yes feel homesick and miss their mothers and fathers and wish to go back. So then we have trained Spirits who can help them and teach them and give the guidance and bit by bit, they are able to settle down.

Then of course, we have the Masters, who can go on teaching you about all the arts, of which you have learnt or maybe want to learn or are not able to experience in a lifetime. We have musicians and artists and writers, all who have lived before, all who wish to carry on sharing their work and helping people.

Paul: How do lower entities come into being?

Sojah: *Well, of course, they create their own lower entity. They are born. They do not do what they decided to do. But they go wrong. They are wicked. They are unkind. And when they come over to this side, they can't possibly come to the better realms where there is no disharmony. Anyone who would cause disharmony would not be admitted. Therefore, they must go to the lower realms. They can stay there if they wish, but they are very unhappy people.*

They hang around Earth. They hang around depressed people. They try to reach them if they can and make them worse. If there is any sadness, they revel in it. If you have someone with murder in their heart, they will encourage this. Not always can the person hear them. Again a lot is how psychic you are. But they cannot harm anyone if one does not wish to listen to them.

There is a lot of fear about Ghosts and lower entities. These can only come in and take possession if you let them. The best thing to do with this if you are aware they are around is to ignore and laugh at them. Do not take them seriously, and when they find this out they will leave you and search somewhere else to frighten people.

It is sad, but as you know of people in this world who are like this, when they die, they cannot change. They will still be the same. That is why there are lower entities. Of course, there are even lower regions where people have created wars, starvation, done much cruelty and millions and millions of people have suffered. They are even in much lower regions and there they will stay until they have realised what they have done.

Paul: How can we best manage the forces of evil in our life?

Sojah: *Evil is very strong, Paul as Love is. Like attracts like, and if one thinks evil, then evil will come. Evil can also be created by people's thoughts and actions. These are received on this side by evil Spirits with joy. They will come closer and encourage anyone who wishes to behave in this way.*

You can fight evil by love. It is very hard at times, but hatred brings more evil. Love is the only thing that can keep it at bay.

Many, many people are born into the world and through actions take the wrong course and learn to be evil instead of good. They have to come back to us and learn all over again. Some of them are still in dark places. We try to help them but evil is a very strong force and we are fighting all the time. Some people don't mean to be wicked. These people's actions do not come from the heart. Therefore we do not call them evil, and these people we can help. But many slip by the wayside. You on your side can help by refusing to accept wickedness and send out love.

Paul: Can you say something about the Spiritual changes happening on the Earth at the moment?

Sojah: *Well, of course, we are trying very hard on this side. A lot depends on the ones who are born who have promised to help and if they are following in the path they have chosen. But it is becoming more and more difficult.*

In a lot of cases, children are not being disciplined in the way they should be disciplined. They are being given too much freedom. In the case of thinking, I do not mean they should not be allowed their own mind and thoughts. But they should be taught the difference between right and wrong. They should be taught when they are hurting someone. They should be taught when they are being selfish. All children are like this. A lot is the parent's fault for not teaching them. They grow up in a world where they feel it is there especially for them and nobody else. They do not care about other people and so they live their lives. Because of this - it has gone on for many centuries, and sadly, it is becoming worse instead of better.

A lot of the younger generation are not being taught anything Spiritually at all. They are no longer being sent to the Churches or Sunday schools. The schools of education no longer preach anything about any of the religions or about love or Spiritual love. Therefore, they do not know these things. And without it, one day, the world will crumble. It will be over run by evil and no one can stop this.

That is why we are trying so hard to bring about a new Spiritual awareness. I am only one of many Spirits working in this way. All you can do is your best and believe me, if you give your life and your best, then that is something for which you will be greatly rewarded when you come over to this side.

We can only try. We cannot stop wars. We cannot stop people from being wicked, because they are born with a free Will, you see. If, every time they behaved dishonestly or wickedly they were struck down, they would not be living a free life. So therefore, other people and other beings have to suffer.

Sometimes though, there are certain people who choose to be born wicked. But these are special people - and they know that at the end of this life span they will be forgiven. You see, some are born to cause disruption, to cause learning. It may sound complicated to you, but there has to be someone to start things in the first place. But this is not always so.

In many cases, it is the Spirit that has taken the wrong path, become over greedy, over zealous, and cared for no one but themselves. And that is what unfortunately, the world is becoming at the moment. It is not easy.

In the end, energy or God will end the world if it does not become better, because it cannot go on, poisoning the Earth, poisoning everything and disrupting everyone. One day it has to end. But we are doing our best on this side to try and save people so that when the time comes, they will come over to us, understanding and caring.

Paul: You have spoken sometimes of the possibilities of a Spiritual revolution in the next century?

Sojah: *Well, you must see for yourself, Paul. Since you have taken up your work, how many more people now are doing similarly. How many more workshops, how many more Healing Sanctuaries, how many more people working for Spirit are there, than there were, say 10 years ago. So look in thirty years time. Yes, there will be a Spiritual revolution. I cannot promise you whether it will even be in your lifetime. But people are going that way and you can see now it is building up.*

So look to the future. Once there is a breakthrough it will be almost like Christianity over again. A light, a new awakening and people will try to live more loving, more caring and stop all this greed, selfishness and cruelty. But it won't happen overnight. But I honestly predict to you that this will be so, because it is the only thing to save your world.

Paul: What will happen to religion in the future?

Sojah: *Well, people will form their own religion. There are still good Christians. Therefore the Christian religion will never die if people are happy living under the Christian religion. They are doing good; they are helping others; they are doing what Christ preached. And that will survive.*

But too many cult things are beginning. Too many are trying to take the wrong path. These we hope will be trampled underfoot.

Religion will always be there because again, it is like art, like music. You choose what you wish to hear. Some may be happy listening to pop music and jazz. Someone else will be happy listening to classical music. It is all music, but you are choosing with what you feel best.

This is what happens you see. You find your own path and the way that you feel is Spiritually awakened and love. It may not be a church. The churches will not be burned down and destroyed. But people will find other ways of worshipping and loving. But religion will always be there, as it has been since time began.

If you go back to Druids and before that, they too had their religion. It was destroyed later on, but it was there. People must always follow someone, and believe in something. Otherwise they do not survive.

Paul: What happens to animals in Spirit?

Sojah: *They are reincarnated the same as humans. They live life spans but not quite as long. They do not die. They have souls. Anyone who tells you they do not are wrong. They have their animal kingdoms and they live in peace and harmony once they come to this side.*

Pets, like dogs and cats or whatever who love a certain human, will want for that person to come and they too can be united on the other side and spend eternity together if they wish.

Also, animals of course have always spoken with their minds through telepathy so this is nothing new to them on this side. You do not realise when you speak to a dog or a cat that they are reading your mind. There are many who say, "He knows exactly what I am saying' or 'she understands every word.' Your pet does not understand words because he has not been taught to read or write or understand, but he reads your mind and picks up your thoughts. He knows when there are good thoughts; he knows when there are bad thoughts, wicked thoughts, angry thoughts, loving thoughts, and will respond accordingly, as I'm sure, if you have had a pet dog or cat, you will know.

Again, you can have a good animal and a bad animal. An animal who has not been very happy, who has caused a lot of destruction, when it comes over to this side - well it will have to go back and try again.

They are learning in their own way. But I think I have explained before, they are usually Group Souls. It is very difficult to explain this to you. As I've said before to you, animals are more or less born in packs - not one animal born alone. And therefore they are used to being together, even if separated, their Soul is one if you understand me.

Paul: So what is the relationship between the animal and the human kingdom in Spirit?

Sojah: *It depends on the Spirits that wish to be with animals. Animals are left to live their own lives in the Spiritual realm. But if someone has loved an animal, then they can be together. You can travel to the animal realm any time you wish. There will be no more viciousness. You can meet a lion or a tiger and they will no longer harm you because you see, physically, they do not need food and therefore they do not need to kill.*

Animals are really much fairer than human beings. Most animals would not kill, unless it was to survive. Unfortunately human beings kill for other reasons also. There is much to learn from animals. There is goodness there that some human beings do not have.

Paul: Could you tell about Astral travel - what it is and how we can learn to do that responsibly?

Sojah: *Well again, as I have said before, it rests with the individual, and how they go about this. A lot that prevents Astral travelling or remembering Astral travel is fear. People are afraid that if they leave their body they will not get back into it, or that something will take over while they have left.*

None of these things can happen. But if they believe it, then they will fear it, and I am afraid they will never be successful at Astral travelling.

The important thing is relaxation. But as I have said before, never do it when you are tired, if you wish to remember where you go, because if you are tired, you will fall into a deep sleep. You will still Astral travel, but you will not know, not remember when you wake up.

The time for Astral travelling is when you feel more energetic and at peace with yourself. And you can lie quietly on your bed, sit quietly in your chair and then begin to imagine at the beginning that you are feeling some sensations. What is really happening, is that the Spiritual body is slowly sliding out of the physical body. There is sometimes a warning when this is about to happen, and you feel it first in the head and the back of the neck. You may even in your head feel a loud crack. This is nothing to be alarmed about. This is the beginning of the physical body and the Spiritual body separating.

The first time you may be afraid. You find yourself suddenly floating above your body and you don't know what to do. If it is the first time, do not go far. Float around the establishment you are in, looking down at things. Float to the top of your wardrobe and you may be surprised to see something there that you lost a year ago and did not know where it had gone because you have never seen the top of your wardrobe. These things prove that if when you awaken in the morning you then climb up and look on to the wardrobe and find the very article you saw in your Astral body, there is your proof that you have travelled.

A lot don't believe it. They think they have been dreaming. But again, it is part of the pattern, it is part of the plan. You could not survive in your world, if you were not able to come home and relax and be in Spirit, just like you could not sit forever in a classroom without a break.

But Astral travelling is difficult for some and easier for others. And for those who find it, it gives much joy, because they can travel where they wish, learn much, and also share joy with other Spiritual beings who are travelling also.

A lot of psychic people do know the difference between a Spiritual body, and one they call a sleep walker, knowing that this person is not dead but is travelling in their sleep. They are a different texture and a different colouring and people who are studying this, understand and know immediately what they are looking at. Quite often, if they see someone appear in their room and they know it is a sleep walker, they will say 'Go back to your body', because naturally, they do not want to be spied upon. If it is a Spiritual being well they will ask why they have come, or if it is someone they love, they will chat to them. But there is a difference in the substance and outline of a Spiritual being from someone who is travelling in the Astral.

Paul: What role do Spiritual guides play when we travel in the Astral planes?

Sojah: *Well, if you ask them to be there and if you try to remember, they will be waiting for you as you leave your body. Then if you wish for them to do so, they will travel with you. They will help you. Any problems you have, you wish to discuss with them while you are in the Astral, then they will be very glad to help you also. But quite often, you are entitled to your own privacy to enjoy your own Astral travelling as you will.*

Then your Spiritual guide will leave you and let you go on your way. But your body will always be guarded and you will always be safe. If there is ever anything threatening your body, immediately you will be reeled in as you reel in a fishing line. That is why some people wake quite suddenly, alarmed, with their heart beating and possibly their head aching, thinking 'Whatever was that?' You have been brought back into your body too quickly. Sometimes it is difficult to get comfortable again that night.

The best thing to do if that happens is to try to gently slide out of your body again and move back in slowly. But your Spiritual guide is there to help you when you need assistance. But as I say, your guide will also let you go your own way if you wish.

Paul: That is all the questions I have now Sojah

Sojah: *Well, I think we have done very, very well today. I hope I have answered to the best of my ability the questions you have asked me. Thank you.*

Stories from the Dead

During one very interesting channelling session with Marjorie, Sojah allowed three different Spiritual beings to tell their stories of what happened when they died, and left their physical bodies on Earth. The following is what they each had to say.

Gretchen

My name is Gretchen and I came over to Spirit quite early. I was only a young person of twenty four. I had tuberculosis and I knew I would die because I had this disease at a time when there was little help towards curing my complaint. I was afraid because I knew I would die. I had not had any religious teachings but I had a friend who had also TB. She was in a sanatorium with me. She used to talk to me about what she believed in Spirit. And I listened. But still I was afraid.

I want to tell you this because there was nothing for me to fear. It was the most marvellous experience. I suddenly left my body and in front of me was a beautiful person. And I suddenly recognised this person and knew we had been together many times. He simply took my hands and we left behind my body which by this time had suffered much.

It was wonderful to go with my Spiritual friend. I found myself in a beautiful place and then I saw not just one person I knew, but suddenly I remembered I had lived other lives and I was able to see my families and parents from other lives who were there waiting for me.

And since then I have progressed and felt that all my suffering was perhaps worthwhile to receive such joy and harmony. I just wanted to tell you and then you would know.

Ronald

My name is Ronald and I did not believe in anything. I decided that when one died, that was the end and there was no existence of any kind. I found myself stood by my bed and I was amazed that I was standing up because I had been ill and was quite old, and I had not stood up in this way for some time.

I was very confused. And even more so when I looked and saw myself still lying on the bed. But then everything seemed to go black and I floated around in a haze. It was not very nice. But I did not seem to be able to find my way.

In the end I shouted 'Will somebody help me?' And immediately the fog began to clear and there were arms outstretched, and they said 'We have been trying for ages to reach you, but you would not believe we were here and you did not ask for help.'

So I was glad that I did. And now I am happy and fine. I just wanted to tell you this.

Rosemary

My name is Rosemary and I was a very religious person brought up in a Catholic Church. I believed when I died that I would see God and Jesus and all good Christians. I was not afraid to die because I was sure I was one of the chosen ones and everything would be all right.

It was not quite like that. I was received with love and help. But I did not see God. But I did feel the presence of Jesus, and at first I did see the crosses and the statues and all the things I expected to see.

And yet somehow, it did not feel right and I was confused. And then one day, someone came to help me and they said 'Your mind is too much on one channel, and you are blocking the others. Cast out what you have believed and just look at what you see.'

And it was marvellous. All the images and symbols fell away. In its place were many people wishing to share love and kindness. And I learnt that this is what it is all about - that it does not matter what denomination you believe in. It is all one and it is full of love and understanding.

Chapter 19

Challenges of Our Modern World

Sharing Spiritual Experiences With Others

Sometimes, inner experiences that come to us may make a profound difference to the way how we relate to our life. Experiences like making contact with our Spiritual Guide, recalling a past life or even opening to a deep feeling of peace or love, may affect us in this way. Such experiences may radically change our perception of what feels important to us. From this, we may want to shift our values and make changes in our life so that the essence of these experiences can be honoured and nurtured. But this is not always easy.

When we meet with loved ones and friends after going through such experiences we may sense them to be still in the 'old ways' and this can bring with it a dilemma. We don't want to feel separated or isolated from our loved ones. So, when we have had an important inner revelation we need to be able to share it. However, to feel safe, we need to feel that if we share our precious inner experience it will be understood and accepted. Otherwise, we could feel very hurt and rejected.

To share important inner transforming experiences contains a risk. We need to sense when it is appropriate to do so. It needs courage to make that step.

I have known people who have refused to share their inner life with their partner or loved ones because they were afraid of the trouble it would cause if they did so. People making this choice have tended then to go back into their shell, and dismiss the experiences they have had, so then they can continue the comfortable and secure life they had before.

It may be difficult to have a partner or loved one who is hostile to your Spiritual beliefs or values. Yet it may be counterproductive to try and convince this other person to share your outlook. Everyone is entitled to their own beliefs and way of approaching their life. But this also means that you are entitled to your beliefs and Spiritual outlook too.

If it does not seem possible to be compatible Spiritually with your partner it may be necessary to release that partner and find a companion with whom a relationship can be more constructive. However, it may not always be right or desirable to leave a relationship for these reasons alone. Patience and time may be needed for your partner to more fully accept you and the way you relate to Spiritual life.

If you have a group of friends with whom you conform to particular modes of behaviour as a means to keep you together, it may feel difficult to break out of these patterns if those ways of being no longer fit how you feel inside.

However, unless you are true to yourself with your friends or with anyone else whom you love, this will cause an inner conflict within you. As a result of this, you may feel stress, unhappiness or emptiness.

Many people are very frightened to do anything which may be outside the pressures of their peer group. There is an instinctive tendency in us where we want to be like everyone else. It needs a certain degree of daring and trust to go beyond this. Ultimately though, if we are not true to our deep inner needs as individuals, I believe we will not make progress Spiritually.

Our energy will remain strongly connected to those we love whatever we do. So, if we make some important steps in our life, to live our life more true to the inner qualities and values of our Soul, then this shift may on a subtle level help those we love to the steps they need to make too. Knowing this, we can feel free but also more confident that we may not be left alone or acting selfishly.

Demands From the Society We Have Created

For many people in our modern world, life seems to proceed at a very fast pace. People are rushing, trying to cram as much activity, efficiently, into the shortest space of time possible, straining to meet deadlines and cope with all the many expectations around them. At the workplace people are pushed to meet evermore challenging targets from the companies with whom they work. It is a competitive world. Time with family and loved ones is usually squeezed out at the end of the day when people feel tired and exhausted. Then there is always the media, controlling, manipulating, influencing people's behaviour toward the latest fashion of thought, social outlook and dress. With consumerism people are encouraged to buy and spend more and more money to be happy and comfortable. In the city there are flashing lights, noise and buzzing activity never ceasing.

Who really wants to live like this? These kinds of society structures do not allow much inner space for genuine inner reflection. A lot of people caught in these systems spend most moments just struggling to survive and keep up with it all.

More and more people go to Doctors complaining of stress, not knowing what to do with themselves. Once people get used to the daily grind of these kinds of bustling activities, this can be like an addiction and then they can go into panic, not knowing how to cope without it.

But it is in quiet inner spaces where people can find peace. When we are very busy our Spiritual guides cannot get through to us. We need to slow down and become still to find the meaning in our lives. Then we can realise what is important to us.

If we become aware that our lifestyle needs to change, we may need time to adjust to that. Our nervous systems can only cope with so much. Changes may come best in small steps while we check inside what is the right way for us to go forward.

Our Relationship to Money

One of the main driving forces pushing our society in the direction it is going, is the pursuit of money and profit.

Some people with no openness to Spiritual beliefs try to grab from life all they can. They say that they only live once and they therefore want to make the most of it, regardless of how it affects anyone else. These people can attain positions of great power and influence, and they only care about themselves. How unjust and corrupt it can seem when people with this motivation gather to themselves vast sums of money. But this does not make money bad.

For people whose main object in life is to generate money, they may never be satisfied. They will be perpetually aware of what they lack, seeing this in material terms, and wanting more and more. Comparing themselves with others, they will tend to view anyone else as a rival and want to have everything at least as good as them. This is where money can become a vehicle for greed and exploitation. But I believe that people will only find peace when they begin to give as much as take.

Money is basically an instrument of exchange, to bring into balance giving and receiving. To honour the societies we live in, we need money to survive. And if we do not have enough money to adequately meet our basic needs of food, clothing and shelter, then we will suffer. To be able to get the money that we need, we have to value our worth for what we do and the services we offer. This is important for our dignity. The challenge for all of us is to find harmony between our inner path and meeting our material needs adequately.

The Abuse of Drugs

For many people, life in our material world can feel like a prison. They don't want to be here. Especially when people are taught, or they come to believe, that the material world is all that exists, then life can be very frustrating. Through Spiritual and emotional deprivation life can feel to have no meaning or substantial purpose. It is understandable then that people coming from this base seek for forms of escape from the boredom and miseries of their mundane life.

Therefore, it is not surprising that drug taking is very attractive and popular with young people particularly. The opportunity to get 'high', to have 'good feelings' or even strange visions can be very exciting. However, it is the drugs that produce these effects. Sooner or later the effects of the drugs will wear off and then it may feel even more awful to be imprisoned in mundane Earthly life. Then more drugs may be needed to repeat the experience so they can get away again. Often the quantity of drugs needs to be increased to be able to repeat the quality of the first experience. So soon it is very easy for these people to be going on a path towards drug addiction.

Drugs can produce some very interesting experiences of altered consciousness. They can open doorways to a perception of inner psychic worlds, but this is attained through distorting the psychic/energetic body of the person and pushing it open in ways that it would not normally do so. Inevitably, this can cause long-term damage to the psychic/Spiritual body of people if drug use is sustained.

Often, when I have worked with people who have been excessive drug users, I have found their inner life to be very chaotic and confused. They can still pick up psychic experiences, but images tend to flitter around and usually they can not concentrate very well. What they experience internally is typically not substantial and they can seem to have lost clear contact with the inner sources of their being. These people may need much Spiritual Healing to help restore their inner psychic body to health again.

In past times there were Shamans who would use drugs for special ceremonial purposes. This drug taking would be accompanied by Ritual, prayer and spiritual support. The Shaman would seek visions in service to the community, and would have undergone years of training to know how to cope with these experiences.

However, that is not how people use drugs today. They use them just for their own pleasure and for nobody else but themselves.

In a Healing circle and through Spiritual attunement and meditation people can get 'high' from experiences of Spiritual love and caring. But these experiences will last and they help people to become more loving and at peace with themselves. People can then feel more connected to Spirit and feel more supported to live in our material world and choose to do what is needed to be done here. Surely this is a better way.

Chapter 20

Conclusions

We all have healing journeys that we have to make through life. These may take on many different shapes and forms for each of us. Although we can feel very alone on our journey, because no one can live our lives for us, I believe that we are supported and we can reach out for help.

There is an inner dimension of life that is very important. People tend to neglect this in our modern society. However, it is from within that we find peace.

In the beginning, people need to satisfy their wants and desires, but this is not necessarily sufficient for us to be happy. By caring for others and having our attention on what others need rather than ourselves, we can learn about love. By extending this to a caring for all life forms, we can learn more about our place in the Universe. And love goes wide as well as deep. There is so much potential for us when we stop thinking just of ourselves and reach out to embrace others.

It is not always easy to learn to do that, and our own needs are important to honour too. But the joys of life come through sharing, not from isolation.

When we think only of ourselves, pain and suffering can be so big. Our whole world can then be so narrow and really the interests of our Self are then so small. Pleasures can be very empty unless there is a sense of communion.

So when we open to experience our past lives or the inner child within us, we are considering and becoming aware of the foundations of that which has happened to make us who we are today. When we seek help and inspiration from Spiritual sources, from our Spiritual guides and inner teachers, we are gaining access to our Soul and greater Self, which in essence is connected to all life. This is not some idle curiosity. Nor can this be separated from other aspects of our ordinary life. The deeper the knowledge we have of ourselves, the more we can act from a place of truth, facing our future and making our contribution to it. This knowledge is bound to bring increasing respect for all forms of life including the Spirit of the Earth which is our physical home.

In writing this book, I am urging a more meditative, contemplative and healing life for people. Apart from changing names to protect the identity of those involved, all the stories I have written about are factual accounts of experiences I have witnessed and shared. I hope that in reading these accounts and teachings it may be possible to unlock and open inner doorways for you, my readers.

Author Contact

The author may be contacted at:

Paul Williamson
PO Box 121
Lancaster
LA1 5GS
England

Please enclose an SAE or two International Reply Coupons

FREE CATALOGUE

Capall Bann is owned and run by people actively involved in many of the areas in which we publish. A detailed illustrated catalogue is available on request, SAE or International Postal Coupon appreciated. **Titles can be ordered direct from Capall Bann, post free in the UK** (cheque or PO with order) or from good bookshops and specialist outlets. Do contact us for details on the latest releases at: **Capall Bann Publishing, Freshfields, Chieveley, Berks, RG20 8TF.** Titles include:

A Breath Behind Time, Terri Hector
Angels and Goddesses - Celtic Christianity & Paganism, M. Howard
Arthur - The Legend Unveiled, C Johnson & E Lung
Astrology The Inner Eye - A Guide in Everyday Language, E Smith
Auguries and Omens - The Magical Lore of Birds, Yvonne Aburrow
Asyniur - Womens Mysteries in the Northern Tradition, S McGrath
Begonnings - Geomancy, Builder's Rites & Electional Astrology in the
     European Tradition, Nigel Pennick Between Earth and Sky, Julia Day
Book of the Veil , Peter Paddon
Caer Sidhe - Celtic Astrology and Astronomy, Vol 1, Michael Bayley
Caer Sidhe - Celtic Astrology and Astronomy, Vol 2 M Bayley
Call of the Horned Piper, Nigel Jackson
Cat's Company, Ann Walker
Celtic Faery Shamanism, Catrin James
Celtic Faery Shamanism - The Wisdom of the Otherworld, Catrin James
Celtic Lore & Druidic Ritual, Rhiannon Ryall
Celtic Sacifice - Pre Christian Ritual & Religion, Marion Pearce
Celtic Saints and the Glastonbury Zodiac, Mary Caine
Circle and the Square, Jack Gale
Compleat Vampyre - The Vampyre Shaman, Nigel Jackson
Creating Form From the Mist - The Wisdom of Women in Celtic Myth and
     Culture, Lynne Sinclair-Wood
Crystal Clear - A Guide to Quartz Crystal, Jennifer Dent
Crystal Doorways, Simon & Sue Lilly
Crossing the Borderlines - Guising, Masking & Ritual Animal Disguise in the
     European Tradition, Nigel Pennick
Dragons of the West, Nigel Pennick
Earth Dance - A Year of Pagan Rituals, Jan Brodie
Earth Harmony - Places of Power, Holiness & Healing, Nigel Pennick

Magical Guardians - Exploring the Spirit and Nature of Trees, Philip Heselton
Magical History of the Horse, Janet Farrar & Virginia Russell
Magical Lore of Animals, Yvonne Aburrow
Magical Lore of Cats, Marion Davies
Magical Lore of Herbs, Marion Davies
Magick Without Peers, Ariadne Rainbird & David Rankine
Masks of Misrule - Horned God & His Cult in Europe, Nigel Jackson
Medicine For The Coming Age, Lisa Sand MD
Medium Rare - Reminiscences of a Clairvoyant, Muriel Renard
Menopause and the Emotions, Kathleen I Macpherson
Mind Massage - 60 Creative Visualisations, Marlene Maundrill
Mirrors of Magic - Evoking the Spirit of the Dewponds, P Heselton
Moon Mysteries, Jan Brodie
Mysteries of the Runes, Michael Howard
Mystic Life of Animals, Ann Walker
New Celtic Oracle The, Nigel Pennick & Nigel Jackson
Oracle of Geomancy, Nigel Pennick
Pagan Feasts - Seasonal Food for the 8 Festivals, Franklin & Phillips
Patchwork of Magic - Living in a Pagan World, Julia Day
Pathworking - A Practical Book of Guided Meditations, Pete Jennings
Personal Power, Anna Franklin
Pickingill Papers - The Origins of Gardnerian Wicca, Bill Liddell
Pillars of Tubal Cain, Nigel Jackson
Places of Pilgrimage and Healing, Adrian Cooper
Practical Divining, Richard Foord
Practical Meditation, Steve Hounsome
Practical Spirituality, Steve Hounsome
Psychic Self Defence - Real Solutions, Jan Brodie
Real Fairies, David Tame
Reality - How It Works & Why It Mostly Doesn't, Rik Dent
Romany Tapestry, Michael Houghton
Runic Astrology, Nigel Pennick
Sacred Animals, Gordon MacLellan
Sacred Celtic Animals, Marion Davies, Ill. Simon Rouse
Sacred Dorset - On the Path of the Dragon, Peter Knight
Sacred Grove - The Mysteries of the Forest, Yvonne Aburrow
Sacred Geometry, Nigel Pennick
Sacred Nature, Ancient Wisdom & Modern Meanings, A Cooper
Sacred Ring - Pagan Origins of British Folk Festivals, M. Howard
Season of Sorcery - On Becoming a Wisewoman, Poppy Palin
Seasonal Magic - Diary of a Village Witch, Paddy Slade
Secret Places of the Goddess, Philip Heselton

Secret Signs & Sigils, Nigel Pennick
Self Enlightenment, Mayan O'Brien
Shamanica, Martine Ashe
Spirits of the Air, Jaq D Hawkins
Spirits of the Earth, Jaq D Hawkins
Spirits of the Fire, Jaq D Hawkins
Stony Gaze, Investigating Celtic Heads John Billingsley
Stumbling Through the Undergrowth , Mark Kirwan-Heyhoe
Subterranean Kingdom, The, revised 2nd ed, Nigel Pennick
Symbols of Ancient Gods, Rhiannon Ryall
Talking to the Earth, Gordon MacLellan
Taming the Wolf - Full Moon Meditations, Steve Hounsome
Teachings of the Wisewomen, Rhiannon Ryall
The Other Kingdoms Speak, Helena Hawley
Tree: Essence of Healing, Simon & Sue Lilly
Tree: Essence, Spirit & Teacher, Simon & Sue Lilly
Through the Veil, Peter Paddon
Torch and the Spear, Patrick Regan
Understanding Chaos Magic, Jaq D Hawkins
Vortex - The End of History, Mary Russell
Warp and Weft - In Search of the I-Ching, William de Fancourt
Warriors at the Edge of Time, Jan Fry
Water Witches, Tony Steele
Way of the Magus, Michael Howard
Weaving a Web of Magic, Rhiannon Ryall
West Country Wicca, Rhiannon Ryall
Wildwitch - The Craft of the Natural Psychic, Poppy Palin
Wildwood King , Philip Kane
Witches of Oz, Matthew & Julia Philips
Wondrous Land - The Faery Faith of Ireland by Dr Kay Mullin
Working With the Merlin, Geoff Hughes
Your Talking Pet, Ann Walker
Menopausal Woman on the Run, Jaki da Costa

Environmental
Gardening For Wildlife Ron Wilson

FREE CATALOGUE
and
FREE MAGAZINE

Get a copy of our free detailed catalogue and register for your free* copies of *Inspiration* - the free Capall Bann magazine full of inspirational articles, reviews of music and books and news.

Just send your name and address to:

Mailing List
Capall Bann Publishing
Freshfields
Chieveley
Berks
RG20 8TF

* *Inspiration* is mailed out free within the UK, to have the magazine mailed overseas please send four IRCs. Our catalogue is sent out free worldwide.